FOLLOWING THE GENERAL

Why Three Coaches Have Been Unable to
Return Indiana Basketball to Greatness

Terry Hutchens

TERRRY HUTCHENS PUBLICATIONS
Indianapolis, IN

Cover designed by Phil Velikan
Front cover photo of Coach Knight used with the permission of alamy stock photo

Cover and Interior photos provided by Indiana University Archives

Packaged by Wish Publishing

Printed in the United States of America
10 9 8 7 6 5 4 3 2 1

Distributed in the United States by Cardinal Publishers Group.
www.cardinalpub.com

To all of you out there – and you know who you are – who have supported me and encouraged me in my journey as a sports journalist. The business has changed but your support has never wavered.

Table of Contents

Introduction & Acknowledgements

What seems like two lifetimes ago, I wrote a book in 1995 about the Indianapolis Colts called *Let 'Er Rip*. Jim Harbaugh was on the cover and wrote the foreword. It was the story about a magical Colts team that came within a trapped pass in the end zone in Pittsburgh (did someone say Aaron Bailey?) in the AFC Championship game of making it to the Super Bowl. I was the Colts beat writer at the time for the *Indianapolis News* and was contacted by a publisher after that game and asked if I would write a book about the season. I agreed to do it and that was that.

My experience writing a book was enjoyable but it wasn't something I really saw myself doing again. In fact, I didn't write my second book, *Hep Remembered* until 2007, shortly after former IU football coach Terry Hoeppner died of the effects of brain cancer and I wanted to do my part to keep his legacy alive.

And then I caught the bug. The last few years I've published two books a year. All of a sudden this work, *Following the General*, is my 11th book. I feel like an addict. I can't stop myself. I keep thinking about other titles I want to do. Last year I wrote my first children's book, *Hoo-Hoo-Hoo Hoosiers* and had a blast with it. I want to write another children's book or two as well. Maybe next year.

We'll see, but for now I have No. 11 behind me. I think my favorite book I ever wrote was *Hoosiers Through and Through* which looked at the best IU basketball players of all-time who hailed from the state of Indiana. I wrote a book called *Missing Banners*, that I co-wrote with Tom Brew, that looked at all the years in IU history that Indiana came close to hanging another national championship banner but came up short. And now *Following the General*, I kind of think will enter into my list of my favorite topical books.

I've been thinking about this particular book since about 2012 but I told myself I didn't want to write it until three permanent head coaches (in this case Mike Davis, Kelvin Sampson and Tom Crean) had all completed their tenures. And to be honest, after Tom Crean and Indiana made the 2013 run that was stopped short in the Sweet Sixteen by Syracuse, I still thought I might never write this book. That's because I really thought Tom Crean might be able to find that sustained level of success that has been missing at Indiana for nearly 25 years. That's right. This isn't a post-Bob Knight problem exclusively. The reality is the last six seasons of Knight at IU were not a lot to write home about. They were all NCAA Tournament years but never did IU make it out of the first weekend in Knight's final six seasons in Bloomington. And really, Knight wasn't able to put up that elusive sixth national championship banner in his final 13 seasons at IU.

So I waited five more years after my initial thoughts of the book in 2012 but when Crean was fired in March of 2017, I told myself it was time to get writing.

As I read back over the entire text, I'm reminded that it may be a little Tom Crean heavy. But I'm not sure how to do it much differently. Crean was at IU the last nine seasons and when you're the most recent guy I think you'll find that most people feel comfortable talking about him the most. Plus, when you have a guy like Sampson who was only at IU less than two years and people remember it as a dark time in the program's history there's only so much that can be said. There's quite a bit on Mike Davis, a guy that I have a tremendous amount of respect for the way he tried to exist within the fishbowl that was Indiana.

I've had amazing cooperation along the way. I think I reached out to about 65 or so people and asked if I could interview them for this project. As of my last count, I've talked to more than 50 and that number includes a lot of big name, national media people, a lot of local media in both the print, radio and TV sectors, a couple of former coaches including former Purdue boss Gene Keady, a couple of IU athletic directors in Fred Glass and Rick Greenspan and more than a dozen former Indiana players. Many of them I interviewed on either May 8 or May 9 as I sat in a condo in Hilton Head and just cubby-holed myself away for a few days. And then others were sprinkled through June, July and even a couple in August as I was completing the project and was looking for specific quotes to fill specific holes.

Most of those interviews lasted 30 minutes or more and I tape recorded them and have gone back and listened to them several times. I must say there was some really incredible insight provided by some really solid sources. So I just want to say thanks to all of you collectively for agreeing to be a part of my latest project.

There are several people I would like to thank for all they do to help make my book writing experiences rewarding and meaningful. I'll begin with Holly Kondras, my book handler, who takes my writing and puts it in book form. She has also been a valuable friend in recent years with both advice and instruction on how to self-publish my books. This is the fourth book I've self-published and there's no way I could do it without her assistance. I wouldn't want to even try.

I want to thank Tom Doherty and his staff at Cardinal Publishing for their support as well. When I'm not using them as my publisher, I use them as my self-publishing distributor. I appreciate the things they do to get my books in front of the necessary consumers.

I want to thank my current employer, CNHI, and specifically my corporate boss Kayla Castille and my local boss, George Bremer, for giving me permission to continue to write my books. It's something I enjoy and since my last 10 books in a row have been on Indiana University football or basketball, I think it grows my brand and that of CNHI Sports Indiana.

I want to thank a few good friends who help me in different ways in the writing process. I'll start with my co-author on my other book that is being released this fall by Triumph Books out of Chicago titled, *An Indiana University Basketball Fan's Bucket List*. My co-author is Bill Murphy who has always been a delight to work with. We had talked over the years about doing a book together and I'm glad we did. I hope we can do another one sometime. I want to thank my pal Amy Coble at the IU Varsity Shop at Assembly Hall. She puts up with my warped sense of humor but has also been a valuable resource for both Bill and myself, allowing us to sign our books before most every home basketball game just outside the door to the Varsity Shop in the West Lobby of Assembly Hall. I love walking into the Varsity Shop and seeing seven or eight of my books on display. It makes it all worthwhile. I also want to thank my support group friends like Kirk Jenkins, Steve Sears, Brian Sears, Knute Lentz, Bob Boynton, Dave Lubovich, Dave Frey, Jerry York, Jeff Smith, Kevin Wyatt, Chris Smith, Dave Carter, Kevin Hunt, Dave Murphy, Bill Lorah, Dale Armbruster, Steve Demas, Tom Bertelotti, Matt Watson, Chris Barnes and Kevin Mulholland. You guys know how you support and I just want you to know I appreciate it.

I want to thank my cornerstone support group at home for all of their love and encouragement. That includes my wife, Susan, and my sons Bryan and Kevin. Thanks guys for bearing with me on all of my book projects that tend to consume a lot of time in the summer.

The last people I want to thank are the men who have Followed the General at Indiana. Mike Davis, Kelvin Sampson,

Dan Dakich, Tom Crean and Archie Miller. This book focuses mainly on Davis, Sampson, Crean and Miller but I make mention of Dakich's contributions in an interim role in 2008 as well. You may not agree with all of the opinions in this book. In fact, I'm sure you won't. Please understand though that I tried to be fair. The one thing I can say for all of you is you have been great coaches to work with and I appreciate the friendship we have built up over the years. Specifically to Archie Miller as he begins his first season in Bloomington, I look forward to working with you as well as I begin my 20th season covering Indiana University football and basketball in the fall of 2017.

Thanks everyone for your contributions in helping me tell the story of those who have Followed the General, Bob Knight, at Indiana.

Foreword
by Steve Lavin

When author Terry Hutchens initially approached me to write the foreword for his latest project, *Following the General*, I was intrigued with the opportunity yet interested to learn more of his thinking. Terry pointed out that in his view, my career experience following an iconic coach at UCLA shaped a timely perspective worth sharing for the foreword in this book given the subject matter is examining the daunting task basketball coaches face at Indiana University following in the footsteps of Bob Knight's larger than life legacy. After brief period deliberating I agreed to take my maiden voyage writing a foreword for *Following the General*.

FOLLOWING A COACHING WIZARD

From 1996-2003 I was head coach of the UCLA men's basketball team, making me the seventh successor in a line of Bruins coaches that have followed in the footsteps of icon John Robert Wooden.

Coaching at UCLA was an opportunity of a lifetime yet presented some inherently unique challenges, including being compared to the greatest coach in college basketball history.

For the sake of context, let's look back and consider Coach Wooden's astounding achievements as the Bruins coach of 27 years. He won 10 NCAA Titles over a 12 year period. Other notable accomplishments during Coach Wooden's dominating run include four undefeated seasons, a winning streak of 88

games, a record of 620-147 (.808), and seven consecutive seasons that concluded with a Bruins national title game victory.

After the most successful run in college basketball history, John Wooden retired in 1975. Since his retirement nine different successors have assumed the helm of the Bruins program. Each Coach that followed in Wooden's footsteps has been ushered in with hopes of returning the Bruins to the glory years of the 1960's and 1970's, yet predictably no successor has measured up to UCLA's unparalleled expectations.

Practicing and playing home games in Pauley Pavillon under the 11 National Championship banners that hang from the rafters above Nell and John Wooden Court serve as a constant reminder of the unprecedented standard of excellence all Bruins coaches are measured against.

From the time of John Wooden's retirement in 1975 up to his passing in 2010, he actively followed UCLA athletics. He especially enjoyed attending men's basketball games. Remarkably, in Coach Wooden's retirement he sat in the stands of Pauley Pavilion as a fan for 35 seasons - a longer period of time than the 27 seasons he sat on the bench directing the Bruins as head coach.

I can still vividly recall the palpable energy and buzz generated by Coach Wooden's arrival to Pauley Pavillon when attending home games. Once in the building, Coach and his daughter Nan would gradually make their way over to the aisle seats located directly behind our team's bench. Inevitably, adoring fans would line up to shake his hand, take photographs or get an autograph. Coach was most gracious with his time as he genuinely enjoyed engagement with people.

From a personal standpoint it was always a thrill to get the Coach Wooden good luck handshake or friendly wink, wave and nod from him just prior to Tipoff. This was Coach's authentic way of conveying he was rooting hard for our team to perform well. Those were just a few of the pinch me, am I awake or dreaming treasured moments from my time at UCLA.

Prior to my Bruins head coaching tenure I served as an assistant to Jim Harrick at UCLA. In 1995 Coach Harrick led our team to the National Championship and an overall record of 32-1. Incidentally, Jim Harrick is the only Bruins Head Coach other than John Wooden to have won a National Title at UCLA. Coach Harrick pushed all the right buttons in 1995 as our three Senior's Tyus Edney, Ed O'Bannon, and George Zidek provided inspiring play and outstanding leadership throughout a magical season that put the Bruins back on top of the College Basketball world.

In 1996 one year removed from an NCAA Championship and a National Coach of the Year Award Jim Harrick was fired. At the time of Coach Harrick's dismissal, I was the assistant with the most years of experience on staff at UCLA, consequently the administration elevated me to an "interim" head coach as the school began a national search for a permanent replacement.

Our team struggled on the court in the early stages of the 1996-97 season, as the firing of our leader Jim Harrick understandably created a period of emotional volatility contributing to a difficult transition for our entire basketball family.

By mid January of 1997 the staff and players began to exhibit a greater comfort level with one another, consequently we began to accumulate wins as our team climbed the PAC 10 conference standings. In February, with our team in first place, UCLA President Charles Young halted the national coaching search, lifted the "interim" tag and appointed me the schools 11th Men's Basketball Head Coach.

In retrospect, I now recognize it was a blessing that my appointment as a 32-year-old head coach happened in the midst of our season. There was no time to be overwhelmed with reflection or existential thinking as our team was performing well and had its sights set on a National Championship.

We continued our winning ways in February and March winning our final 11 games. Along the way we captured the PAC 10 championship and made a run to the NCAA Regional Final. Our season ended in the Elite 8 as we were defeated by the Minnesota Gophers at the Alamodome in San Antonio.

I'm especially grateful for the efforts of the 1996-97 team as it was the players and staffs efforts along with Coach Wooden's advocacy that led to me becoming head coach at UCLA for seven seasons.

During my tenure as Head Coach at UCLA our teams earned six consecutive NCAA tournament berths, including six straight seasons of 21 or more wins, five Sweet 16 appearances and an Elite 8. In my final season (2002-03) we had a losing record (10-19), therefore I was fired in March of 2003. I understood the schools decision as Final Four appearances and National Titles are the expectation at UCLA because Coach Wooden was able to deliver incomparable levels of achievement during his final 12 years as Head Coach.

I look back upon my time at UCLA most fondly and consider those twelve seasons on staff from 1991-2003 to be some of the best years in my life. I started on staff as an entry level volunteer coach then moved up the ranks to the third assistant to the second assistant to the first assistant to the "interim" Head Coach to the permanent Head Coach and eventually to the fired Head Coach. Serving in seven different roles within the same organization over a twelve year period shaped a helpful perspective forged by a bottom to the to the top and then to the chopping block journey.

One of the many memorable days spent with Coach Wooden took place shortly after I was fired by UCLA in the Spring of 2003. We had not had an opportunity to connect in person since before my termination. I drove out to Coach's apartment located in Encino on White Oak Boulevard to pick him up  before heading to an early dinner at Fromins Deli, one of his favorite haunts.

It was always good to spend time with Coach as he had a gift for teaching without preaching. We made small talk on the drive to Fromins. After arriving, being seated, and then ordering our food, Coach leaned over and said in a soft voice, "Steve, I want to share something with you, and my hope is you won't take this the wrong way. Only a former UCLA coach can fully appreciate what I'm about to share with you." Coach then paused, I can still picture him leaning toward me from across the table as his 92 year old piercing blue eyes were twinkling ever so brightly. Naturally, my mind was racing. 'Was there something down the stretch in my final weeks at UCLA, that I messed up? Did I say something in my final days to the press that had been less than exemplary?' Over my 12 years at UCLA Coach Wooden had shared so many helpful lessons that resonated in profound ways. 'Being humble in victory and gracious in defeat.' 'The most powerful form of teaching is rooted in one's actions and deeds - leading by example.' 'The best thing we can do for those we love is to not do for them what they are capable of doing for themselves.' These were a few of pearls of wisdom Coach had shared with me. I have a stack of yellow notepads containing his teachings, adages, observations and quotes from numerous meetings at his apartment. He was an awe inspiring human being.

So now here we are at Fromins Deli and I'm thinking during his pause, 'What did I do or say in my final days at UCLA to disappointment Coach Wooden?" The silence is deafening, his deadpan expression giving away no clues, he then smiles and says, "You're much better off!'' After a few seconds of processing, we both shared a hearty laugh. Coach had a knack for knowing just what to say at precisely the right moment. He had the perspective and foresight to realize my end at UCLA was actually a new beginning. At that moment Coach was a friend, mentor, teacher, and prophet. His wealth of knowledge appetite to learn more shaped a sage perspective and he truly enjoyed sharing his wisdom to help others navigate life's inevitable challenges.

A few weeks after the meeting at Fromins with Coach Wooden, Bruin alum Bill Walton reached out to me and asked if I was free to get together. Walton proceeded to invite me to go on an early morning Saturday walk on Venice Beach. The brisk paced walk and wonderfully eclectic and entertaining banter was a welcome diversion, as it served to my mind off of being out of work. At the conclusion of our walk, Walton shared that a colleague of his at ESPN/ABC named Mark Shapiro was hoping to meet with me to gauge my interest in working for the networks as a college basketball television analyst. I enthusiastically accepted the offer from ESPN/ABC and spent seven enjoyable years in broadcasting.

Ben Howland followed me at UCLA and his teams had a highly successful run, including three consecutive Final Four appearances. In fact, Coach Howland was fired in 2013 following a season his team earned a PAC-12 championship and berth in the NCAA tournament.

Interestingly, Howland's successor was Steve Alford who played basketball at Indiana University under Bob Knight. Alford is the ninth successor since John Wooden retired in 1975.

He has a uniquely informed perspective and expertise when it comes to the subject of coaching icons as he played for Bob Knight and now is working at UCLA in the shadows of John Wooden's unparalleled legacy. Coach Alford is winning, recruiting well, and his teams play an entertaining brand of basketball.

The decades pass but the refrain remains the same. Coach Wooden set an incomparable standard of achievement during his time at UCLA hence in some form or fashion his nine successors have come up short in the eyes of most fans, alums, administrators.

It's been 42 years (1975) since Coach Wooden retired from UCLA and seven years ago (2010) he passed.

I miss Coach Wooden too.

CHASING BOB KNIGHT

As a student-athlete attending Chapman University in the 1980's with aspirations to become a basketball coach, I began writing letters to college coaches throughout the country asking for career advice. Surprisingly Bob Knight, Gene Keady, Mike Krzyzewski, Tim Grgurich, Mike Legarza, and Mike Dunlap were coaches kind enough to respond with helpful direction. The aforementioned individuals helped encourage and fuel my dream to coach college basketball.

After corresponding for a year through letter writing Coach Knight was gracious enough to grant me access to sit in and observe Hoosiers practices, video sessions, and team meetings for a three week period during the 1987-88 season.

One of the highlights of my visit was sitting on the Hoosiers team bench at Assembly Hall for a game against the Michigan Wolverines at Assembly Hall. The all access experience of the seeing up close the pregame talk, fierce action on the court, halftime and timeout strategic adjustments was as good as it gets.

My experience at IU was crash course on coaching college basketball. Thankfully I was able to offset lodging expenses by sleeping on the couches of some hospitable IU players and managers. Long time stalwart athletic trainer Tim Garl, Craig Hartman, Brian Sloan, Kreigh Smith and Mike D'Alisio were especially helpful and hospitable.

At the time of my visit, Indiana University was defending National Champs and the Big Ten was in the midst of what most would consider a Golden Era of basketball for the conference.

I'm grateful for the opportunity to have been able to study Coach Knight and his staff's exceptional teaching methods. It was my time with the Hoosiers and subsequent inspiring visit that same season to observe Gene Keady's Purdue Boilermakers at work that served as a basketball baptism of sorts - a pivotal learning experience that was a catalyst for chasing the dream of becoming a Division 1 basketball coach.

Clearly, Indiana University holds a special place in the history of college basketball as Coach Knight achieved unparalleled success. Coach Knight's intellect, appreciation of history, gift for teaching, competitive drive and larger than life persona set him apart from most all peers of his generation. Three NCAA Titles, an Olympic Gold Medal, an NIT Championship and being inducted into the Hall of Fame.

When Indiana University parted ways with Bob Knight in 2000 it brought to a close one of the most successful tenures in the history of college basketball leaving a coaching legacy behind that no subsequent Hoosier coach has been able to live up to.

THOSE WHO HAVE FOLLOWED

Mike Davis, Kelvin Sampson and Tom Crean were the first three coaches at IU to follow Bob Knight.

Archie Miller is the fourth Coach and most recent to follow in Knights footsteps, taking the helm at IU in March of 2017.

Miller has a tremendous basketball pedigree. He checks all the boxes when considering the traits of successful coaches. He is an outstanding teacher, strong tactician, diligent recruiter and has a natural engaging manner when communicating with people.

Miller was able to refine his craft as Head Coach at Dayton and his efforts led to a very successful run, elevating the Flyers to one of the country's elite mid major programs.

Miller is a terrific hire and will be an outstanding fit at IU. He has the talent, skill, work ethic and ideal temperament to lead the Hoosiers back to sustained national prominence.

1

Following a Legend

There is nothing remotely easy about following a legend.

Whenever a coach is asked to follow in the footsteps of one of the great coaches in the game, the odds are just stacked incredibly high against him. There are always going to be endless comparisons. And basically anything short of winning a national championship – and quickly – is going to be unacceptable.

CBS Sports college basketball analyst Clark Kellogg said following someone like Bob Knight was even a greater challenge than most because of the way Knight was put on a pedestal in the state of Indiana.

"I don't know if there was ever going to be a natural fit to follow someone like coach Knight because he was so unique and so beloved and in some ways polarizing but by and large was revered and worshipped in Indiana," Kellogg said. "It was to a level that would probably be comparable to Woody Hayes at Ohio State in football. It's just a little bit beyond the norm and in many ways not rational.

"Anybody following that type of personality, that type of successful leader, that type of well-respected coach is going to always run into the inevitable and impossible comparisons."

Zach Osterman, the IU beat writer for the *Indianapolis Star*, questioned how often does it ever work, especially in college, that a coach can immediately successfully follow a legend.

"It just rarely works," Osterman said. "Perhaps you can point to Alabama football as a success story as a program that can't get it back until they get a guy who was so strong willed on his own. Nobody says Nick Saban is doing it Bear Bryant's way."

And he's right. Alabama may indeed be the case study that Indiana ultimately follows. Paul 'Bear' Bryant left the school in 1982 and it really wasn't until Nick Saban came on board in 2007 that the Crimson Tide got their guy.

In between, you had a plethora of coaches. Ray Perkins, Bill Curry, Gene Stallings, Mike DuBose, Dennis Franchione, Mike Price and Mike Shula. And those coaches had successes but it took a strong personality like that of Saban to really allow him to establish his own identity at Alabama and put the Tide back on the pedestal the program believes it should enjoy.

And there are other examples, too. Kentucky basketball has had a lot of pretty good coaches since Adolph Rupp left the program in 1972. But John Calipari, since arriving in 2009, has seemed to take things to a different level.

"And nobody is saying John Calipari is doing it Adolph Rupp's way," Osterman added. "You almost have to go find someone is so strong of a personality that they can do it their own way instead of constantly trying to measure up to the legend."

At Indiana, it almost wasn't fair that Mike Davis was "the guy" to follow Knight. And the others who have tried – Kelvin Sampson, Dan Dakich (for seven games) and Tom Crean – have had limited success but have been unable to maintain it over an extended period of time.

"It's just almost a given that when you follow a legend that that's just not going to be a successful transition," said IU basketball historian Bill Murphy.

Steve Alford once said that he didn't want to be the coach that followed Bob Knight at Indiana. He wanted to be the coach who followed the coach that followed Bob Knight.

And it makes sense. Rarely do things go well for a coach who follows a legend.

It was certainly the script that played out for Mike Davis at Indiana.

Depending on how you look at it, Davis was either in the wrong place at the wrong time or vice versa. He was in his third season as an assistant on Knight's Indiana staff when Knight was dismissed by the university.

When that dismissal took place in early September, five weeks before the first official day of practice and almost two months to the date when Indiana would open the season against Pepperdine in the preseason NIT, Indiana had to act fast in bringing on a replacement.

Enter Mike Davis into the picture and a six-year attempt at following a legend was about to begin.

• • • • •

It wasn't the first time that an IU basketball coach had attempted to follow a legend.

It had happened at least one other time and an argument could be made for two times.

But let's have a quick IU basketball history lesson here.

Everett Dean got Indiana basketball on the map in the 1920's and 30's. When he left following the 1938 season, Dean was Indiana's all-time winningest coach with a 162-93 record.

The next coach, however, would be the first to take on what I would term "legendary" status as the head coach of the Hoosiers. Branch McCracken, the IU coach who helped hang the school's first two national championship banners in 1940 and 1953, would spend 24 seasons on the Hoosier Hardwood. His final season was 1964-65 and IU was 19-5 that year.

Whenever I need to be educated on some IU basketball history, especially pre-Bob Knight, I go to my good friend and co-author of my other book out in the fall of 2017, *An Indiana Hoosiers Bucket List*. Bill wrote a book on Branch McCracken

3

entitled *Branch* and he's my go-to author for IU basketball history questions.

"People tend to think of history as something that happened in the last five years," Murphy said. "They don't seem to look at the whole scope of things."

That may be the high school history teacher in him talking there, too, but the point is a valid one. And when you look at Indiana basketball history though, you'll find that IU pre-Everett Dean wasn't very good. They never could hold a candle to rivals like Purdue or Butler in particular. But the Dean era changed all of that. Dean led IU to its first ever co-Big Ten title in 1926. He would end up leading Indiana to two more Big Ten crowns.

Next up was Branch McCracken, who came to IU for the 1938-39 season after spending eight seasons as the head coach at Ball State. Much like Bob Knight would do thirty plus years later, McCracken brought in a new offense. It was a run-and-gun style offense with lots of movement up and down the court.

"Branch did that because he thought for one the easiest way to score was on layups and the other was that basketball was supposed to be entertaining to the fans," Murphy said. "It was a big hit right away and very entertaining. People loved the Hurryin' Hoosiers."

Murphy said McCracken had a basic philosophy and one that has been successful when used by others, including Bob Knight, over the years.

"Branch's philosophy was to get good kids, to get Indiana kids and to have this fast break style of basketball that in many ways revolutionized the game of basketball at that particular time," Murphy said. "I think the thing that made Branch so successful is that he recognized that Indiana was a hot bed of talent, that kids played harder for their state school and then he used his offensive system that utilized high percentage shots but also in getting quick offense and quick shots."

When McCracken left IU following the 1964-65 season, the next coach up was Lou Watson. Had Bill Murphy wrote this book, he might have called it Following the *General and the Sheriff* as that was McCracken's nickname.

Murphy said that Watson was well received by the Hoosier faithful despite not having head coaching experience. Clearly it was a different time than when Davis replaced Knight but also a completely different set of circumstances. McCracken left on his terms and Knight did not.

"Everybody was happy when Lou Watson was hired to replace Branch," Murphy said. "But it was a different time. College basketball at that time was still college basketball. Today, college basketball to me if I had to define it would be almost semi-pro. They don't get paid but it's a business.

"Branch McCracken said he wanted Lou Watson to be his successor and so he was. That's what was done back then. And so everybody was fine with it."

I must admit I found a lot of interesting similarities between the guys that have followed let's say three legends at Indiana – Everett Dean, Branch McCracken and Bob Knight.

The three men who have followed them in order were McCracken, Lou Watson and Mike Davis.

So here's the first interesting comparison one that can be made comparing Branch McCracken and Mike Davis. Now there probably wouldn't be a lot of comparisons made between the two overall, and I'm not saying that. McCracken won 249 more games than Davis did in his career. And when they followed legends at IU, McCracken had been a head coach at Ball State for eight seasons and Davis was about to begin his first head coaching job.

Still, a great comparison can be made between the two if you look at their second seasons on the job.

In McCracken's second season, in 1939-40, Indiana won its first national championship. Conversely, in his second season in Bloomington, Davis took the Hoosiers to the national

IU President Myles Brand, Vice President Terry Clapacs and Indiana coach Mike Davis on the day Davis was named the IU coach. In the back to the left is assistant coach John Treloar and in the middle is IU athletic director Michael McNeely. Behind Davis is his wife Tamilya.

championship game in 2002. IU didn't win but it played for the title that year.

I just have to wonder if anyone said back then that McCracken won the title with Everett Dean's players? (Sorry I couldn't resist that one). The truth, however, is that the leading scorer for McCracken that title year was All-American Marv Huffman who was a senior. And as a sophomore, he had indeed played for Everett Dean.

The next interesting comparison that I find is between Lou Watson and Mike Davis.

Both had been assistant coaches for the coach they ultimately replaced. Watson had been an assistant for McCracken for 10 seasons and Davis had been on Bob Knight's IU staff for three seasons.

Another thing that they had in common was that both ended up coaching six seasons in their attempts at following a legend.

Davis was more successful than Watson, though as the latter had four losing seasons in his first five. Davis, on the other hand, made the NCAA Tournament in four of six seasons.

The third and final legend following comparison would be Lou Watson and Tom Crean.

This is more of an indirect comparison though as Crean was a few coaches removed from following Bob Knight but the situation is still interesting.

Everyone knows the mess that Crean inherited when Sampson was fired and Dan Dakich cleaned house before he left the building and kicked a few players off the team that were arguably bad eggs in Jamarcus Ellis and Armon Bassett. Basically, Crean returned two players from the year before. Kyle Taber, a former walk-on who had earned a scholarship the year before, and walk-on Brett Finkelmeier. Taber had scored 28 points the year before and Finkelmeier had scored two.

That means Indiana had 30 points returning from a team that scored 2,476 the year before.

Lou Watson had similar issues with the team that Branch McCracken had ended his career with. But his losses were all due to graduation. Still, McCracken's final team went 19-5 and was considered one of the best in the nation. But he had seven seniors on that team. And when the players returned the following season for Watson, they returned a total of 154 from a team that scored 2,200 the year before.

So Indiana went 25-8 the year before Crean came on board to a shell of that team. Crean's first year IU was 6-25. McCracken's final team went 19-5 and Watson's first squad went 8-16. So Watson followed the legend and Crean did so indirectly as the third coach to follow Bob Knight.

Watson's final season was 1971 when the Hoosiers, thanks mostly to All-American George McGinnis, went 17-7.

IU's coach that followed Watson? Bob Knight.

But as I said, like Watson, Davis would spend six seasons attempting to fill shoes that were several sizes too big. He would win 53 more games than Watson did but he would fail in one specific category: Like Watson, Davis was unable to bring Indiana basketball back to a sustained level of success. Yes, he had one great year where the Hoosiers came within one game of hanging the elusive sixth national championship banner. But he also had back-to-back seasons where Indiana finished 14-15 and 15-14.

And at a school where making the NCAA Tournament had become a given under Bob Knight, mediocrity – even for just a season or two – would never be acceptable.

• • • • •

Former IU athletic director Rick Greenspan, who wasn't the athletic director at the beginning of Davis's tenure but was at the end, had a real interesting take on Davis.

"Mike Davis was fired the day he was hired," Greenspan said. "And I'm not sure that Mike didn't know that as well as anybody."

Greenspan said Davis just had challenges that no one else has had since.

"He was probably in the most challenging position of anybody that I could think of off the top of my head that followed a legend," Greenspan said. "He was hired in a crisis process, following a guy who didn't want to leave and a man who had a tremendous following in the state. And IU hired a guy who had never been a head coach or had experienced that level of scrutiny and accountability and expectations and quite honestly let's face it, he was a black guy in the state of Indiana.

"You put all of those things together at that time and I think you've got a remarkable deck stacked against you."

But Greenspan echoed comments made by many others when talking about Davis being in that position.

"So if you're Mike Davis how do you not accept that job?" Greenspan said. "Without being political but in some ways the best analogy I can think of is that you hire a guy that has no experience, has never been a military leader and never been a politician and all of a sudden you say, 'Hey, do you want to be president and then almost in the same breath, how are you going to handle this thing in North Korea?"

Don Fischer, the longtime play-by-play voice of Indiana football and basketball, said Davis simply had one major thing working against him that there was no way that he could ever get past.

"Mike was dealing with the fact that he was following a legend," Fischer said. "It's pretty simple. He was the first guy to follow a legend that in many people's minds was fired without good reason."

Indianapolis Star IU beat writer Zach Osterman said he felt that because of the way Davis came into the job, he never really had a chance to create his own identity.

"There just always seemed to be the feeling with Mike that that ghost of coach Knight was never going to leave him or whoever was in the job at that time," Osterman said.

Piggybacking off of Alford's comment about no one wanting to be the guy that followed Knight, former IU All-American Brian Evans said it really was as simple as no one really wanted to be first in that race.

"I just think (Davis) was thrown into one of the toughest jobs ever," Evans said. "Look at all the people and some of the great names that followed John Wooden at UCLA. I think following somebody like Coach as the university kind of decompresses from everything that was happening, can you imagine being a first time coach and doing it at that program?

"It's borderline not fair."

When John Wooden left UCLA, Gene Bartow was the next man up. He lasted 28 months and actually took the Bruins to a Final Four but the pressure of following Wooden was very real. And unlike Davis, Bartow at least had some Division I college head coaching experience before he followed the Wizard of Westwood. Bartow had been the head coach at Central Missouri State, Valparaiso, Memphis and Illinois before he headed West to take on the biggest of challenges in following Wooden.

In a 2010 interview with the Associated Press, Bartow spoke of the pressure that he faced as the UCLA coach.

"At UCLA, every time you lost it was a major catastrophe, so that was different than what I had at Memphis or anywhere I'd been," Bartow said.

He eventually left for a combo athletic director/head basketball coaching position at Alabama-Birmingham. At the time, the move gave him a considerable pay bump but more than that he was able to emerge from the shadow of Wooden.

Bartow went on to compile a record of 366-203 in 17 seasons at UAB. But when you mention Bartow's name it's often first associated as the man who followed Wooden.

And UCLA has had a total of nine coaches, as of the writing of this book, who have tried to follow the legendary Wooden. One of those was Steve Lavin, a former Purdue Indiana assistant under Gene Keady who coached the Bruins from 1996-2003.

There are other examples, too.

When Dean Smith left North Carolina after 36 seasons, he was replaced by Bill Guthridge, who had been on Smith's staff as an assistant for 30 years. He spent three seasons as head coach before retiring in 2000. That was a little different because in many ways Guthridge was an extension of Smith. It wasn't until Carolina hired Matt Doherty in 2000 that it experienced what it was like to truly follow the legendary Smith.

Doherty, who had played for Smith, was seen as the kind of person that could help get Carolina basketball back to the rich tradition it had enjoyed for so many years. But after three seasons, Doherty ultimately resigned after feeling incredible pressure on and off the court to uphold the Carolina tradition of success.

In Doherty's final two seasons with North Carolina, the Tar Heels failed to reach the NCAA Tournament or win 20 games.

The pressure to succeed a legend was simply too much.

It will be the same challenge facing whoever ultimately follows Mike Krzykewski at Duke or now Roy Williams at North Carolina.

The bottom line is that it's an impossible situation.

It was definitely an impossible situation at Indiana where Knight had just been dismissed after 29 seasons as the head coach. It didn't help that Knight wasn't able to leave on his own terms either and resented the way that Myles Brand and the IU administration relieved him of his duties.

That's another great difference between the coaches who tried to follow Wooden at UCLA and those who tried to follow Knight. At UCLA, the followers had Wooden's support and he was around and there wasn't a negative shadow in the background. At Indiana, Knight wanted nothing to do with anything IU and went out of his way to shun the Hoosiers at every opportunity. Not having that kind of support just made the transition that much more difficult.

I asked Jon Crispin, an analyst with the Big Ten, that very question. Crispin played two seasons at UCLA under Steve Lavin. I asked him if you could somehow feel Wooden's presence in the building back then much like Indiana basketball fans seem to talk at times about the ghost of Bob Knight in Assembly Hall.

"The difference is this," Crispin said. "I've always been a fan of Bob Knight but he's partially responsible for this. John

11

Wooden was able to alleviate a lot of that pressure (on future coaches). He was able to do so because he was present. Because he was there and said, 'I fully support Steve Lavin.' They would talk a lot. He would come to our games. He spoke to us at practice. We really all got to know him. It was great.

"But he never undermined the coach. He never had a negative influence on our program or on any aspect of it."

Crispin said that's clearly the big difference between following a legend at UCLA and trying to do so at Indiana.

"That's the biggest difference," Crispin said. "Bob Knight is not around to show support for whoever is there. He's not around to say, 'Hey guys what they're doing right now is really what it takes.' He's not going to say that. So right now it's really just new coaches coming in trying to live in this glorified version of the past. That's all it is."

Perhaps, but there is one big difference between John Wooden at UCLA and Bob Knight at Indiana — Wooden left on his own terms. Knight was shown the door. Now, am I of the opinion that Knight should bury the hatchet and come back to receive his due from the Indiana fans that continue to worship him? Absolutely. I used to always say that if they were ever to have an event like that, they should really hold it in a building like Lucas Oil Stadium that could manage the mass of people that would show up.

But as time has gone on and Knight has continued to come off more and more as simply a bitter old man, I've wondered if Assembly Hall would be about the right size venue for something like that. And there might be some empty seats, too. Not sure how many people would sit in the balcony for that for example.

•••••

Still, at his greatest time, when Knight was roaming the sidelines in Bloomington the state of Indiana in many ways belonged to Bob Knight. If you didn't live in Indiana or weren't closely familiar with the program, it's hard to comprehend the lofty place Knight occupied within the state's borders.

But it was iconic-like. For 29 years, Bob Knight WAS Indiana Basketball.

He was the face of the program. Sometimes a good face and other times a not so good face. But always THE face.

With Bob Knight as IU's pilot, you knew a few things would happen:

- His team would always be well prepared for every game it played
- They would do the little things well
- Kids in the state wanted to play at Indiana
- He would follow the rules
- He would graduate his players
- And year in and year out, Indiana would represent on the basketball floor

The reality is they were simple premises but something Indiana basketball fans everywhere took for granted. But in their defense, why wouldn't you? When you reach a certain level of success, you simply expect your team to be in the winner's circle each and every season.

It's the same situation in place today for fans at Duke, North Carolina, Kentucky and Kansas. The rare exception to the rule is that one of those teams will be on the outside looking in come tournament time. They have all reached the mountain top and are in no hurry to come back down.

Indiana was in their company once but has slipped down the side of that mountain.

Back in Knight's days at IU, the NCAA Tournament was pretty much a given. Knight's final 15 seasons at Indiana, the Hoosiers were in the Big Dance every year. That was true in 20 of his final 21 seasons and 24 years overall. Indiana put up national championship banners three times under Knight – 1976, 1981 and 1987.

13

But again, if you were an Indiana basketball fan you did not tune into the NCAA Tournament Selection show worrying about whether your team was going to be in the field or not. Instead, you tuned in curious to see what your seed would be and whether or not your first round site would be somewhere you could find a way to travel to and see the game in person. Often times, you were expecting to have to do some research on whatever double-digit seed you were about to face in the Dance.

That was the life of an Indiana University basketball fan.

Most years, Indiana was a No. 8 seed or better. Only once under Knight – in 1995 – were the Hoosiers outside of the top 8 and that season the Hoosiers were No. 9.

Indiana had good players during that time. Make no mistake about that. Guys like Kent Benson, Quinn Buckner, Scott May and company were dominant names in the mid-70's. A few years later it was Mike Woodson and then players like Isiah Thomas, Ted Kitchel, Randy Wittman, Ray Tolbert and Landon Turner.

The next grouping had household names in the state of Indiana like Steve Alford, Keith Smart, Dean Garrett, Ricky Calloway, Eric Anderson and Jay Edwards. In the 1990's it was Calbert Cheaney, Alan Henderson, Damon Bailey, Brian Evans, Greg Graham and Andrae Patterson. Later it was A.J. Guyton and Luke Recker toward the end of Knight's Indiana career.

But the constant throughout was the General himself resided in Bloomington – Bob Knight.

To repeat an early point, the reality is that to many people Bob Knight WAS Indiana Basketball.

If you went to an IU game at Assembly Hall, your attention span was split between two spots. You would watch the action on the floor but at the same time you always had an eye trained on Knight, looking for a reaction. If someone made a careless pass, you glanced over at Knight to see what he might do. If someone made a hot dog play (which they rarely did out of

14

fear for their lives) and you sensed that the General might not like it, you were quick to check it out. If an official made a bad call, everyone would look at Knight to see what he might do.

If the official was Ted Valentine or Ed Hightower or any number of old school conference referees, you might even watch Knight more than you watched the flow of the game.

But that was the impact that Bob Knight had on Indiana basketball. In many ways, he was larger than life. He truly deserves the legend moniker.

In fact, when Knight was ultimately dismissed in September of 2000 by then Indiana University president Myles Brand, there were a lot of Indiana basketball fans that had to answer a simple question in their minds: Were they truly Indiana fans or were they really more Bob Knight fans? In other words, would they be happy to follow the Hoosiers no matter who the next coach would be, or would they be more apt to find a way to watch Texas Tech play so they could watch the General roam the sidelines?

For many, it was not an easy decision (partly because Texas Tech wasn't on TV as much). Some believed they were truly IU fans but after a few seasons of watching the product on the floor changed their mind and found other things to do on the nights that Indiana played basketball. Some continued to follow IU but just opted to bitch about it year after year when expectations fell short and the level of coaching wasn't as high as it once had been.

But make no mistake, there was truly a great divide. Indiana Basketball became a fractured fan base. That fracture was trumpeted and exposed even more by the onslaught of different social media platforms that didn't exist when Knight was the coach at IU. Still, it was a difficult time for those who had bought all-in to the game that Knight was coaching.

To this day, it's always interesting when as an Indiana fan you encounter what I would call a non-Indiana fan on the street

Quinn Buckner (left) and Scott May (right), members of the unbeaten 1976 national champions, converse with Bob Knight during practice.

and you happen to be wearing something that identifies you as being a follower of the Hoosiers.

In that instance, what does an IU fan hear?

Someone might mention the nickname "Hoosiers" as to non-IU fans, it's a name that some people just like to say. They may even say "Hoosier Daddy?" or something along that line.

They could mention a former player but they usually don't. If you're wearing candy-striped warm up pants, which a lot of true IU fans do, there may be a reference to that. Or if it's clear that you're an IU basketball fan by something you're wearing, someone could mention the five national championships or specifically the unbeaten 1976 IU Hoosiers, who as of 2017 were still the last unbeaten national champion in history.

A true historian of the game might say something about Keith Smart's shot to beat Syracuse for the 1987 national championship, or younger fans may remember Christian Watford's shot in 2011 that knocked off No. 1 Kentucky. That memory is imbedded in the minds of a generation of young people because it was played a zillion times on ESPN for more than a year.

But in terms of percentages, you would have a smattering of people who might mention one of those examples from above.

And then about 90 percent will always mention Bob Knight, or Bobby Knight as many will say.

They won't mention Branch McCracken unless they are really old and that's too bad because McCracken had a profound early effect on Indiana basketball, too. He was the man responsible for the first two IU NCAA basketball championship banners.

No, the majority of people who think of Indiana basketball also think of Bob Knight.

Now, they may think of him throwing the chair, or grabbing Neil Reed by the throat or any number of countless explosions he had in press conferences or on the court with officials.

The point is that Knight has always been a larger than life personality when associated with his 29 seasons at Indiana from 1971-2000.

Whenever someone like that leaves their former school, there's always a buzz as to who will be the next coach to follow in his footsteps. This is true whether it's on that coach's own terms for guys like John Wooden at UCLA or Dean Smith at North Carolina, or on someone else's terms for people like Joe Paterno at Penn State or Woody Hayes at Ohio State.

Bob Knight would be in the second category, too, but for an entirely different set of circumstances. He was the beloved coach, who went about his business the right way, graduated his players, ran a clean program but ultimately was let go for what Brand termed "uncivil, defiant and unacceptable behavior."

But once that legend is gone, and the university attempts to move on with a new coach, that's when things really get interesting. Often times, the expectations are lofty and in some cases completely unattainable. The reality is that in some cases those expectations aren't just on the first person that followed the legend but for many years after that. Basically, until someone comes in and achieves close to the same level of success as the legend, then the ghost or shadow of the legend will always loom large over the program.

That's the case still today at Indiana. Bob Knight has been gone for 17 years as of the time of the writing of this book in 2017, and yet some people haven't let go.

• • • • •

Mike Davis was the first to attempt it, but as I wrote about earlier in the chapter, Indiana should never be your first head coaching job. And despite one year where he almost reached the promised land, the Davis years were pretty uneventful.

"I think Mike just maybe had too much early success," said IU basketball historian Bill Murphy. "That second year and going where they did it just kept going downhill from there. And then I just think Davis just couldn't recruit good enough classes. The thing we kept always hearing with Mike was 'Help is on the way,' 'Help is on the way.' And he just couldn't keep it going."

Kelvin Sampson turned out to be the epic fail but just because he cheated. His two seasons as coach resulted in NCAA Tournament appearances. If he just could have followed the rules and kept his nose clean there are a lot of people, several who were interviewed for this book, that believe IU would now be in search of seventh or eighth national championship banner. Just in terms of being a great coach, Sampson may be the best that Indana has had in the post-Knight era.

Murphy certainly believes that to be true.

"Sampson was a good coach," Murphy said. "Sampson, had he not cheated, and had he recruited the right kids he could have still be there today and IU could have had a successful run. He won 21 and 25 games and finished third in the Big Ten both years.''

Dan Dakich took over for seven games to fill out Sampson's second season but he was never a permanent Indiana head coach and so doesn't get a lot of air time in this book. Some will argue that Indiana has had four head coaches since Knight, and five when you count the hiring of Archie Miller in March of 2017. But this is where I disagree and have a different take. When I think of the coaches that have followed Bob Knight at Indiana I think of the ones who actually had a chance to return Indiana basketball to a sustained level of success.

Mike Davis had that chance. He coached 194 games in six seasons as the Indiana head coach, winning 115 of them. Kelvin Sampson had that chance, too, but because of his own indiscretions left Indiana after 58 games and before his second full season was up. The third coach, Tom Crean, had nine seasons to return Indiana basketball to that sustained level of success but he was ultimately unable to have the consistency required by those making the decisions on who should be the IU coach.

Dan Dakich was the IU coach for seven games. Five in the regular season where he closed the Big Ten schedule by winning three of the last five. Indiana, despite being a No. 3 seed, had a quick cup of coffee in the Big Ten Tournament and lost in the first round thanks to a shot by Minnesota's Blake Hofarber at the buzzer and then the Hoosiers advanced to the NCAA Tournament as a No. 8 seed. There, in Raleigh, N.C., Indiana played No. 9 seed Arkansas on March 21 and lost in the first round, 86-72. Twelve days later, athletic director Rick Greenspan thanked Dakich for his service and hired Tom Crean as the next Indiana basketball coach.

But my point with Dakich is that unlike the other three coaches that I focus on in this book, he never had a chance to turn the Indiana program around. He did his service which was to finish out the season. He was basically a caretaker for

19

the program until someone else was hired. His entire time as IU's interim coach lasted 39 days. Sure, he did some things that he deserves credit for, too. He kept the program together at a difficult time. And then he made some tough decisions with a couple of players that were bold moves at the time but needed to be done. Dakich did everything he was supposed to do. He coached the seven games and he tried to show Greenspan that he was the right guy to take over, and ultimately the IU athletic director decided otherwise and hired Crean. But Dakich never had a real chance to turn Indiana around and thus I believe it's difficult to offer much analysis to his brief stint as the IU head coach.

With each of the other three, there is simply enough of a body of work to properly analyze what worked and what didn't work in their time trying to bring Indiana basketball back to relevance again.

After Dakich's interim stint, the third permanent IU coach was Tom Crean, the man credited for cleaning up Sampson's mess and getting Indiana Basketball back on the map again. His first three years were building the Hoosiers back and his last six were a combination of a huge high when IU was the No. 1 overall seed in the NCAA Tournament to a couple of lows – one where IU missed out on the tournament all together and another where it bowed out in the first round of the NIT.

Of all the coaches who have followed Knight, Crean is the one who came the closest. Two outright Big Ten championships in a four year span and three trips to the Sweet Sixteen are pretty good on a resume over his final six seasons. But while the highs were plenty high, the lows were simply too low. And ultimately that led to a change.

And so you had three coaches who all set out with the greatest of aspirations to be THE GUY that made people not think as much about Knight. I won't go as far as to say that they would be THE GUY that made people forget coach Knight. That will never happen at IU and it shouldn't. Knight achieved a sustained level of winning year after year and he did it the right way. No cheating, good fundamental basketball, he graduated his players and had players that were not only good on the basketball court but also in the class room and in representing themselves well in the community.

And as 2017 begins, the fourth coach, Archie Miller, will attempt to do what the first three were unable to accomplish – get Indiana basketball back to a sustained level of winning. Can he do it? There are a lot of people who think he has a good shot because of his basketball pedigree and what he did at the University of Dayton in making that program one that was in the national consciousness in Division I basketball. Only time will tell, but Miller will be the fourth contender – the fifth if you count Dakich – to return Indiana basketball to that sustained level of winning.

And let's talk about that sustained level for a moment, too. In order to properly write a book like this, we need a definition for a sustained level of success at Indiana.

Because as many people will point out, Knight's last six seasons at the University were much different than his first 23. In those last six seasons he never made it out of the second game of the NCAA Tournament and never out of the first weekend and on to the Sweet Sixteen. His NCAA Tournament record in those final six seasons was 2-6.

Still, there were several points that still occurred that make up the definition of a sustained level of success. They would include:

- Indiana made it to the NCAA Tournament each of those years
- Indiana always finished at .500 or better in Big Ten play in each of those years
- Indiana won at least 19 games in each of those seasons
- The players followed a system and executed that system

- Defense and valuing the basketball were significant elements in the process
- Players graduated and there were no significant off-the-court problems like you would find with future IU teams
- IU teams generally had a state of Indiana flavor to them
- Indiana basketball was viewed as being one of the blueblood programs in college basketball. It was considered right up there with North Carolina, Duke, Kansas and Kentucky

Part of the proof of that success was that Indiana basketball fans never had to give Selection Sunday a second thought. They always knew they would be in the tournament.

But that was also back at a time when a true legend was roaming the sidelines in Bloomington. And in the 17 years that have followed, a handful of guys have tried to get Indiana basketball back to that sustained level of winning and have yet to make it happen.

Will Archie Miller be the guy that becomes the exception? Only time will tell.

2

What Made Bob Knight So Successful at Indiana?

If you were to ask a dozen people what they thought was the primary reason Bob Knight's teams were so successful at Indiana University, you might get 12 different answers.

The media perspective might be much different than what you would hear from those who participated in Knight's practices every day. The view of an opposing coach might be very different from what one of Knight's own assistants might think.

But you hear common themes. You hear about how prepared Knight's teams always were for an opponent. You hear how Knight didn't always have the greatest players but how his players were able to function as one within his system and become a great team. You hear that he had a simplistic approach to the game that was built on a repetition of fundamentals and being able to read and react both offensively and defensively within the structure of his system. You hear that recruiting came very easy for Knight, especially in the state of Indiana where players felt as if it were an honor to head to Bloomington and play for The General.

They are all good points and all valid ones. The truth is that Knight's success in 29 seasons at Indiana came from a variety of different reasons.

But it all began with a simple approach. And there were two things within that simplicity that stood out above the rest: Playing good defense and running the motion offense.

Do those two things to the best of your ability and you'd have a good chance to be successful. Different Knight teams at Indiana were known for different things but they all were known for being able to play good defense and for running the motion offense effectively.

Steve Risley played for Knight from 1978-81. He was a senior when the Hoosiers won the second of Knight's three national championships. He said the blueprint for Knight's success at Indiana was the repetition, the attention to detail and the simplicity of his approach.

"Coach Knight's theory was that he would rather be great at two things than good at a bunch of things," Risley said. "I don't think it was ever any secret that we were going to play man-to-man defense and we were going to run motion offense."

For Indiana basketball players everything was a product of repetition. The basic principles of the motion offense and man-to-man defense became a fabric of their lives. Over and over they would do drills to where they could do everything they needed to do in their sleep. And they were a lot better at doing it than opponents were at stopping it.

Indiana became fundamentally sound every season at switching, being in defensive position, blocking out, ball transition, ball denial in the passing lanes, setting screens, running off of screens and the list goes on and on. It may sound like basic stuff but IU celebrated the fact that it could do the basics better than an opponent.

"We were so proficient at doing those things that it didn't matter that you knew what we were doing because we were better at doing it than you could ever get to be at stopping us," Risley said. "And the reality is that we knew that you would never spend the amount of time necessary to be good enough to stop us."

Indianapolis sports talk radio show host Kent Sterling said he thought Knight and UCLA's John Wooden had similarities in their approach to the game.

"With coach Knight it was all about simplicity," Sterling said. "I feel like Knight's system was similar to John Wooden's approach and that's that he preached to kids to do the same things, the same way every time. So you ran motion and you ran man and that's all you had to be great at. I think it's really difficult to be great at something unless you do it exclusively.

"And I think that also helped his recruiting. He didn't have to recruit a kid who could play a zone well. He was trying to recruit good man-to-man defenders and that's what Indiana was."

Bob Lovell, who spent 12 seasons as the head basketball coach at IUPUI from 1982-93 back when they were the Metros, agreed that with Knight it was all about his system. And Lovell said there were no surprises.

"His system was predicated on he was going to outwork his opponents and he was going to take care of the things he could take care of," Lovell said. "Indiana wasn't going to turn the ball over, they were going to get on the glass and they were going to defend. And back then you worked to get the best shot without worrying about a shot clock. You were going to get the best shot however long it might take.

"Because it was that simple, Knight was able to go to practice and just focus on those things. He was a taskmaster, everybody knew that. But what the players came to realize, too, is that they didn't want to disappoint him and that can be a big motivator."

Risley said the standard was man-to-man defense and motion offense but with every opponent IU played there were variations of it.

"Like obviously somebody would read where (Steve) Alford was going to come off a screen shoulder to shoulder every time," Risley said. "Teams would watch film and they would figure that out. And then (Knight) would run variations coming off a screen.

25

"That's where Knight was a master in a way that Tom Crean could never be," Risley said. "He could make deviations and changes like that within a 30-second timeout. And he could pick up on what they were doing instantly. With Bob Knight every timeout was a working timeout. There were so many times when I would see teams especially in the Crean era when it wasn't a working timeout. It was just a timeout to slow momentum. But under Knight every timeout was a working timeout. That's why Knight didn't waste a lot of timeouts because he didn't see the need to call one because there was nothing to work on at that point and time."

Talk to players who played for Knight at Indiana and one thing you hear over and over is the simplistic nature of the way Knight wanted to do things.

When you think of Knight, most people think of this complex basketball mind that was always thinking one or two steps ahead of his opponent. He was a strategist. Basketball was a chess game and Knight was making all the right moves. He was pushing the right buttons and then his vision for what he wanted his team to be was playing out before his eyes.

Don Fischer, the voice of Indiana basketball for all but two of Knight's 29 seasons at Indiana, saw it more up close and personal than most. For 27 seasons, Fischer did a pregame show with Knight for every game he coached at IU. He also had a weekly radio show with The General.

"If you could get past some of the comments that he would make to you about how stupid you were about the game, you could really figure out how smart he was about it," Fischer said with a chuckle. "If you could separate those feelings and just listen to what he was telling you, he was just brilliant in regard to coaching. He was just a guy that you had to revere whether you liked him personally or not. You had to revere his abilities as a basketball coach and his understanding of the game."

The General – Robert Montgomery Knight

It was easy to walk away from dealings with Knight feeling as if you had been in the presence of the smartest guy in the room but often it was the simplest of techniques and philosophies that made Knight so successful at Indiana.

Kirk Haston, who played on Knight's final teams at IU, likened Knight's system to that of a golfer who doesn't have to worry when he's on the driving range about his swing but rather can focus on the more specific details and shots to make his game better.

"When I know I don't have to worry about my full swing, I can go out and practice at the golf course and I can work on a flop shot, or I can work on a bunker shot or I can work on chipping the ball onto the green," Haston said. "It's all the little stuff that you might not be doing if you had to worry about the big stuff all the time.

"With Knight's system, we never had to worry about the big stuff on offense and defense. It was just like we had that stuff set up every game ready to go. It was like eighty percent of our game plan was ready every game. Then you can get into really good details about what teams were doing, what personnel was doing, you could really focus on that stuff because you didn't have to think about your own stuff."

Pat Graham, who played at IU from 1989-94 and was a part of the heralded recruiting class of '89 that among others included Calbert Cheaney, said the system became second nature.

"It's just repetition, repetition, repetition," Graham said. "Every guy knew what the other four were thinking at all times and that's how we could use the motion offense to beat a team like Michigan."

Haston said the principles that Graham talked about were the beauty of Knight's system.

"I think the hidden beauty of his system was that it really freed us up to not have to worry about things, once our minds did something and our bodies just took over reflectively where we needed to go when an action took place," Haston said. "It took a lot of hours and drills and maybe getting yelled at a couple of times but once you got it down it really minimized the amount of things you had to worry about. All you had to worry about was the two or three reactions you faced to each upcoming scenario."

Todd Leary, who played for Knight from 1989-94 and was a teammate of Graham's, said IU ran the motion offense in practice to the point of exhaustion. He said everyone's least favorite drill was a 5-on-zero segment that Knight would have them do over and over.

"I didn't get the point of it at first but after a while you figured it out," Leary said. "It was really just to get it so that it came natural to you in any situation."

Lovell, the former IUPUI coach who for the last 20 plus years has been the radio host of Network Indiana's Indiana Sports Talk, said running the motion offense wasn't easy.

"Running motion offense is hard. Teaching motion offense is hard," Lovell said. "But everybody knew what they were getting into when they came in. And his foundation has been emulated by thousands over the years both in this state and around the country."

Joe Hillman, who played for Knight and was a member of the 1987 national championship team, agreed that running motion was difficult but he said it demanded of IU's players that they were disciplined as far as not taking a bad shot or turning the ball over.

"Coach just created a team that was hard to play against," Hillman said. "I'm not just saying this about Indiana, but about teams in general, and that's that teams aren't hard to play against any more. Our system was hard to defend but it was also hard to run because it was all predicated on cutting and going where the defense wasn't at and it took a while to learn that.

"That was not just if I passed it here, I screened here, that was all about the reading and recognition that had to happen. You had to have good players and you had to have smart guys. I think now everyone recruits just the best player. I think so much of recruiting today is focused on getting the most athletically gifted player and thinking 'Let's get him and then we'll make him a basketball player. It was different with coach Knight."

Jake Query, the afternoon co-host of the Query & Schultz Show on Indianapolis afternoon sports talk radio, said the system that Indiana played simply had its fan base very confident in what would happen if the IU players were able to execute it successfully.

"I think growing up and watching them I always assumed that Indiana had a chance in any game because their players knew better what they were supposed to do than the opponents players knew what they were supposed to do," Query said. "And now I think I've come to the epiphany that the reality is Indiana won games because Indiana knew more what the opponent was supposed to do than the opponents did.

"So in other words if Indiana is playing Iowa or Indiana is playing UNLV or somebody that runs a system other than the motion offense and a man-to-man defense, Indiana's players were tutored on that other teams' system so well that the other team could not do anything that Indiana did not anticipate."

• • • • •

Pat Graham said one of the toughest questions he gets asked about his playing days under Knight is to explain the motion offense. He says he was there five years and every year it was a little different.

"One year we had Matt Nover who was a really hard guy to guard in a motion offense," Graham said. "When we lost Nover, we played the motion a little different way. When we lost Calbert (Cheaney) when I was a senior, we didn't run the same motion offense that we had ran with Calbert in the previous years. Every year was a different type of motion offense. You could still label it motion but it was different."

Graham said the best way he could describe the motion would be to look at the five guys on the floor and if you could hit the pause button and see everyone in statue-like poses as the offense would begin you would know everything you needed to know.

"Let's say I had the ball, I would be able to look at each of those other four guys and be able to say, 'if he does this, then I'm going to do that, or if he makes that cut, then this is what I'm going to do.' You knew what the other four guys were going to do almost before they did it."

Joe Hillman said another thing going for IU was that the motion offense just made the Hoosiers difficult to guard.

"The reason we beat better teams when I was at IU is that we were hard to guard," Hillman said. "I've always said if you took a team like Kentucky with all their great players and took all of their great ability and you ran what we ran it would be impossible to guard those guys. You think back to coach Knight's most talented players, most athletic players. When they ran that stuff that we ran, you couldn't guard them. Look at Calbert Cheaney. You couldn't guard him. Isiah was a different guy. He was just so much better but even in our championship game when we got Smart involved running off picks.

"That was kind of the start of the three-guard stuff when I was there with Smart kind of running around in the championship game and being hard to guard. He had played almost that whole year with the ball and then we kind of got into the finals, and it was like look at this guy running off of screens."

Hillman said college basketball today is too simplified. He said that's not a good thing either.

"Unless you have the best players I don't think you're going to win consistently," Hillman said. "And Knight never had the best players. Now the year he won he had some talent. In '81 he obviously had great talent and the same in 1975 and 1976 but in '87 we didn't have the best players. In '89 we certainly didn't have the best players. But it has gotten to the point now where if you don't have the best players and you're not running anything different than anyone else it comes down to who has the best players.

"I think that's where Indiana has fallen into line. They are trying to recruit the best players and then put them in a system that everybody wants to play where you run around, shoot 3's and drive to the basket, where if you did what Knight used to run, you're going to run it. People used to say that Knight ran this structured offense. No he didn't, we had tons of freelance. But we took good shots. And we were always at the top of the Big Ten in scoring. It wasn't like we were walking the ball up. We were just efficient."

The simplistic aspect of the offense was that depending on what the defender did, you knew exactly what you were expected to do. And it wasn't like there were dozens of possibilities on most actions. In fact there were usually just two or three. For example, in the Indiana motion offense if they executed a down screen there were really just three basic options. A defender could either go underneath the screener, chase and follow over the top or switch.

If the defender went underneath the screener, IU players were taught to flare out. If they chased over the top and went around, players were taught to curl. If they chose to switch, IU's players believed they eventually would get the best of them because it was too difficult to continue to switch the amount of times that IU was screening on each possession.

Todd Leary, who played for Knight from 1989-94, said his coach knew that the strategy would work with constant repetition.

"If they're switching they have to execute a perfect switch four different times down the court and that sounds easier than it really is," Leary said. "There is communicating and timing and both guys seeing it and everything else. That's where I think coach Knight was taking advantage of the numbers and saying if you executed it enough, they were going to screw it up eventually."

One thing Indiana would do on offense early in a game especially was it would pass the ball a minimum of four or five times not only to get the offense flowing but also to tire the defense that was trying to fight through so many screens.

"The first time down the floor, you would set a screen and the defense would be all set and ready and gung ho," Leary said. "They've decided they're going to chase hard or they're going to go underneath the screen hard and they're going to do all of that. That's the first time down the floor.

"But after they fight through two, three or four screens, every time down the floor they don't give the same effort on that second or the same on the third."

And that's where ball movement would really come into play as a tool to wear an opponent down.

"Sometimes against lesser teams like we might play in the Indiana Classic or the Hoosier Classic, we would intentionally pass the ball around like eight times even if we were wide open just to watch how tired they got," Leary said. "The coaches didn't tell us to do that but as players we would just do that to kind of dick with them a little bit and see them on film and see how tired they got defensively.

"And physically, it's much more tiring to be in a defensive stance and fighting through screens than it is offensively."

Todd Meier, a senior on the 1987 national championship team, said there were four things that stood out to him that Knight always preached: fundamentals, simplicity, execution and toughness.

"From Day 1 in practice until we played in the Final Four, we were practicing screening angles and cutting," Meier said. "We just focused on doing it right every time. We would do fundamentals and shell drills every day. At the start of every day we did some type of fundamental drills."

But Meier also remembers the simplistic nature of Knight's offense.

"With coach Knight it was a simplistic approach," Meier said. "When we did game plans there would be something on all of the opponents' key players. There were maybe three or four things that showed strengths and weaknesses. On his game plans there were three things on offense you needed to do and three things on defense you needed to do. And that was the game plan. The tough thing was executing those very tough, specific points, whether it was fundamentals or a simple game plan or how do you play a specific player. But that was what was important to coach. You do it right every time and you do the basics and that's going to lead you to winning."

One thing that wasn't a big part of Knight's system was having a playbook that resembled the Yellow Pages. Brad Stevens has one of those playbooks and he has been successful both at the college and professional levels. But Knight had his system of offense that was the motion offense and he basically dared opponents to find a way to beat him.

"We didn't run any plays," Leary said. "We had a couple of sets. We had a triangle and a post exchange and motion. Other than that, we didn't have any plays or any sets. And the triangle and post exchange those were just sets. The triangle had three guys inside and the post exchange had three guys outside. Two guys would work on their own inside in the post exchange and three guys would stay outside. They didn't have to stay in their area but they wouldn't go through the lane. The triangle was the opposite. The triangle would have three guys inside and they would all move inside and the two guys outside would just stand outside the 3-point line basically.

"To think that Indiana won as many games as it did and he won those national championships and ran the same thing over and over and over again, all the time, is pretty incredible. Because in today's world that just doesn't make any sense. These guys have 55 sets when they go into a game."

Brian Evans, who played for Knight from 1992-96, said with Knight it was all pretty simple.

"Let's build an offense that other teams are going to have to prepare for with nonspecific movements and patterns," Evans said. "They're going to have to have a week of practice where they're going to have to do some things that they've never done before. For every other game they're going to try to get their second team or scout team to memorize plays but with us there were no plays to memorize so you're kind of throwing them off.

"It was kind of like playing against Syracuse in the last 20 years. You have to practice that week to play against something that you don't ever practice against. And how do you simulate that in practice when you only have three days to do it?"

Evans said he appreciated the way that Knight communicated what he wanted his players to do. He said when he was a redshirt freshman he had a meeting with Knight where the veteran coach asked him if he wanted to play in games? Of course Evans responded that he did.

"He said, 'Well, you need to get your notebook out and I'm going to tell you how you can play on this team," Evans recalled. "And he had two really simple things. He said if you rebound the basketball you can play on this team. And if you set screens and get Calbert Cheaney open you can play on this team. He said if I just did those two things I was going to play. And he just boiled it down to that. It was that simple.

"I think he gave all the players kind of a recipe to play there and made it real simple. You didn't have to do 10 things, you had to do one or two things."

35

Don Fischer said that simple point was one of the things he thought separated Knight from the majority of coaches of his time.

"He was tremendous at understanding what a player could do and what he couldn't do, both his own players and opposing players," Fischer said. "And then in the case of opposing players, what he was able to do to take advantage of that situation. I thought that was his greatest attribute as a basketball coach because he could break down film, figure out where the weak spots were on a basketball team, what players could and could not do and then take advantage of those things.

"To me, that's what made Bob Knight special."

Clark Kellogg, the CBS Sports college basketball analyst, said what stood out about Knight was his understanding and knowledge of the game. That helped him keep things simple, too.

"He saw it very simply and clearly and he was able to teach it that way," Kellogg said. "I think all of the really good coaches have some of those qualities. But it was simply his way of teaching the game. At some points, he earns a certain amount of respect from his players that allows him to get the most out of them. I don't think it's real complicated. He had a high standard of what his expectations were, the respect and credibility or fear from his players that they would execute what he was teaching and produce great results."

Kellogg said he didn't want to discount the quality of players that IU had under Knight, too.

"There aren't many Mount Rushmore's of coaching without players that make somebody's Mount Rushmore, too," Kellogg said. "So it's a combination. But I just think his teaching of the game, the demands he placed on his players. I think they knew that he was serious about the important things which you saw in how they played and how they represented the school. But it was just his understanding of the game. We heard him talking about it when he was analyzing games for a little while. It was always interesting to listen to how he saw it."

Pat Graham agreed that his former coach was special. He said he has to laugh when he hears people suggest that a big reason for his success was that Knight's Indiana teams were so much more talented than their opponents.

"Are you kidding me?" Graham said. "Very few times in the Big Ten did we line up at the jump ball and go 'We've got more talent than that team.' If you're talking physicality and jumping ability and strength and quickness, I would say very few times. The success we had was because of that motion offense."

Graham said the absolute same was true on defense. It wasn't that IU had the biggest and strongest players, it was because they had a system in place and they believed the system would work.

"Defensively, I always laughed and said none of us could have guarded a phone booth," Pat Graham said. "Very few of us any way because we just were not good one-on-one defenders. Chris Reynolds was. Jamal Meeks was. Greg Graham was. But damn near after that, Evans, Calbert, me? No. But with team defense we were pretty good. You knew your strengths, you knew other guys' strengths, you knew teammates' weaknesses and you were just ready for anything. We played that motion offense but we kind of played a motion defense, too. And it helped us compete."

Leary agreed with Graham's assessment.

"You'd look at us on paper and yeah, Alan Henderson was super talented and Calbert (Cheaney) was super talented but you get past that and I don't know how you could think we could match up with some of the teams that we played against," Leary said. "That's where I think coach Knight was so great to get us to buy into the whole idea that if you run the system it doesn't matter what they do. They're going to score. We're not going to hold them scoreless but it doesn't matter what they do. We're going to be in the game and have a chance to win."

• • • • •

Indianapolis sports talk show host Jake Query was an Indiana basketball fan growing up. He said the one thing that always stood out to him about Indiana basketball was that at the end of close games, no matter who IU was playing, he felt supremely confident that because Indiana had Knight on its bench it had a huge advantage over the opposition.

"I remember always looking down to the bench and seeing Knight sitting there and feeling a sense of security in knowing that when it comes right down to it he's going to know exactly what strings to pull to win this game," Query said. "And strangely enough when they wouldn't, I never, ever thought it was his fault. And that was part of his grip on the entire state of Indiana. Nothing was ever his fault.

"It was the feeling that he had everything under control and that he was the first move on the chess board every time. He didn't react to others, they had to react to him."

Mike DeCourcy of *The Sporting News* and as of 2017 a studio analyst on the Big Ten Network said he doesn't think it's any coincidence that the last time that a school won a national championship without a first round NBA pick was Indiana in 1987.

DeCourcy said Knight's success had a lot to do with not only the players he was able to attract to Indiana but ultimately what he was able to get out of those players.

"You have to start with the general understanding that there really has never been anyone who elevated his players more than Bob at his best," DeCourcy said. "I thought that was really evident at Texas Tech. When he left there, you knew that whoever was following him was walking into a disaster because you looked at the five guys he was winning with and thought 'No one else could win with those guys.'

"That's not to diminish the fact that he had some phenomenal players in his time at Indiana but they were all elevated a little bit more. But that's who Bob Knight was. You give Bob Knight five guys and he was going to make a good team of it. In some cases, he was going to make a great team of it."

Knight clearly had some great teams at Indiana. If you're an IU historian, the names just roll of your tongue. And while there were great players for sure, they formed to make great teams.

Everyone wants to talk about 1976, Knight's first national championship team that as of the writing of this book did something that no one else has ever done since. The Hoosiers were an unbeaten national champion. There's no doubting that was a great team. Scott May, Kent Benson, Quinn Buckner, Tom Abernethy and Bobby Wilkerson leading the charge. But there were also a lot of guys that played significant roles on that team, too. Players like Wayne Radford and Jimmy Crews come to mind.

But go back one season before that to the team that many believed was Knight's greatest team – the 1974-75 Indiana Hoosiers. That team won its first 31 games, including all 18 in the Big Ten season, and if Scott May hadn't sustained a broken arm the Hoosiers may have won back-to-back national championships. It's coulda, woulda, shoulda but still it was a GREAT Indiana basketball team. And that team had other great pieces that would graduate before IU won it all in 1976. Take a guy like Steve Green, who led the Hoosiers in scoring in both 1974 and '75. And don't forget the super sub, John Laskowski, another player whose name is etched in Indiana history as being a great team player.

You could make the same claim to the guys that played in the early 1980's that they were a part of great teams. Sure Isiah Thomas was a GREAT player it his own right but Indiana won the national championship in 1981 because of the sum of all of its parts. Guys like Ray Tolbert, Randy Wittman, Landon Turner and Ted Kitchel. But there were other great players on those teams that played important roles, too. Guys like Jimmy Thomas and Steve Risley.

The same was true in 1987. Yes, Indiana had a GREAT player in Steve Alford but once again it was the sum of all its parts. Daryl Thomas, Dean Garrett, Keith Smart, Ricky Calloway and Joe Hillman all come to mind. But even guys like Steve Eyl, Brian Sloan and Todd Meier and the list goes on and on. Indiana was great because it had great TEAM players.

The same was true in the early 1990's even though those IU teams did not win the ultimate prize. Still, when you think of Calbert Cheaney, Alan Henderson, Eric Anderson, Damon Bailey, Pat Graham, Greg Graham, Matt Nover, Chris Reynolds and on and on you think of great teams.

It was the sum of all parts. That was what made Indiana basketball special.

Former *Indianapolis Star* columnist Bob Kravitz said IU always played good, disciplined basketball under Knight.

"I think it was discipline through fear," Kravitz said. "He played a beautiful style of basketball that we just don't see anymore. The whole thing with movement, and moving without the ball, and ball screens and things that just seem to have gone away. Back at some point he was getting the best players. He got Scott May and Kent Benson, Bobby Wilkerson and people like that. It was a combination of really getting Indiana kids plus it was a style of basketball that just traveled well and it was beautiful to watch and really difficult to defend."

Different people interviewed for this book had different takes on what made Knight so successful. Leary said he believed the one single thing that Knight did better than anyone else was preparation.

Leary said when his talented recruiting class arrived on campus in '89, a class that included the likes of Calbert

Bob Knight gives instructions to IU All-American Steve Alford.

Cheaney, Greg Graham, Pat Graham, Chris Lawson, Lawrence Funderburke, Chris Reynolds and himself, they were immediately presented with some of Knight's favorite sayings. Things like 'Failing to prepare is preparing to fail', and 'It's not the will to win, it's the will to prepare to win.' Leary admitted that initially those words went in one ear and out the other.

"But as time went on you would start to see it work," Leary said. "And you'd start to see you were taking things away from other teams. And you'd start to see that they are not prepared to the same level that you feel like you guys are prepared for. When you see it works like that, it just snowballs. And you know how kids are, when they see something that they think works then all of a sudden they're like addicted to it and want to do it more and more and more. That's what I bought into with coach Knight and that's what I think separated him apart from other good coaches.

"There are a lot of really, really good coaches but he's in the great category because of the little things he could do that would separate him and preparation was a big one. I don't think we ever walked into a game and felt like that they might trick us with something weird."

Leary said he knows that was what the culture was when he was there as a player. When he returned as the color commentator on the IU Radio Network with Don Fischer in the early 2000's when Mike Davis was the IU coach, he never had the same feeling.

"I like Mike Davis a lot but I never felt like that team was overly prepared when they went into a game," Leary said. "But guys like Dane Fife, Tom Coverdale, Jarrad Odle and those guys that were ultra competitive and probably carrying over some of that preparedness from their time with Knight, were able to bridge that gap a little bit.

"But I thought once that leadership had left the program I don't think Indiana had the same culture anymore than it did when coach Knight was there."

The preparedness theme was also top on the list of former IU All-American Brian Evans, who played for Knight from 1992-96.

"I just think in every facet of that job, I think that Bob Knight out-prepared the competition," Evans said. "That means in building a practice plan for the day and a practice plan for the week when you might have a couple of games. Basically, how much work can we get done in those off days. I think it was true in film work. I think he had our managers better prepared than any other coach had their managers prepared. I think he had our assistant coaches working harder than the competition.

"I think he finished it up by sleeping less, working more and just being efficient with his time."

Pat Graham, Indiana's 1989 Mr. Basketball from Floyds Knobs, Indiana, said the best compliment he could pay to Knight was simply that the coach's success began with the quality of players he recruited.

"Bob Knight recruited good kids," Graham said. "He recruited good families. He recruited good students. He didn't recruit bad kids. And so when you got a group of 10, 11, 12 or 13 guys together in the locker room and they were all pretty good players but especially they were all pretty good kids, then you had something. They were all organized and they were disciplined and they knew what hard work does."

Graham said that Knight told his mom and dad during the recruiting process that he recruited parents as much as he did players.

"Everyone automatically thinks of Knight as this brilliant basketball mind and while that was true, people forget that the cornerstone to his success was doing one of the most simple things you could do which was go get good kids," Graham said. "Coach Knight believed if kids came from good backgrounds that would translate to their ability to be successful and to be able to handle the demands he had on you as a player at IU. I was (at Indiana) five years and we had very few discipline problems. And back then if you recruited that type of kid that he went after, you probably were going to have some success. I think that's one of the biggest things that was lost when he left."

Risley said Knight always recruited good players and then often times in his system they were able to form a great team.

"I believe a great team will always be a collection of great players because the team functions as one," Risley said. "Knight had talented players. Great players? I guess that depends on how you want to define great players. How many of Bob Knight's players ever went on to be bonafide NBA superstars? Knight never produced an overload of those. Isiah (Thomas) was an exception but Isiah was great when he came to IU. Other than that even the Scott May's of the world were great players on a better team. IU made Scott (May) a great player. But at IU the team was always bigger than the individual.

"Knight had talented players who were fundamentally sound who became great players because they worked in his system. Yes, Knight had great players but not because they were like Magic Johnson, Larry Bird, Kareem Abdul Jabbar great, they were great because they collectively formed a great team. That's why the greatest college basketball team of all time was the 1976 undefeated Indiana basketball team. It was just a great team comprised of great players."

Mike Marot, the Associated Press writer from Indianapolis who has covered Indiana for two decades, said Knight was special because of the things he could do with players.

"I always thought that the most impressive part about Knight was that he got more out of his guys than anybody else could get out of those guys," Marot said. "And his ability to draw that out of a player that he brought in, whether they were a highly touted recruited guys or middle of the pack recruited guys or even lower recruited guys, he always had the ability to get so much from them.

"I just felt like they were always overachievers and I always believed that was his greatest contribution to the game. He took sometimes not the best kids in the recruiting class, made them into a team, and then made them winners."

• • • • •

One thing that players point to that played for Knight was how much of a tactician he was during a game. He was always quick to make a change or a small adjustment during the flow of a game. Timeouts were a precious commodity and players knew they needed to be attentive and listen because Knight would use his timeouts as teaching moments.

An opposing team might think they had found a way to stop Steve Alford because they saw that every time he came off a screen he would do so shoulder-to-shoulder and an opponent might believe they could find a way to cheat on the screen and better defend IU's sharpshooter. Then Knight would take a timeout and make a quick adjustment.

"That's where Knight was a master in a way that Tom Crean could never be," Risley said. "He could make deviations and changes like that within a 30-second timeout. And he could pick up on what they were doing instantly. With Bob Knight every timeout was a working timeout. They were so many times when I would see teams especially in the Crean era when it wasn't a working timeout. It was just a timeout to slow momentum. But under Knight every timeout was a working timeout. That's why Knight didn't waste a lot of timeouts because he didn't see the need to call one because there was nothing to work on at that point and time."

As good as Knight's teams were consistently from the time he stepped on campus in the fall of 1971 through the Big Ten championship season of 1993, there was clearly a dropoff at some point in the final six or seven seasons he coached at Indiana.

And again, the basic premise of IU's success was still present. At the very least, Knight was still getting Indiana to the NCAA Tournament every season – the Hoosiers just weren't going anywhere once they got there. The days of deep NCAA Tournament runs left IU about the same time that a guy like Calbert Cheaney left the building following the 1993 season.

In 1994, IU was a respectable 12-6 in the Big Ten and won 19 games going into the NCAA Tournament. As a No. 5 seed in the tournament, IU beat No. 12 Ohio and No. 4 Temple to reach the Sweet Sixteen where it lost to ninth-seeded Boston College. So it was still a Sweet Sixteen run but even those days would end in 1994 for Knight.

His final six seasons at Indiana, the Hoosiers never made it out of the first weekend of the tournament. In the first three years of that run (1995-97) IU was a first round victim each season. The Hoosiers lost to Missouri in 1995, Boston College in 1996 and Colorado in 1997. In both 1998 and 1999, IU won the first game but lost in the round to get to the Sweet Sixteen. In '98, Indiana lost to Connecticut and the next season to St. John's. Knight's final season, in the 1999-2000 campaign, the Hoosiers lost by 20 to No. 11 seed Pepperdine in a late game in Buffalo, N.Y. in a first round elimination.

Several people weighed in for this book on why they thought Knight's final six or seven seasons weren't as successful as the first 22 or 23.

One constant theme was that perhaps Knight wasn't as involved in the recruiting process – or maybe didn't really enjoy it – as he had earlier in his career.

Ken Bikoff said Knight may have just gotten tired of the recruiting process. He referenced 'The Legends Club' by John Feinstein where Duke coach Mike Krzykewski (a Knight disciple) said he took on more of a "closer" role in terms of recruiting at Duke at some point too.

"So it's going to happen to anybody," Bikoff said. "I think years and years of begging 17 year old kids to come and play for you has to take its toll. I think once you get older maybe you don't have the same kind of energy that you once did for that. So you relegate those tasks to younger assistant coaches who are going to be looking for different things that maybe Knight himself would have early in his career.

"I think that's what may have led to some of Knight's struggles in the mid-to-later parts of the 1990s. Indiana was recruiting players that instead of fitting what Knight wanted them to do it evolved into the thought that we can coach them into what we want them to do. And that ended up being not quite as successful of a formula."

Bob Kravitz wondered the same things.

"First of all I think he got a little bit lazier as he got older," Kravitz said. "I think if you talk to people who knew him they would tell you that. But the way the social climate has changed, kids aren't going to put up with that militaristic B.S. anymore. Once upon a time they took it as a show of strength to say I can play for this guy, I can play for anybody, I can play for Bob Knight.

"I think now they understand that they can be seen on TV no matter where they go. And they could play somewhere where they didn't have to quote unquote put up with the abusive tactics of the General. They can get as much exposure anywhere that they go. There is more and more emphasis now on getting NBA ready. Maybe there's some sense that the Knight system didn't get them as ready to play in the NBA as some other places."

Indianapolis sports radio talk show host Kent Sterling used the word "bored," in talking about Knight at Indiana after about 1994.

"This is going to sound odd, but I really thought coach Knight kind of got bored with being extremely successful with really good players and he wanted to challenge himself to see how good he could be without them," Sterling said. "I think he found ways to not have great players. I think he found a way to screw up some recruiting triumphs he could have had. I think he would have loved a challenge like having two scholarship players and a bunch of walk ons."

Risley said he thought there were a lot of different variables as to why Knight struggled a little bit at Indiana in his final six seasons. He said though, that some of the things he learned at that time, probably helped him at his next stop which was Texas Tech.

"He wasn't putting the effort into recruiting and maybe getting a little fat and happy to be honest," Risley said. "And I think what happened when he went to Texas Tech I think it woke him up. I think when he got let go, he actually said 'I'm a basketball coach.' And he went back and probably did some of his greatest coaching at Texas Tech.

47

"Getting that program into the tournament was a feat. It wasn't the level of success we saw at Indiana but the growth of success that we saw at Texas Tech was probably every bit as good of anything he ever did at Indiana."

Risley believes that once Knight had that experience at Texas Tech, he was satisfied and could walk away from coaching.

"I think he said 'I need to prove that I'm still a basketball coach' and once he proved that again I think he said that's enough," Risley said.

3

A Different Time
in College Basketball

To be fair, in order to compare the situations of current coaches in trying to follow Bob Knight at Indiana you have to understand the differences in the game of college basketball from when Knight was coaching at IU compared to his successors.

It's a different world in so many ways. From a basketball perspective, it's not quite like going from a peach basket to a metal rim but it's close.

The bottom line is that Knight lived in a completely different world than coaches experience today.

Let's begin by throwing out a few examples of things that Bob Knight never worried about when he arrived in Bloomington in 1971.

- AAU Basketball didn't get real popular until the 1990's.
- Only a few teams were on television regularly.
- Kids weren't thinking NBA first
- There weren't as many one and done's
- Recruiting was completely different
- Specifically if Knight wanted a kid from Indiana, he generally was going to get him
- There was no Internet or social media as we know it today

The list truly goes on and on. College basketball is just a different animal today than it was in 1971 when Bob Knight left Army to become the new Indiana head coach.

Now, in the words of former Indiana University athletic director Rick Greenspan, that doesn't mean that you should discount Bob Knight's success in any way. He said it's not about that. It's simply a lot more about with a changing game, changing culture and climate, it can just be a little more difficult today to maintain a long run of sustained, consistent success.

"This is not to take away from coach Knight's level of success because as a strategy guy and a basketball coach he was phenomenal," Greenspan said. "And frankly, back in his day he didn't have an equal. But if were coaching in today's game I wonder if we would all say the same thing because of how different the game is today."

Bob Lovell, the host of Network Indiana's popular syndicated Indiana Sports Talk program throughout the state of Indiana, spent 12 seasons from 1982-93 as the head basketball coach at IUPUI.

He said something else that existed back then was that coaches could coach without a lot of distractions or outside noise. Basically, they were allowed to do their job.

He said back then what a coach said was gold.

"Coaches were just looked at a lot differently," Lovell said. "The coach was right. I was brought up in a culture back then and coached in a culture back then that what the coach said was the law. There was no discussion. There was no AAU coach telling me to do something a certain way."

I get it. I played high school basketball in that kind of culture. We had the discipline with our buzzed haircuts and the coach was clearly the King. There was no backlash and if there ever was, the entire team would pay for it in running what we called lines or some people call suicides. Whatever the term, you don't want to do it and you certainly don't want to do it in payment for a teammates' transgressions. I will say

Bob Knight with assistant coach Dan Dakich.

this the fear of not wanting to say or do something that was going to cause your buddies to run was a powerful motivation. But it all came about because the coach was the King.

Plus Lovell said players just seem to have been more bought-in back in the time when coaches like Knight were dominating college basketball.

"I think guys bought in more," Lovell said. "You bought into the whole culture of giving up your ego and doing what you had to do for everybody else. I think it would be hard to replicate that today to be honest."

And being "the guy" in your state definitely had its advantages. Lovell remembers once Bob Knight made the motion offense and tough, half court, man-to-man defense the staples of his program, everyone else was quick to come along.

"If you think about it when Knight came to IU, in some ways the state of Indiana became a motion offense and man-to-man basketball state because he was the guy," Lovell said. "All of a sudden whatever he said was gospel. You may disagree with it but you were going to do it. The other thing is that there weren't any comments coming from moms and dads and others. No, he was the coach. Whatever he said was the law and that's not the case anymore."

Lovell said in many ways he believes it was easier to coach "back in the day." Recruiting was something a coach did that involved himself, a high school coach and mom and dad. And Lovell said people were just more reasonable with their expectations of the process.

"I think recruiting was a whole lot easier back then because you didn't have all of these forces at work against you," Lovell said. "You didn't have moms and dads with unrealistic expectations. You didn't have AAU coaches. You didn't have all of that working against you when you were trying to recruit a kid. Now a days, when you're going after a quality kid, it's like he has an agent, he has a publicist, he has this, he has that. And now instead of just talking to the kid, you're talking to his AAU coach and an advisor and all of these other people and you're thinking 'How did we get to this point?'"

There's no question that the emergence of AAU has had a dramatic effect on how different college basketball has become today.

Malcom Moran, the former lead college basketball writer for *USA Today* who also worked at the *Chicago Tribune*, the *New York Times* and *Newsday*, said a big difference in the game today is how AAU coaches are perceived as being more important in many ways than the local high school coach when it comes to the recruiting process.

"One element that I think is pretty clear is just that the way the influence is structured now with so much more of the AAU coaches and the entourages and people that fit that category as opposed to high school basketball coaches," Moran said. "I think that influence takes the whole enterprise just that much farther away from anything that has to do with education."

I suggested that it was almost more important to have the relationship with the AAU coach than it is the high school coach.

"I would remove the word 'almost'," Moran said.

Another big difference is coaching salaries. With the way salaries are handed out today, you don't have to coach at a place like Indiana to make a comfortable living. There was a chart done by USA Today that showed coaching salaries for the 68 programs that were in the 2017 NCAA Tournament. A total of 41 of those coaches were making more than $1 million per season.

And it wasn't just the big boys either. Gregg Marshall at Wichita State was earning more than $3 million per season. Gonzaga's Mark Few was at $1.6 million. Both Chris Mack at Xavier and Will Wade at VCU were at $1.4 million per season. The days of having to climb the ladder to play at a Power Five Conference in order to collect a big pay day are obviously over.

Former Indiana athletic director Rick Greenspan said he believes this has caused for a major shift in parity in the college basketball world, too.

"You now have highly capable players going to play for highly capable coaches at places like Butler and Dayton and Xavier," Greenspan said. "Places where they might not have that long and rich history but some of those places, their last 10, 15 or maybe 20 years of competitive postseason success are better than that of a place like Indiana.

"So you've got regional coaches who are very good and very talented but have been compensated at a high enough level that they don't feel like they've got to run out and get that next job. They feel like 'I'm going to stay at Dayton or I'm going to stay at Butler because I'm making a million or a million and a half bucks, whatever the case may be.'"

That's a big difference Greenspan said to the "old days" where salaries were considerably less.

"Back then people were thinking that they needed to get to a big name place to coach so that they could make enough money to send their own kids to college," Greenspan said. "Obviously, that's not the case anymore."

The reality, Greenspan said, is that some of those places can almost be more appealing that the pressure you're going to be under and the expectations like somewhere like Indiana.

"There's longevity, there's familiarity, and in Butler's case there's that attitude that we've got there before and we can get there again," Greenspan said. "If you like a smaller place maybe, and you're OK with less fanatical support, that can be a good spot for you."

• • • • •

Brian Snow, the national college basketball recruiting analyst for Scout.com, said the difference in television exposure has changed recruiting completely.

"It's totally different," Snow said. "When you think about it, when Bob Knight was recruiting in the 70's and 80's and what have you, what were there six schools on TV consistently? Now every game is on TV. You just don't have that brand awareness that you used to have for a premium school like an Indiana.

"Now you do because look around the area. Every game Butler plays is on TV. Every game Xavier plays is on TV. Every game Louisville plays is on TV. Every game Michigan State plays is on TV. So these kids are exposed to so much more than they were in the 70's and 80's because of cable television, TV rights and everything that comes with it."

Snow said it's a little different these days when you're walking into a kid's living room. In the old days, a premium school like Indiana had a big advantage but now the playing field has been leveled.

"You can't just walk in and say, 'We're Indiana, you know who we are. Who the heck is Oregon?'," Snow said. "Today the kid might say, 'Oh, I've watched Oregon 22 times this year.'

"It's just the reality."

It was a long journey from the way things were done when Knight was at Indiana. Back then to a paraphrase the old E.F. Hutton commercial, 'When Bob Knight talked, people listened.'

Basically, if you were a good player in the state of Indiana and Knight came calling, you were there.

Former Indiana University athletic director Rick Greenspan said it was a lot like the situation with a certain college football legend from down south.

"It was the same as Bear Bryant calling a kid in Alabama," Greenspan said. "It's every kids dream. And it really was the same in Bryant's day. Kids would turn down full scholarships to other places if Bryant would let them walk on. Texas was like that, too, for a while in football.

"And I'm not saying this is easy by any means but if you're in a state that is great producer of talent it certainly gives you a major leg up."

Bob Lovell couldn't agree more.

"If you were a kid in Indiana and IU offered you a scholarship, bam, you were there," Lovell said. "Nowadays, that's not the case. Every kid is going to be on a national stage so a lot more is going to go into their decision as to where they want to play college basketball."

The fact that the world is such a bigger place for kids today has to be a part of it, too. The reality is that a lot of kids are yearning to get away from their hometowns or in many cases their states to somewhere else for college. Why should college athletes be any different and just want to get out of state? This could also be a reason why IU coaches have had trouble keeping Indiana kids in the state of Indiana in recent years.

"Kids today have so many more opportunities, so many more avenues where they can go," Lovell said. "Think about it. If you're a kid growing up in Indiana a lot of kids want to leave home. They want to get out of the state. I see that. I hear that all the time. So now you turn that around and you say, yes a lot of people say that but you're not allowed to say that if you're a basketball player. You have to stay at home.

"I understand the dilemma that people have on this. When I recruited kids, what I would tell them was that more than likely wherever you go to college, you're still going to come back and live in and around where you grew up. Or at least within a certain proximity. And if you go somewhere else for four years, now you're out of sight and out of mind. If you stay around here, people are going to hear about you and read about you and talk about you and you can say you played at Indiana when you go to get that job and make up your resume. I don't know if it was necessarily true but it seemed to work."

Malcom Moran said it would be interesting to look at recruiting just with regular college students and not even athletes.

"For a regular college student that made a decision in the early 1970's (when Knight arrived at Indiana) as to where they wanted to go to college as opposed to now, think about how much more frequently kids are going out of state and in some cases going a significant distance," Moran said. "It's not nearly the obstacle that it was viewed as forty-something years ago. It's just really no big deal.

"I think for institutional ego purposes it's nice to say they need to recruit Indiana players. They don't have to you know. I mean Isiah Thomas was pretty good. So was Scott May and Quinn Buckner. Were there people complaining back then when those guys were in school that we don't have enough Indiana players?"

But again it was a different time in recruiting, too. It was a time when Knight might only target five or six players because he was pretty sure he was going to get commitments for the three or four that he needed.

Brian Snow, the national recruiting analyst from Scout.com, said those days are long gone.

"If Indiana tried to do that now it just wouldn't work," Snow said. "Kentucky, Duke and Arizona have had as much success recruiting as anybody in the last 10 years and they wouldn't be crazy enough to target five guys for three spots. It's just not a reality at this point and time. Because there is so much competition."

Steve Risley, who played at IU from 1978-81 and played on Knight's second national championship team with the Hoosiers in '81, may have said it best.

"It was an honor just to get asked to play at Indiana back then," Risley said. "It was a freaking honor."

How big of an honor? Risley had already committed to play basketball at Notre Dame. Digger Phelps had recruited him. Risley had played basketball and quarterback in football and had an opportunity to play both at Notre Dame. He was talking to both programs.

As for Indiana, Risley said he had never heard from Knight. Knight hadn't been at any of his games. But all of that changed with one phone call.

"He calls my house one day and I answer and he talked for about 30 minutes and then he said, 'I'd like to have you come play ball at Indiana," Risley recalled. "And I said 'Yes.' I accepted on the spot. I never talked to my high school coach, my parents, or anybody. I told him I had kind of verbally committed to Notre Dame and he asked if I had signed anything and I told him I had not.

"And he said, 'Don't worry about it. I'll take care of that.' And that was it. It was every kid's dream to play at Indiana. You didn't even think about all of that stuff with him beating kids up mentally and berating them on and off of the court. Who cares? You just want to go play for the best."

Mike Marot, the Indianapolis Associated Press writer who has covered Indiana for more than two decades, said the notion that players came to Indiana because it was an honor to play for Knight is simply something that has been lost over the years in Bloomington.

"Part of it is that the AAU stuff has opened up the world and provided so many different opportunities for these kids and so many times kids don't want to stay near home," Marot said. "But you know what there are still some special kids that do. Take Collin Hartman. He came to Indiana and lot of people didn't think he would make it. Now he's closing out a five-year (as of 2017) and he's one of the most beloved kids in the program.

"I'm guessing it was an honor for him to play basketball at Indiana University. I think that's pretty safe to say."

Marot said Hartman was an Indiana kid who wanted to stay in state and felt like he had something invested in the state. He said now you tend to get kids that don't have as much invested in the state.

"And there was something about Knight's personality that made them feel that way," Marot said. "It was like if he's recruiting you that really means something.

"I don't know if there has been anyone here since then that that has been the case."

• • • • •

Today, kids really don't even have a feel for what Indiana basketball once was. The example I use, and I think I use it a couple of times in this book, is just very simply if you were to ask a kid today if he had ever heard of Isiah Thomas, without hesitation he would tell you that Thomas in the current hot shot guard for the Boston Celtics. He might know that the kid played at the University of Washington.

But THE OTHER ISIAH? No chance.

Indianapolis Star columnist Gregg Doyel remembers a conversation he had a few years ago with an IU player, Stanford Robinson.

"I asked him what he knew about IU's tradition before he came to Indiana and if that maybe was why he had come to IU?" Doyel said. "He said he didn't know anything about it. He didn't know anything about it until he got here.

"He said he was on campus before he even realized what Bob Knight had done at IU. But for me the fact that was even possible for a great recruit, one who was good enough to go to IU, to not know anything about IU until he got is really a mouthful."

Robinson wasn't even aware there were five national championship banners hanging in the south end zone of Assembly Hall.

That's a prime example of how things have changed in recruiting. ESPN.com's Jeff Goodman said players back then might react a lot differently to Knight's approach than perhaps they would today.

"A lot of it was just the reputation he had built up," Goodman said. "The combination today is if you have the coach, the brand and the program it's hard to beat and that was the case with Knight. But it has all changed so much. Nowadays there would be a lot more kids and people that don't want their kids playing for Bob Knight but back then that wasn't the case. Back then accountability was still something that was prevalent.

"Now the culture has changed. Bob Knight probably would not be as successful right now in this day and age because holding kids accountable worked with certain kids and their parents and their people around them. I just think he had done it, he had already established himself as a hell of a basketball coach and back then kids wanted to play for Indiana basketball."

Knight could potentially have had other problems in today's game, too. I've always tried to imagine how Knight would have handled all the negative feedback he likely would have received on social media if someone objected to a substitution pattern or his failure to have recruited a certain kid.

Some will maintain that he probably would have just ignored it or he wouldn't have even been on Twitter to have seen it in the first place. But the problem there is that someone is always on the lookout it seems, from a media relations standpoint or that of an assistant coach, to bring negative comments to the attention of a coach.

And just knowing Knight the way I did for a short period of time, it's hard to imagine that he would have been real comfortable with being second-guessed by someone on Twitter. It was bad enough when it was a media member that he had no affinity for but if it was just some guy sitting behind his computer on Twitter trying to egg Knight on, can you imagine how that would have played out?

Now, Knight did have a small exposure to Twitter and Facebook for that matter when he was at Texas Tech but not during his time at Indiana. Facebook launched in February of 2004 and Twitter was founded in March of 2006. He was a little pre Instagram though as that site launched in October of 2010.

Malcom Moran said he doesn't think it would have been a good fit for Knight to have had to endure criticism via social media platforms over the entire course of his career. Fans can be brutal. Just check out some of the memes that have been made on former IU coaches who have fallen out of favor with the fan base.

"I think it would have been very difficult for him," Moran said. "He would not have enjoyed being second-guessed, I can tell you that. The sense of control that a coach could build was much more easily constructed in those days."

As Moran pointed out there was no talk radio back then. Sure, Knight had his own weekly radio show with Don Fischer but even that he grew tired very quickly of people calling in and challenging his coaching strategy. After a few bad shows, Knight finally did away with the call-in segment and only allowed questions that would be mailed in ahead of time. And even those would be hand-picked and approved by Knight before the show.

"I mean now in Indianapolis you have competing talk radio outlets and you have influential people who must be paying attention because they are guests on the show," Moran said.

Alex Bozich, who founded the Indiana fan site 'Inside the Hall' in 2007, said there used to be a bigger emphasis on having a good relationship with high school coaches in the state. Bozich said he's not saying that's not important today but there are bigger factors in play.

"With the AAU circuit taking the prominent role that it has it's nothing for kids to be playing for programs that are based in different states," Bozich said. "Kids today move around to different programs and in a lot of ways they're catered to and in a whole different way than how they were when a guy like Bob Knight was coaching at Indiana.

"If they don't hear what they want to hear from the coach they may just go somewhere else. Whereas it may not have been that way before. I think the AAU angle is really a thing that has changed college basketball."

Bozich said again there are just too many factors in place.

"With social media and recruiting rankings and all of that it has become about how kids can brand themselves and get their own message out," Bozich said. "They can pretty much go anywhere. It used to be if you were a great player growing up in Indiana the expectation was that you would go to Indiana but today you can really go anywhere.

"I just think the mindset of kids today is different. I think we're in a society where kids are more worried about their brand and the exposure they can get rather than going to play for Bob Knight."

Former IU player Pat Graham, Indiana's Mr. Basketball in 1989, said one thing that set Knight apart in his recruiting approach was the kind of player he recruited.

"He told my mom and my dad that he recruited families as much as he did players," Graham said. "And I believe he did that. Good kids, good families, good parents, I think his recruiting style fit that type of basketball in that age when he was so successful.

"In the 1990's all of a sudden you had social media, and cellphones and the Internet and that's when everything changed," Graham said. "And all of a sudden kids from Indiana started seeing other places."

Former ESPN college basketball analyst Andy Katz said you can't compare the two eras of college basketball without putting it in proper context.

Katz said the dawn of social media changed basketball the way that IU fans grew up knowing it to be.

"It was all pre something happening in another state that everybody knows at the same time," Katz said. "Everything happened in kind of its own little vacuum. Kids growing up in Indiana wanted to play in Indiana. Today, an Indiana kid, or a Kentucky kid or a North Carolina kid, they have access to every single program in the country, they can see things and everything is so global that the attachment to your local school doesn't have the same strength or power.

"It's just a different world. Today, if you're from Gary, Indiana, coaches can see you play every game because it's all available on line almost at every level."

Katz said back in Knight's time he could have a kid's full attention. Today that's an impossibility.

"At that time, Knight was able to kind of capture the minds of every prospect because that was all they knew and that was kind of their world view."

Katz said another big difference is that in today's game everything is about getting to the NBA. Back then, not so much.

"I think we've lost that time when you wanted to enjoy the college experience," Katz said. "Not everyone but a lot of people have lost that. Coach Knight wasn't coaching at a time where everything was about getting to the NBA. It was about the experience of becoming a teammate, building a team, becoming a man. All of those things have changed dramatically because of the way in which everything is so geared toward the NBA."

Lovell said it's another example of how things are different than when he was the head coach at IUPUI, too.

"Nowadays kids are thinking about two things," Lovell said."They want to get to the NBA and they want to know which program is going to showcase their talents more."

Katz said today kids are thinking about themselves first.

"That was the beginning of the migration if you will of everyone being NBA-centric," Katz said. "It's also the beginning of the time when players had much more access to information about every other program. You can't put a price tag on how that changed the thinking process."

It was a different time in college basketball. But Indiana basketball was a household name not only in the state of Indiana but nationwide. When ESPN first debuted in the fall of 1979, it was a good time to be an IU basketball fan. And Indiana was on television all the time. Today everybody's on television all the time. But back then, the name Indiana and that of its coach Bob Knight, especially with those from within the state, carried a tremendous amount of weight.

4

Is Indiana Basketball A Blueblood Program?

The blueblood discussion regarding Indiana basketball is always a good one.

And I think in a book like this one, when you're talking about all of the things that IU basketball aspires to be, it's more than a fair question.

Bottom line: Is Indiana University basketball a blueblood program?

If you're outside of the state of Indiana, or for that matter just a small section of the state of Indiana, the answer is probably no. IU just hasn't had the success in the last 30 years to warrant such a designation.

But still, if you ask the right diehard Indiana basketball fan or even some folks in the media, you might be surprised at their answer. There's a lot of people who truly believe that IU still deserves to be in that conversation.

Some will say maybe on the fringe or the second tier of schools. Perhaps a second tier would include teams like Arizona, Wisconsin, Michigan, Michigan State, Florida, Villanova and Louisville. Would Indiana be more comfortable in company such as that?

The standard blueblood response normally includes North Carolina, Duke, Kansas, Kentucky and in some circles UCLA … and then Indiana.

If this was 1987 or even the early 1990's, there would not be a question. Indiana would have three national championships since 1976 and would have appeared in a Final Four in 1992 and an Elite Eight in 1993.

Back then, Indiana was always in that conversation. The Hoosiers were always considered to be one of the faces on college basketball's Mount Rushmore.

But that was a different time. That was Bob Knight's time. Now, you're 30 years removed from that last national championship and since that Final Four in 1992, Indiana has only played in one more in the last 25 years.

And when you really look at the numbers that have been put up by those other blueblood programs in the time since IU's last national championship in 1987, the evidence is staggering.

Just since 1988, those other five programs (including UCLA) which I mentioned as bluebloods have won 14 national championships. IU, as we mentioned, has not been able to put up that sixth national championship banner in school history.

The Final Four numbers for those other five schools are equally staggering. Those five schools have been to a total of 39 Final Fours since 1988. IU has been to two.

Another interesting factoid there is that since 1988, only one Final Four has not included at least one of those blueblood programs. And interestingly that was 2013, a year when Indiana was the No. 1 overall seed and got knocked off in the Sweet Sixteen by Syracuse. The Final Four that year included Louisville, Michigan, Syracuse and Wisconsin.

But when you look at a breakdown of those five other blueblood programs compared to Indiana since 1988 you really don't need any other evidence, at least not in terms of on-the-court performance.

Since 1988, the five bluebloods have looked like this:
- North Carolina (11 Final Fours, 4 national champion-ships – 1993, 2005, 2009 and 2017
- Duke (10 Final Fours, 4 national championships – 1991, 1992, 2001 and 2010

- Kentucky (8 Final Fours, 3 national championships – 1996, 1998 and 2012
- Kansas (6 Final Fours, 2 national championships – 1988 and 2008
- UCLA (4 Final Fours, 1 national championship – 1995

So you could probably exclude UCLA from the list except that the Bruins have made it to four Final Fours following the most impressive run of championships in NCAA history when UCLA won 10 national championships from 1964-75. When you figure that stat alone, you could easily justify continuing to keep the Bruins on the list.

What Indiana fans will counter with is that IU has everything possible that it needs to get back to being in the conversation for a blueblood program but now it just needs the coach to get them there.

The things that IU believes it has in its corner are:
- Facilities that include an updated Assembly Hall and Cook Hall, a state of the art practice facility
- A budget to pay its coaches in line if not higher than other blueblood programs
- A fanatical fan base that travels the world to see the Hoosiers play
- One of the best recruiting bases anywhere with the talent coming out of the state of Indiana
- Those five banners that serve as a constant reminder to all Indiana fans of what was once and could be again

That last one, however, kind of sums it all up. In many ways, the rest of the college basketball world believes that Indiana is living in the past. College recruits today were born in the 1999/2000 time frame. So unless they have an IU fan in their ear, there's a good chance they have no idea what Indiana basketball once was.

I think it should be mentioned, too, though that this is not necessarily just an indictment on the three permanent coaches that have followed Bob Knight at Indiana. Those three coaches have not been able to put up a banner in Assembly Hall in 17 seasons. But the reality is that Knight himself was unable to win another title in his final 13 seasons in Bloomington. And in his final six seasons at IU, Knight's teams were unable to make it out of the first weekend of the NCAA Tournament.

• • • • •

In talking to people for this book, I found several who had interesting commentary on whether they believed Indiana basketball could still be in the conversation to be considered a blueblood program.

IU athletic director Fred Glass, not surprisingly either, is of the opinion that Indiana should still be in the blueblood conversation. And I get that. As several people talked about in the pages ahead, it's good to aspire to be that lofty of a program. But Glass believed it was more than an aspiration.

When Glass made a statement at the time of the Archie Miller hiring that the expectation for Indiana basketball was to perennially run deep in the NCAA Tournament and to hang national championship banners, he was accused by some in the national media of living firmly in the past.

"One of the guys literally said that I should have a Members Only jacket on because I'm still living in the 80's," Glass said. "And that my ambition to go deep in the tournament and win a sixth championship and be thought of in the same breath as Kentucky and Duke and North Carolina was crazy and I just reject that.

"There is no reason why we can't be there and should be there. And I don't apologize for that."

A former Indiana athletic director, Rick Greenspan, said he thought it absolutely made sense for Indiana basketball to aspire to that lofty goal and he thought it was a relatively realistic and admirable goal at that. But he stopped short of calling IU a blueblood, too.

"Now, if you were to say that about Indiana football that a realistic goal was to perennially be a top five program then that's not realistic," Greenspan said. "That just leads to frustration, disappointment and to everybody getting fired every five years."

As for Glass's way of thinking, Greenspan said he understood it to some degree but called it a nostalgic way of looking at things.

"Nostalgia matters but it doesn't matter all that much to kids that are 17 or 18 years old," Greenspan said. "So nostalgia is fine but you know what, that doesn't make you a blueblood. Having the resources, having the facilities, having the budget and having a great fan base, that doesn't make you a blueblood either. Those are factors that play into it.

"Being a blueblood comes from competitive, consistent, sustained success over the tenure of multiple coaches."

Clark Kellogg, the college basketball analyst for CBS Sports, said like anything else it's a process. Programs that have been on the outside looking in for a while need to take baby steps to get back to that elite level again.

"I think it should be more about playing and performing at a championship level so you have a chance and not necessarily thinking you're entitled to be a blueblood program," Kellogg said. "You clearly want to aspire to the very best that you can be and we measure that by national championships."

But Kellogg said you have to be careful though when you start defining champions only in terms of a championship.

"You can have a champion culture and a champion performance and not win championships," Kellogg said. "Yet, that's the ultimate so you strive for it. You don't lose sight of it but it can't be the be all, end all."

Kellogg said a program like Indiana needs to return to that consistent, sustained level of winning again before it can think of itself in blueblood terms.

"You want to put yourself in position to consistently challenge and be in position for Big Ten championships which puts you in a good position to have a chance on the national stage," Kellogg said. "But there are not a lot of teams – we can count them on two hands and maybe a foot – that are winning national championships."

As Kellogg said though, Indiana does have some cache in its corner. But that's not enough.

"Indiana has the resources and it has the past history to recapture some of that but that can't be the driver," Kellogg said. "It has to be a process of let's just get back to the consistent flow of being in the top of the Big Ten. And then after that you go for national success. And we're going to do it the right way.

"So we're going to strive for that but that's not going to be the way we ultimately define ourselves. I think that's something that all programs should get a handle on quite honestly but certainly there are a handful of programs like Duke, Carolina, Kansas and Kentucky."

Kellogg said he thinks it's pretty obvious when it comes to Indiana in this context as to what the goal should be.

"You need to put yourself in position to re-enter the conversation," Kellogg said. "I think that is what the goal should be. Then you just let the chips fall where they will after that."

Malcom Moran, the former college basketball writer for *USA Today* who also worked at places like the *Chicago Tribune*, *New York Times* and *Newsday*, believes in some ways time has passed the Hoosiers by. "First of all, 30 years is a legitimate sample size," Moran said, "and it includes more than a decade of the Knight era. And as you look at tournament performance, number of head coaches because I think if you're going to have a checklist of blueblood qualities, stability would rank high on my list."

Moran said to look at other blueblood schools and compare how many coaches they have had in the last 17 years. He said the Indiana number could be four or five depending on if you include Dan Dakich, who coached the Hoosiers on an interim basis at the end of the 2007-08 season after Kelvin Sampson was fired.

Obviously Duke has only had Mike Krzyzewski since 1980. Kansas has had either Bill Self or Roy Williams since 1988. Kentucky has had three: Tubby Smith, Billy Gillispie and John Calipari, and North Carolina has had Roy Williams and Matt Doherty. Even UCLA, a program you think of that may have had some turnover, has only had three coaches in that time span. That would be Steve Lavin, Ben Howland and now Steve Alford.

"To me the whole aura of blueblood status does not match the performance over 30 years," Moran said. "It doesn't come close. They have the trappings but they haven't had the performance."

And Moran doesn't buy the whole argument that Indiana perhaps belongs in the next tier down of schools that you could argue are in a top 10 list of the best programs ever.

"This might seem like semantics but either you're a blueblood or you're not," Moran said. "I don't know if there are degrees. And if you're looking at the period of say over the last 20, 25 or 30 years, I would think Michigan State definitely belongs on that list. I would say Arizona definitely belongs on that list. They've won and they've consistently competed at a high level.

"But for Indiana since 1987, I don't think you can justify them being anywhere near that list."

•••••

Zach Osterman, the IU beat writer for the *Indianapolis Star*, had an interesting take on why he thinks that IU is hand's down a top 10 program in the country for certain and has the potential to possibly re-enter the elite once more.

71

Osterman explained an exercise that he believes proves his point. (It's kind of long but stay with us here).

He said if you wiped the slate clean on all 14 Big Ten programs and all you had was facilities, fan base, budget, recruiting base and administrative support and then lined up the 14 coaches in the Big Ten and asked them to pick where they would like to coach, he believes they would come to the same conclusion. He said somehow you would have to tell one that since he's the best coach he would pick first, and the next best would pick second, etc...

"I believe that coach picks Indiana because I believe in a vacuum that Indiana is the best job in the conference," Osterman said. "It has the second most Big Ten titles of all time, the most All-Americans, the most NBA draft picks, and half of the conference's national championships in the sport. And as long as those things still exist and as long as those people who set expectations for the program can still treat Indiana that way, then those expectations are legitimate."

Osterman said he believes Indiana has a top 10 facility, top 10 fan support and a top 5 recruiting base.

"It's in one of the three best conferences in the country consistently," Osterman said. "It has a fan base that is incredibly rabid and hyper but is extremely passionate. It has more tradition than anybody else in the Big Ten can boast. As long as those things exist, people at Indiana have a right to expect that this is consistently an elite program.

"Maybe not one of those top four but certainly always in the top 10," Osterman said. "When you're talking year after year who are the top 8-10 programs in the country, Indiana is always in that group. I think that's a fair expectation."

Osterman said and then maybe one day you regain your lofty status at the top.

"Maybe at some point you do break into that top four if you get it right and somebody else starts to get it wrong," Osterman said.

72

Bob Knight and his team during the national anthem.

Osterman said he believed the blue blood programs nationally were the big four: North Carolina, Duke, Kansas and Kentucky. And he thinks Indiana belongs either in the conversation or just outside of it.

"Are people realistic in that Indiana can compete for the Final Four every year? No, of course not," Osterman said. "But I think if you look around the country there are four programs that are established as above the rest. That's North Carolina, Duke, Kansas and Kentucky. Behind those is a group that includes Syracuse, Louisville, Michigan State, UCLA and I think includes Indiana. There are probably a couple of others I missed, too.

"And if you were somehow were able to add up a sum total of who has the best facilities, who has the best fan base, who has the most tradition they can lean on, who has the best recruiting base and who plays in the conference that will put them in the most advantageous position then Indiana has to be in that conversation."

You can make the argument that having the right coach can take you a long way into the blueblood conversation. If you have the resources, budget and fan base but don't have the right coach leading your program it can be difficult to be successful. North Carolina suffered through Matt Doherty before landing Roy Williams. Kentucky had Billy Gillespie right before John Calipari.

Alex Bozich thinks the same could be true at Indiana if Archie Miller indeed turns out to be the right guy.

"When you look at the resources and the fan support that Indiana has had I think they can get back up there but I don't think for a variety of reasons that they've had the right guy since Knight," Bozich said. "And even in Knight's last (six) years, he was average at best. It has been a long time.

"Everyone likes to point to the banners and obviously they do mean something but after a while ... it's fun to talk about and it's good for fans to have pride about most kids you talk to don't care anymore than Indiana won a national championship in 1987."

Bozich said there are two ways to look at it: potential vs. reality. His basic point was that Indiana has the potential but the reality is that its not a blueblood program.

Bozich said he did a study of Big Ten teams in 2016 and compared different programs using his own set of criteria. And Indiana ranked fifth among Big Ten schools.

"So are they a top 10 program based on what they have done in recent history? I don't think there's any way you can argue for that," Bozich said. "Now should they be a top 10 program based on what they put into it and what is available to them resource-wise and the in-state talent in the area? Like I said I think there is the potential to be there as a top 10 program but is there the body of work and recent history that would suggest that they are right now?

"Absolutely not."

Bob Lovell, the host of Network Indiana's Indiana Sports Talk program and a former head basketball coach for 12 seasons at IUPUI, said if the criteria is a top five or six program then he doesn't think Indiana belongs in that group. Top 10?

"I do think Indiana is a top 10 program and I don't think that is that bad," Lovell said. "But I believe with the facilities they have, the budget they have, the fan support that they have that they can absolutely get back to that place again. I'm not sure how soon but I believe they can. The proof is in the classic pudding.

"If you're an ESPN programmer and you're putting together a high profile event does Indiana get invited to those events? The answer is no. In terms of people who are decision makers or image shapers or however you want to say it they're not a top five program. But I think they can be within a few years and get back to where they were. I really believe that."

• • • • •

Mike Pegram, the longtime publisher of the popular IU fan site Peegs.com, said he believes Indiana is a selective blueblood program.

"I would just say it is a blueblood program in certain respects," Pegram said. "I think in fan support it's a blueblood and that's a big thing. Indiana fans travel well and they support their team. And when they bring in a recruit for Hoosier Hysteria or for a home game, it really shows because fans know of the recruits and they appreciate them being in the building."

Pegram admits though that in the overall scope of college basketball, things have changed a bit on the Indiana front.

"But Indiana doesn't have the name recognition right now because of a lack of Final Fours and success in the tournament and any consistency in the top part of the Big Ten standings," Pegram said. "But you can't dismiss what it means to have the full support of the fan base whether it's a real game or not. That is something that is hard to match with the exception of just a few places in the country."

Another thought that kind of piggybacks off of the blueblood idea is whether Indiana basketball fans simply have an unrealistic opinion of where their program should be. It has been 30 years since a national championship. There have been two Final Four appearances since 1988, too. And yet IU fans, every time the Hoosiers earn a top 10 national ranking like they have in 17 seasons since 1988 are quick to believe that this could be the year that the drought ends.

Take the 2016-17 season for example after Indiana opened the season in Honolulu by knocking off No. 3 ranked Kansas and a few weeks later beat another No. 3 ranked team in eventual national champion North Carolina in the ACC-Big Ten Challenge. The win over Kansas got the fans excited, but then a loss to Fort Wayne brought them back to reality. Then came the win over North Carolina and hopes were up again.

Indianapolis sports radio talk show host Kent Sterling said talk at this point of a sixth national championship banner is simply false optimism by fans yearning for something that is still a ways off in the distance.

"Even after the wins over Kansas and North Carolina, anyone who watched that team knew how far off that team was in the scheme of things," Sterling said. "You just knew that other teams were going to be able to progress through the year in ways that Indiana couldn't do."

I spoke to a few players about the whole idea of whether Indiana fans have unrealistic expectations and most of them believe that there's nothing wrong with aspiring to greatness.

"I understand the expectations because we're a blueblood program," said Christian Watford, who played for Tom Crean from 2010-13. "You look at Kansas and they're always in there. The same with Duke, North Carolina and UCLA has been there, too.

"But the expectations are achievable when you look at other programs. I could see it if the other blueblood programs weren't doing it but they're constantly in the mix every year so why shouldn't Indiana be in there?"

Jarrad Odle, who played for both Knight and Davis in his four seasons at IU, said unrealistic expectations simply come with the territory in college basketball.

"I think every fan of every school has unrealistic expectations," Odle said. "I think they expect a Final Four or a national championship every year. But on the other hand, I wouldn't want it any other way because I think that fan or that fanatic that is part of our fan base is what makes it so fun.

"It's not supposed to be a cakewalk and if it was then every school would be able to get to the top every single year. I don't think it's unrealistic because that's the way it has always been and always will be at Indiana. "

Lance Stemler played two seasons at Indiana and Kelvin Sampson was his coach both years. But he continues to be a big supporter living in Southern Indiana. He acknowledged that the expectations are high but doesn't think they're unrealistic.

"The expectations are wildly high I would say but I don't think they're anywhere they shouldn't be though," Stemler said. "I think when you have five championship banners and when you are in a state that backs the program like they do, I don't have a problem with it."

Stemler said he believes the fans of Indiana are entitled to think the way that many of them do.

"Coming from Illinois, Indiana high school basketball to me is on the top echelon as far as it goes in high school

IU's all-time leading scorer Calbert Cheaney talks with IU coach Mike Davis.

basketball," Stemler said. "And I think the knowledge base of Indiana basketball fans is extremely high. I think that's where those expectations come from and I think coach Knight built it over his time at IU. I think he put that expectation there and I think that's good especially with the level of talent that is within this state."

Mike Marot, the Indianapolis-based Associated Press writer who has covered Indiana University basketball for more than two decades, thinks the idea of aspiring to something like being a blueblood program is a good thing for the Hoosiers.

"I do think you have to aspire to the level you want to get to," Marot said. "Is it unrealistic? Probably. But fans are always unrealistic to some extent. I mean fans always think their NFL team is going to win the Super Bowl every year. And they don't."

As for the blueblood discussion though Marot said what most seem to agree with that when you're talking Indiana and blueblood you're talking more in the past tense.

"There was a time when Indiana was one of the blueblood programs," Marot said, "but recently has it been a blueblood program? Not really. If you go back to the last national championship year this is a program that gets to the NCAA Tournament on a pretty regular basis, it gets to the Sweet Sixteen a couple of times and that's about as far as they get with the exception of the run in 2002 with Mike Davis and the Final Four team in the early 1990s.

"But can they get back to that level of greatness? Yes, they can get back. All of these programs can get back. But it comes down to fans needing to be patient and I really don't think they have been."

Did Marot just used the words Indiana, fans and patient in the same sentence? That's not something you see very often.

Malcom Moran offered an interesting perspective though, too, when he said that if you looked at the period of Indiana basketball from the early 1960's until the time that Bob Knight arrived at the university, you could have made the same claim that Indiana wasn't a blueblood like it had been in the mid 1950's when the Hoosiers put up their second national championship banner in 1953.

"If someone was evaluating the status of the IU program from the beginning of the 1960's to the beginning of the 1970's you could have said the same thing and if anything, for most of that period, IU appeared to be further away from that (blueblood) level than it is now," Moran said. "It didn't have the facility yet. In terms of national visibility the program really became dormant."

Moran is correct in that viewpoint, too. In the 1950's, IU won 154 games and had a Big Ten record of 95-47. In the 1960's, Indiana won 135 games total and had a conference record of 71-69. The 1950's had four first place Big Ten finishes and one second place. The next decade had one of each.

And then when the blueblood period arrived with Knight in the 1970's and '80's those numbers really took off. In the

1970's, IU was 208-75 overall and 113-47 in Big Ten play. In the 1980's those numbers were 228-86 including a record of 126-54 in conference. The 1990's were solid, too, despite the fact that IU didn't make it out of the first weekend of the NCAA Tournament its final six seasons under Knight.

In the 1990's, Indiana's record was 229-94 and 116-60.

Compare that to the two decades since Knight left IU. In the 2000's, IU had a record of 187-32 and 90-74 in conference. Through the first eight seasons of the current decade, Indiana is 170-110 but has a losing conference record overall at 70-74.

Doesn't sound a lot like a blueblood program any more does it?

"And I wouldn't say it's easier now but it's simple to elevate to elite status today because in the 1960's the league would receive one bid to the NCAA Tournament," Moran said. "So if you get in the NIT you're going to have a good year. But you wouldn't even have a chance to get to the Final Four unless you won your league back then.

"Now in year two or three of the Archie Miller regime, they could be the third or fourth best team in the Big Ten, and be very good, and get on a roll in March and get to the Final Four and people are going to be saying 'happy days are here again.'"

And once again IU fans everywhere will trumpet the program's return to greatness.

"Once again the perception will be 'Indiana is back like they felt it was in 2002,'" Moran said. "The problem then was they couldn't sustain it. When Indiana beat Duke in 2002 and made it to the national title game, and people forget how close that team came to pulling a rabbit out of its hat and winning the whole thing, the perception was Indiana is back and they are on their way.

"But they just couldn't sustain it."

5

Right Guy or Wrong Guy?

Since Bob Knight was fired in September of 2000, Indiana basketball has had a total of five coaches lead its basketball program.

Four of them were permanent head coaches and the fifth, Dan Dakich, coached the final seven games of the 2007-08 season but then was not hired to replace Kelvin Sampson on a permanent basis.

But when you look at the permanent replacements, it is difficult to lump them all into one category because they were all very different.

Using hindsight as 20-20 vision it's easy to look back now on the first three permanent hires and determine whether the move was the right one or the wrong on Indiana University's part.

If I were to put those labels on each of the coaches, it would come out something like this and I'll explain in detail in the rest of the chapter:

Mike Davis: Wrong.

Kelvin Sampson: Wrong

Tom Crean: Right

Archie Miller: Right

Obviously, it's a little too early to tell with Miller, since as of the writing of this book in the summer of 2017 his record as the Indiana coach was still 0-0. He was hired in March of 2017. But the early reaction to Miller has been very positive and so without the benefit of 20-20 vision, we'll put him in the right person category for now.

As for the others, the conventional wisdom goes something like this:

Indiana should never be someone's first head coaching job and yet that was the case with Davis. Most everyone you talk to will tell you that Davis faced an impossible situation and actually still performed at a much higher level that probably should have been expected. And taking that 2002 team to the only post-Knight Final Four and ultimately the championship game before losing to Maryland was an impressive feat.

The reality with Davis though was that he was in over his head. He has admitted as much in recent years in a couple of interviews. As he puts it, his coaching progression should have been from Texas Southern to UAB to Indiana, and not the other way around. It's hard to argue with that way of thinking.

But Davis was a class act and will forever be remembered as the coach who took over for the legendary Bob Knight at Indiana.

As former IU great Steve Alford once said though, he didn't want to be the guy that followed Knight at Indiana. He wanted to be the guy who followed the guy that followed Knight at Indiana.

Again with the benefit of 20-20 hindsight, it's certainly easy to see why you would think that way.

The no-brainer in terms of a coach who will wear the wrong hire tag is Kelvin Sampson. He cheated at Oklahoma, swore that he had learned his lesson and wouldn't do it again and then turned around and repeated the same behavior at Indiana.

When Sampson's tenure ended at Indiana, 26 games into his second season on the job, the Indiana University program was on the verge of being brought to its knees by the NCAA Committee on Infractions. A charge of lack of institutional control was levied against IU athletic director Rick Greenspan and it would take three years for IU basketball to recover.

Kelvin Sampson

The shame is that Kelvin Sampson was a pretty darn good coach. Several people that I interviewed for this book have said they honestly believe that had Sampson kept his nose clean and played by the rules that Indiana would have had another national championship banner hanging by now. But that's completely hypothetical, too.

As for the wrong person tag for Sampson, there were a great number of people who believed before Sampson had ever coached a game that IU had made the wrong hire. They didn't like his history of skirting the NCAA rules book and it was just something that a lot of people didn't understand from the very first.

As former ESPN college basketball analyst Andy Katz said in an interview for this book, on the day that Indiana hired Kelvin Sampson it did the most un-Indiana like thing that Indiana had ever done.

No one could argue with that.

• • • • •

Sampson was followed by Dan Dakich who spent 39 days on the job including 12 days after the season had ended with a thud in the first round of the NCAA Tournament in Raleigh, N.C. With Dakich at the helm, IU had finished the regular season by winning three of five games to finish with a 25-6 record overall and a 14-4 mark in the Big Ten. That final record would be 25-8, however, as IU was upset in the first game of the Big Ten Tournament by Minnesota and then lost to Arkansas in the NCAA Tournament.

I opt not to put a tag one way or the other on Dakich. If I was pressed for one, I would say it was the right move as Dakich did everyone in the university a tremendous favor when he took over the team on an interim basis. Dakich, who had been the head coach at Bowling Green as well as serving as an assistant under Knight for 10 years from 1987-97, had spent one season on Sampson's staff and then was promoted to the interim job when Sampson was fired.

But again, my own feeling is that Dakich had too small of a sample size to really judge or analyze what his potential could have been for bringing Indiana basketball back to a sustained level of success. The truth is he never was given a real chance. Everyone else, the permanent head coaches, were given an opportunity but that wasn't the case with Dakich.

When I spoke to former IU athletic director Rick Greenspan for this book, I asked him about Dakich and wondered if it was a case where he felt that because Dakich had been on Sampson's staff, and Sampson had just broken the rules, that he really couldn't hire someone from that staff? Or was it more than that?

In essence, however, Greenspan defended the decision to bring him along as the interim coach but wasn't definitive regarding why it ended there.

"I knew of Dan a little bit, and I had talked to Dan before that job and I had also talked to coach Knight about him," Greenspan said. "I had spent a reasonable amount of time with Dan once he came back and accepted the interim position. And what I thought, and I think I was absolutely correct in this, is that Dan would be a very honest guy. I thought he was a good interim fit.

"And to me at that point in time, honesty was a trait that the institution absolutely needed. And Dan as everybody knows is outspoken, he can be bombastic, he can be opinionated, he can will people, players and recruits along the way but he's an honest guy. And to me that was critical at that time, but quite honestly it was more critical than it was to some people at the higher levels of the institution."

Twelve days after the 2007-08 season came to an end, Greenspan introduced Tom Crean as the next IU basketball coach. Like Davis, another class act, Crean also faced a situation as Davis did with the odds stacked against him. With Davis, it was the impossible task of following Bob Knight. With Crean, it was the near impossible task of playing a basketball season in just a few short months with only the benefit of one scholarship player and one walk-on. And the scholarship player had been a walk-on until just the previous season.

Crean's first year IU was 6-25 and 1-17 in the Big Ten. His second year there was improvement to 10-21 and 4-14 in the conference and then in year three went 12-20 and 3-15 in conference.

But while picking up a couple of key recruits, including Indiana Mr. Basketball Cody Zeller, a diamond in the rough in Victor Oladipo and a young playmaker in Yogi Ferrell, IU was able to post back-to-back Sweet Sixteen appearances the next two seasons.

Crean's problem at IU was maintaining that consistent, sustained level of success. Ultimately, following an NIT appearance the year after winning the outright Big Ten title in 2016, the university made the decision to let Crean go.

That led to the hiring of Archie Miller who got the Indiana fan base on his side right from the start when he talked about two things being a priority for IU basketball at this time: Playing defense and valuing the basketball. When he added the fact that he wanted to do a better job recruiting the state of Indiana and keep players from the state at home, he had many, many Indiana fans hooked.

The problem, as I mentioned before, is that it's way too early to be passing judgement on whether Miller is the right person for the job.

•••••

Here's a closer look at each of the former IU coaches.

Let's start with Mike Davis, again one of the most likeable coaches I've ever been around. Davis always wore his heart on his sleeve. Sometimes that would get him in trouble. But he lasted in the position and took IU to within one game of winning in the national championship game.

For Mike Davis following Bob Knight it was almost an impossible situation to the 10th power. As former IU All-American Brian Evans said, looking back it almost wasn't fair. Indiana University basketball should never be someone's first coaching job and yet that was the case with Davis.

ESPN college basketball analyst Jeff Goodman said it was a similar situation that Josh Pastner was in when he took the job at Memphis in 2009. Pastner had been an assistant at Arizona under Lute Olson and then served as an assistant for one season at Memphis under John Calipari before he was hired as Calapari's successor.

In Pastner's case, he was 31 years old. At least with Davis, he was three days shy of his 40th birthday when he was hired as the interim coach at Indiana.

"You can compare it to Josh Pastner," Goodman said. "Josh Pastner's first job shouldn't have been Memphis. Mike Davis's first job should have been a mid-major job. And it wasn't. So he wasn't ready for it and he'll be the first to tell you that."

If you look at Davis's pedigree, perhaps he should have started at Texas Southern, then moved on to UAB and one day had a chance to coach at a place like Indiana. Instead, he did it in reverse.

"If his career arc had been the opposite, it could have been completely different," said Dave Revsine of the Big Ten Network. "If a guy like that starts at Texas Southern, goes to UAB and then takes over Indiana maybe we're talking about it very differently. I just remember the circumstances were impossible."

In a 2017 interview that was a part of a special titled "A Taste of Coaching" that aired on the Big Ten Network, Davis repeated basically the same thing. Seventeen years had clearly given the former IU coach the necessary perspective.

"(Indiana) should be your last job, not your first job," Davis said.

While talking with former UCLA and St. John's head coach Steve Lavin during the Big Ten special, Davis admitted it was difficult to see it when he was living it, beginning in the 2000-01 season.

"I was too naive then to see it and understand," Davis said. "But now I look back and I get nervous."

Davis, much like what Gene Bartow had once said about following John Wooden at UCLA, admitted that the pressure was enormous when he coached at Indiana.

"I was under the spotlight," he said. "Every game, no matter what it was, who it was, we had to win. And not just win, but win by 20 points, which is impossible.

"I'm at Texas Southern now. It should've been Texas Southern, UAB, Indiana. Not Indiana, UAB, and Texas Southern."

Davis, who spent three seasons under Knight as an assistant at IU, said the area where he experienced the biggest feeling that he wasn't ready for the Indiana job was in terms of preparation.

"Coach Knight taught me a lot, but it was unbelievable because I wasn't prepared," Davis said. "I knew I wasn't prepared, but I was trying to walk out like I was prepared."

If you were to ask 100 people what they thought the biggest issue that Davis faced when he took over the reins of the Indiana program, probably more than 90 would give some variation of a basic theme that Davis was simply in over his head.

And he was. He had never been a head basketball coach at any level and all of a sudden he was directing one of the most consistently successful college basketball programs in the country.

Indianapolis Star columnist Gregg Doyel said he didn't think there was any doubt that Davis was in over his head but at the same time the university was in a tough spot and given that reality it's not that hard to believe that the coach they hired was going to be someone who very likely might struggle in that position.

"IU was in a tough spot when they promoted him," Doyel said. "They had just fired the guy, the players were talking about revolting and I can only imagine how angry the fan base was. I wasn't (in Indianapolis) yet but everyone was in a tough spot. The administration felt it had no choice to keep this program from literally falling apart and felt that if they didn't do something quickly that everybody might be gone.

"And so they promoted Mike Davis to keep the peace and frankly, hope to get lucky. And they did get lucky for one year. But the farther Mike Davis got away from Bob Knight and the more he impacted player development, the more it was obvious that he was in over his head."

But even if you use the 'in-over-his-head' phrase as a common theme, I've always wondered if his players sensed it when they played for him. Did his players think Davis was in over his head or were they too much into the moment to really know if he was or wasn't?

Jarrad Odle, who played in Knight's final two seasons and Davis's first two at IU, said there was one thing that stood out about playing for Davis – he knew basketball.

"I don't know if we really felt that he was in over his head but I'll tell you the one thing with coach Davis is that he was and probably still is one of the best basketball minds that there is out there," Odle said. "He knows the game like nobody else. But I think at a place like IU you have to be so much more than a basketball coach. You've got to be the media representative and the interview guy.

"With coach Davis, I think it was everything outside of the basketball court that he was overwhelmed with. He always fought that speech impediment that he had and he overcame a lot of it but we could sense that when he would get the most stressed was when he got the most pressure from the media or the fans."

Former Indiana player Joe Hillman, who played on the '87 national championship team, said no one can blame Davis for taking the job. His point: How could Davis possibly have turned it down?

"It was a no-brainer. He absolutely had to take the position when it was offered," Hillman said. "Anyone in his situation would have done the same thing. Heck, if they had come to me and asked me I would have said, 'Yes', without even thinking about it.

"But then when he got there and realized just how overwhelming the job was I just think it was that point that he realized he was in over his head and then it was too late to turn back."

If you polled that same hundred people and asked them what kind of person they thought Davis was, you would get the same percentage that said he was genuinely a really good person. It would be difficult to find too many people that didn't like Davis.

That was certainly the sentiment of the players – and not just the ones that suited up for him at Indiana but past IU players who had played for Branch McCracken or Bob Knight, too. Everyone liked Mike Davis the person.

"I really liked Mike Davis," said former IU standout Pat Graham, a member of IU's vaunted recruiting class of 1989. "Just one-on-one, me and him, I liked Mike Davis. I think Mike Davis got thrown in to a hot tub that I don't know if anyone at his age or experience level could have handled.

"I think those guys really enjoyed playing for him. I was already gone but he was very respectful of me when I would come around. But when it really came down to it, I don't think coach Davis had a clue of what he was really getting into when he took that job. When you're at Indiana, Kentucky, Duke, North Carolina, those kinds of places, that's just a different world."

The first to follow the General – Mike Davis

Todd Leary, Graham's teammate from 1989-94, said basically the same thing.

"You were never going to find a nicer guy than Mike Davis. You just weren't," Leary said. "But to be successful at Indiana it takes more than just being a nice guy. And when you added everything up that's where Davis fell short in some areas."

Longtime Purdue coach Gene Keady said he felt bad for Davis because he was put into a situation where he really didn't have a realistic chance to succeed.

"No one was going to follow Bob Knight and expect to be successful," Keady said. "It was more of a case of trying to find someone to bridge the gap between Knight and some other coach down the line. It was too bad. I really liked Mike. We didn't have a lot in common but I think most of that was our difference in age. But I always thought he worked really hard and did the absolute best he could do in a very difficult set of circumstances."

There's no question that when Davis took over the Indiana job on an interim basis just as school was beginning in September of 2000, the odds were stacked against him. A few days earlier, on September 10, Indiana University President Myles Brand had dismissed Knight following 29 seasons as the IU basketball coach.

While Brand felt Knight's run in with a student who Knight felt disrespected him rose to the level of a violation of the "zero tolerance" policy that the head coach was existing under, many in the IU fan base were up in arms. It was an angry mob-like environment that Davis walked into.

Dave Furst, the sports anchor for WRTV-6 television in Indianapolis, said when it came to Knight at the end you were either one of the people that supported him to the end or you were ready to move on. There wasn't a lot of middle ground.

Some referred it to as the Knight followers were the grape-Koolaid drinking Bob Knight fans. They would follow him anywhere. And many did. For several years in Bloomington, after Knight had moved on to his new job at Texas Tech, there were a lot of people at IU games wearing Texas Tech gear almost as their own personal protest.

"You were either on the Knight train or you didn't like Knight," Furst said. "But there would still be people in the stands who put on the red sweaters and still wished that Bob was the head coach in Bloomington. And that lasted for a long time.

"But Mike had the hardest job of anyone. He had to be the guy to follow The Guy and that had to be a hard gig for anyone. It's like the guy who is going to follow Mike Krzykewski at Duke. Hey, good luck to that guy."

Don Fischer, the voice of Indiana University football and basketball, said so much of what Davis found himself dealing with upon being hired at IU was completely out of his control.

"A lot of the backlash that Mike was dealing with wasn't necessarily against him, it was against Indiana University at that time," Fischer said. "It was more against Myles Brand and the people who were responsible for taking coach Knight out of his position as the head coach at Indiana. So when you looked at it, Mike was dealing with stuff that I don't think he ever thought he would be dealing with.

"Plus, he was in that fishbowl that is Indiana and that's not a good place for a coach who has never been in that position before and essentially learning on the job."

Dave Revsine of the Big Ten Network said with everything Davis was facing it's amazing he enjoyed the level of success he did in his six seasons at the IU head coach.

"You had the circumstances with Knight's firing that a lot of people didn't agree with so you have a fan base that is divided from the get go as to whether you even ought to have a different coach let alone this guy," Revsine said. "He's not an Indiana guy. Knight does nothing to help the circumstances obviously. He doesn't support him at all. I think given everything that was working against him and it was his first head coaching job, it's remarkable.

"In his second year he took them to the national championship game. Imagine if they would have won that game. Would we be telling a different story? It's crazy that it almost worked. Maybe that speaks to the power of Indiana. With everything working against him he still almost pulled it off. I think it points out that he's a pretty good coach and I think we have subsequently seen that he's a pretty good coach."

Former ESPN college basketball analyst Andy Katz said it was a complex situation because Davis was a man who was caught in the middle. The Knight camp didn't want him to take the job and instead stay loyal to coach Knight. But on the flip side how do you, with a clear conscience, turn down the Indiana job if it's offered to you?

"It was an impossible situation," Katz said. "I think he'll admit it was overwhelming and that he didn't handle things well. He didn't do anything wrong in terms of cheating or anything like that but he was sort of his own worst enemy. He was Indiana's first African American coach and so he just had so many different things coming at him.

"Maybe one of the things that worked against him the most was making it to the title game. Because with that came a completely different level of expectation."

One of the most interesting debates that is forever waged when you talk about Davis following Knight is simply to consider what would have happened had the university opted to go a different direction in September of 2000 and not cave in to the players' demands at the time? What would have happened had IU opted to open up a job search at that time and hire from the outside? How much would have Indiana's basketball history been different today?

You could even make the case that Indiana had a chance to take a mulligan when after Davis's interim year, the university had a chance to open up the search again but decided after one season with Davis at the helm that it would stick with the interim coach on a full time basis.

In Davis's first year at IU, the Hoosiers went 10-6 in the Big Ten and made it to the finals of the Big Ten Tournament and eventually lost to Kent State in the first round of the NCAA Tournament in San Diego.

Looking back, CBS analyst Billy Packer predicted – incorrectly as it turned out – that whoever won the Big Ten Tournament championship game would be named the next Indiana basketball coach. Packer made his comment at the under 4 timeout of the conference title game. Indiana was ahead at the time but Iowa, coached by Steve Alford, ultimately won the game 63-61.

A few days after the season ended, however, IU President Myles Brand announced that Davis would return as the Indiana coach.

In a story written by the Associated Press, Brand made the announcement after two days of deliberations "and a morning filled with contract negotiations."

"We don't name basketball coaches very often around here, and when we do we make sure that we make the right choice," Brand said at the time. "This season has revealed the character of Mike Davis. He and the team have represented the university very well indeed."

University vice president Terry Clapacs, a future IU athletic director and one of seven members on the committee that decided Davis's fate, said no other candidates were contacted.

So IU had a second chance but based on how the season had turned out it felt there was no reason to open up the search. The Hoosiers felt that they had their man.

Interestingly, when you go back to Sept. 10, 2000 and read the news accounts of Knight's firing, there's a line in there where IU President Myles Brand says that a "national search" for Knight's replacement would begin immediately.

The reality, however, is that 48 hours later, Clarence Doninger announced on Sept. 12 that Mike Davis had been hired as IU's 25th head basketball coach. Davis would coach his first season with an interim tag.

The high for Davis was obviously the magical run through the NCAA Tournament in 2002 when the No. 5 seeded Hoosiers won five games (including beating No. 1 Duke in the Sweet Sixteen in Lexington) en route to the national championship game where the Hoosiers lost to Maryland.

Many believed at that moment that Indiana was back and had turned the corner again. Unfortunately, as has kind of been the theme with Indiana basketball post-Bob Knight, Davis was unable to maintain a sustained level of success.

The next season IU would win 21 games, go 8-8 in the conference and make the second day of the NCAA Tournament. At some very basic way of looking at it, IU fans were probably still OK with that.

But then the bottom fell out. First it was the 14-15 season where IU was shut out of any postseason play for the first time since the 1976-77 season. Then came the 15-14 season where IU made it to the NIT but lost a first round home game to Vanderbilt.

By the time the 2005-06 season came, Indiana fans were calling for a change. Midway through the season, after a Feb. 11 game at Penn State, the news broke that Davis had resigned. He coached out the rest of the season.

Former IU player Todd Leary was the color commentator on the IU radio network along with Don Fischer during Davis's tenure. He said that preparation was one of the things that really stood out to him about what was different with the IU program when it changed coaches.

"Doing the radio in the early 2000 years, and you know I like Mike Davis a lot, but I never felt like those teams were overly prepared when they went into a game," Leary said. "But when you had Dane Fife, and Tom Coverdale and those guys that were ultracompetitive slash probably carrying over some of that preparedness from coach Knight, that was a big key.

"Once that leadership was gone then I think it became very difficult to have the same culture that Indiana had experienced under coach Knight."

So what happened in those final three seasons of Davis's tenure that was so much different than the success he had enjoyed in the first three years?

Many believe it came down to recruiting and the fact that Indiana was unable to get the kind of players it had thrived on for so many years. Instead, the recruiting focus shifted toward bringing in more elite level players and when in many cases they chose not to attend IU, Indiana was left to play a rugged Big Ten schedule with inferior talent.

Former Indiana player Todd Meier, who was one of three seniors on the 1987 national championship team, said he thought the turning point for Davis was when he no longer had Knight's players in his system.

"I just thought coach Davis did well because he was able to transition with coach Knight's players but it seemed like at some point he lost the hard core, toughness, disciplined aspect of the game," Meier said. "He just had a completely different style than coach Knight. He was maybe more of a player's coach where coach Knight was more 'You're my player and this is how we're going to play basketball.'

"So I'm not sure exactly what it was. It seemed like we lost a little bit of our toughness. Our defense wasn't what it once was. I don't want to take anything away from what coach Davis did, I just think it was a different style. It wasn't coach Knight's blistering, in-your-face, tougher style of basketball."

Derek Schultz, an afternoon sports radio talk show host in Indianapolis, said while a lot of people will try to maintain that Indiana could have gotten a much better coach than Davis in that situation, the reality is that may not have been the case.

Trying to find a coach for a season that was beginning in less than six weeks was not going to be an easy task.

"Given the context of the situation I think it's revisionist history to think that if Indiana opened up that job that 100 people would have been calling begging for it because it was such a tough situation," Schultz said. "What I had always heard and I don't even know if this is true is that (Rick) Pitino was interested. He was with the Celtics at that time and he was interested in getting back.

"I think it's far more likely you would have ended up with a Tom Crean type of coach and kind of what happened with Penn State football and James Franklin replacing Joe Paterno. But I think you would have ended up with someone like that who was kind of a middle tier guy who was willing to take on a challenge."

Schultz said to be honest he's not sure that Indiana could have bridged the gap any better than it did by hiring Davis.

"In hindsight, people's opinion of Davis has greatly improved because I think they appreciate what he went through," Schultz said. "The fact is that yes, it was kind of a fluky run in 2002 but the when you look at the last 20 to 25 years that's kind of the rose among the thorns. That's the greatest memory and certainly the most entertaining run Indiana has had since IU teams started to slide in the mid 1990's."

• • • • •

So that gives you a taste of the Mike Davis era of Indiana basketball. In chapter 6, I'll deal exclusively with the mess that was Kelvin Sampson in a chapter devoted just to his two seasons.

But now let's talk about Tom Crean.

Of the first three coaches that followed Bob Knight at Indiana, there's little argument that Crean came the closest to getting IU over the top.

He won two outright Big Ten championships in a four-year span, something that hadn't been done at Indiana in more than 30 years.

He took Indiana to three Sweet Sixteen appearances in a five-year span, again something that hadn't been done at IU since the early 1990's.

And while many will say that Mike Davis found himself in an impossible situation at Indiana as a young, green coach with no previous head coaching experience attempting to be the first to follow Bob Knight, it can be argued that Crean faced impossible times five.

When all of the dust had cleared and a few players had left the program following the Kelvin Sampson debacle – some voluntary and some through dismissals – Crean found himself with two players returning.

One was Kyle Taber, a 6-7 senior forward who had played in 22 games and averaged 1.3 points the year before. Taber had been a walk-on at Indiana his first two seasons but had been put on scholarship by Sampson his junior season.

The other was 6-foot guard Brett Finkelmeier, a walk-on from Carmel, Ind. who had played in seven games the season before and scored a total of two points.

To put that in perspective, in the 2007-08 season, coached mostly by Sampson and on an interim basis for seven games by Dan Dakich, Indiana had scored 2,476 points.

Taber and Finkelmeier accounted for 30 of those points. There had been 10 players on the roster the previous season that had a higher scoring average than Taber.

In other words, Crean was being asked to rebuild Indiana from the ground up with 30 points total in scoring returning from the season before.

Yes, it was an impossible situation times five. Maybe times 10.

But Crean and his assistant coaching staff navigated the impossible and somehow, within four seasons, had Indiana back in the Sweet Sixteen. From year 3 to year 4, Crean's Indiana squad had improved from a 12-20 season which included a 3-15 Big Ten mark to 27-9 and 11-7 in conference.

During that turnaround season, IU knocked off the No. 1 team in the nation (Kentucky), No. 2 (Ohio State) and No. 5 Michigan State. It was the first time in school history that a coach had guided his team to wins over both a No. 1 and No. 2 team in the same season.

The one thing you hear over and over when you mention Crean is how people are quick to give him credit for returning Indiana basketball to respectability again.

Former Indiana player Todd Meier, one of three seniors on the 1987 national championship team, said Crean will always have a special place in the hearts of former players because of the way he returned IU basketball from the ashes.

"You got to love him and God bless coach Crean for what he did for Indiana basketball no question about it," Meier said.

Brian Evans, a former IU All-American who played at Indiana from 1993-96, said Crean deserves credit for bringing Indiana back. It was an impossible job. But in the same breath he said Crean ultimately just didn't do enough to be the guy for the future.

"Coach Crean brought us back from the dead but he just didn't have enough sustained success," Evans said. "He gave us a huge effort. I mean nobody ever questioned that. He gave a great effort and we've got to be appreciative of that. But we just didn't sustain it. Indiana needs to be like Kansas where we rattle off 30 tournament appearances in a row. We can't be a No. 1 seed and then not make the tournament the next year. And then be a 5-seed and not make the tournament the next year. That just can't be Indiana basketball."

Indianapolis Star columnist Gregg Doyel said Crean inherited a landfill when he arrived at Indiana.

"He wasn't building on the foundation of Knight, he was building on the foundation of a garbage dump," Doyel said.

"And he built it into the No. 1 team in the nation in four years. That's pretty remarkable. That's up there for sure. I think what he did was amazing to get IU back to that level."

Greg Rakestraw, program director at 1070-The Fan in Indianapolis, said when you think about how poor of shape that Kelvin Sampson left the Indiana program in, you gain an even greater appreciation for Tom Crean.

"You can argue that Tom Crean traveled a tremendous amount of ground to get that program to where it was competing for Big Ten championships and going to the Sweet Sixteen on a regular basis," Rakestraw said. "But again, as far as being the guy to get Indiana over the hump that clearly wasn't going to be the case."

Longtime Indiana broadcaster Don Fischer said Crean inherited a program that was basically "at ground zero."

"The program was a shambles when he took over," Fischer said. "He had to make some tough decisions early and let a few people go. He had to get rid of guys because they weren't going to class and progressing academically."

Fischer said what he believed was truly remarkable about what Crean accomplished was that he was still able to recruit good enough players despite having both hands tied behind his back.

"For recruits the question was do you want to go to Indiana and have to deal with that and the struggles they're going to have for the next few years?" Fischer said. "I can't think of a much tougher situation for a coach to come into and have to try to recruit to that situation."

Christian Watford was one of the program-changing recruits that Crean was able to attract out of Alabama. He arrived at Indiana in 2009 and by the time he left following his senior year in 2013, he would rank in the top 10 in school history in scoring with 1,730 points. He made 164 3-point shots including one against Kentucky at the buzzer in December of

2011 that lifted IU over the No. 1 Wildcats and signaled the official return of the IU program.

Watford said Crean's recruiting message to Watford was simple: Do you want to come to Indiana and be a part of something special?

"That's exactly what I wanted to do and I think I can speak for my teammates in saying the same thing," Watford said. "We saw playing for Indiana as an opportunity to help get the program back on the right track again."

Former *Indianapolis Star* columnist Bob Kravitz said he thought Crean was a good pick and a pretty good fit at the time.

"When you think about the fact that Indiana has made the Sweet Sixteen four times in the last 23 years and three of those times are under Tom Crean, I think that's a pretty impressive statistic," Kravitz said. "I think his downfall was that he micromanages. I think he just got on Fred Glass's nerves. I just think his personality which is type A plus, plus ... plus, probably caused some of the problems. I also think that Fred caved a little bit to the pressure from the outside.

"Of the three guys that have followed Bob Knight at Indiana, I thought that Tom Crean was the best fit coming from a fairly major program in Marquette. He had the right personality when he wasn't losing his mind. And I think he was a pretty decent coach. He wasn't a great coach, but a decent coach."

ESPN college basketball analyst Jeff Goodman said if you go back and look at what he wrote at the time that Indiana hired Crean, Goodman really believed that Crean was the right man for the job.

"I thought he was the right guy," Goodman said. "He may have been the second or third choice but I thought he was the right guy to get the program back. I just think Crean's temperament didn't necessarily fit Bloomington the more you looked at it and see how he fit in there.

"And he was never able to have sustained success. He had success here and there but ultimately going to the tournament every other year is not good enough for Indiana fans. And you know what, it shouldn't be good enough for Indiana fans. Indiana is a better program than that. It should be going to the tournament every year unless something crazy happens and they're completely ravaged by one and done's or something happens like what happened with Kelvin and then you've got to rebuild."

But the Crean era of Indiana basketball turned out to be an up and down rollercoaster of a ride. Once IU got clear of the Sampson mess, Crean was in his fourth season with the Hoosiers. He got IU to back-to-back Sweet Sixteen appearances and in fact in 2013, IU was ranked No. 1 in the nation for 10 weeks and was ultimately the No. 1 overall seed in the NCAA Tournament. But IU was upset by Syracuse in the round of 16.

The next year Indiana fell flat on its face and didn't even qualify for postseason play. A few years later, IU basketball was back and once again won the outright Big Ten title in 2016 and made it to the Sweet Sixteen. But the following year, in Crean's final season at IU, the Hoosiers once again followed a big year with a disappointment. This time, IU didn't make the NCAA Tournament again and suffered a first round loss in the NIT.

Jake Query, the Indianapolis sports radio talk show host, said that eccentricity did Tom Crean in at Indiana.

"He was exhausting on the opposite end of Bob Knight," Query said. "Bob Knight was exhausting for being an ass. Tom Crean was exhausting almost for being too nice and just frankly odd. I think it just wore people out including recruits.

"His best recruiting jobs that he did were when he would just scoop in at the last minute. With the exception of Cody Zeller and Yogi Ferrell, the players that Tom Crean got that were the best for him were players that did not have a lot of exposure to him before they committed."

103

Query said in that respect Tom Crean is like egg nog.

"In small doses, every so often, it's really good," Query said. "But all of a sudden when you realize it's too rich for you and you've had enough there's no turning back and it's immediately like 'OK, that's enough. I don't need that again for another year.' That's kind of how it was with Crean I believe. A little bit of it was cool but after a while it just becomes too much.

"It doesn't make it a bad thing and it doesn't make him a bad guy. He was perfect for what they needed for a five year period, but I think Indiana cut the cord at the right time if not later than they should have. But I think it was time for a change."

Query believes that Crean was the right person at the right time but not the long term answer that was going to get Indiana basketball over the top again.

"Tom Crean was perfect for what Indiana needed at that time," Query said. "Tom Crean reminds me a lot of Ron Meyer or Larry Brown. He was a great rah rah guy that gets people to buy in on a short term basis. People bought in and got all excited and he got everybody back together and he rejuvenated the program.

"But I happen to think that what he did a lot of other people could have done, too."

One thing that drives Query crazy is the notion that Crean did things that other college coaches couldn't have done given the same set of circumstances.

"Tom Crean gets way too much credit," Query said. "It's Indiana. He got Cody Zeller to come to Indiana. OK, that's cool. But who's to say that Sean Miller wouldn't have done that, too? Who's to say that Tom Izzo couldn't have done that? We don't know that.

"I know that Tom Crean gets credit for bringing Indiana from ground zero but let's face it, it's Indiana. So when you get on the elevator at ground zero buttons one, two, three and four are already pushed. It just depends on how far past five you get it and he didn't get them a lot past that."

Query doesn't buy the fact the situation Crean inherited was completely impossible because he still believes that when you go after players that Indiana basketball still is able to sell itself. Even in the darkest days after the Sampson mess, Indiana's tradition and history were still able to shine through the gloom.

"People can say what they want about how he inherited very little from Sampson's last team and that's great," Query said. "But this is not Nebraska. This is Indiana. Based on that alone, there are things that could be sold and the history and tradition alone were going to get some play to have some players interested in playing at IU. Now, I give him credit for his enthusiasm and everything else but I think he gets too much credit as if he's the only coach that could have brought them back. That's totally not accurate."

On the day Crean took the Indiana job, one of his most famous quotes when asked why he wanted the job was simple: "It's Indiana," Crean said. "It's Indiana."

That may be true, said former ESPN college basketball analyst Andy Katz, but this is hardly your father's Indiana anymore. Yes, the tradition still exists but this is not the same Indiana that existed when Bob Knight was roaming the sidelines and the program was revered by college basketball fans and up and coming players across the country.

"I have a little bit of a different view of the Crean era," Katz said. "You can argue that he was more traditional in some ways than Knight. He wasn't abusive any way. He recruited very well. Tom dug Indiana out of a massive hole. He had NBA type players come through. He won the Big Ten and got to the Sweet Sixteen.

"In most programs that would be good. But it's Indiana's still sort of skewed view of where they are. I went to Wisconsin and when I was there they were horrible. And now Wisconsin

105

is really what Indiana used to be. That's hard for me to think about because when I went to school there, they never made the tournament and just to make the tournament would be monumental."

Katz said it's interesting to see how the script has completely flipped and how the perception of the two programs is much different than it once was.

"A whole generation now has a completely different view of Wisconsin," Katz said. "It's not the view that I know or the view that I grew up with by any means. With Indiana it just continues to perpetuate this picture of what a program was and should be and the expectations are sometimes a little bit unrealistic. I'm not saying you shouldn't shoot to be a champion. You absolutely should. But I also think Indiana should roll it back a little in terms of what is realistic in the current climate."

• • • • •

Mike DeCourcy of *The Sporting News* has said for years that he doesn't think Tom Crean ever had a chance to truly succeed at Indiana.

DeCourcy said he thinks Crean's tenure at IU was over before his first two seasons were up. The first year under Crean, with a group of players that were not your normal Indiana Big Ten caliber roster, IU went 6-25. The next season IU went 10-21 and the 2010-11 Hoosiers finished 12-20 before the 'Wat Shot' in 2011 against Kentucky signaled the return of IU basketball.

"I think that his tenure there was over before two years were up," DeCourcy said. "And that it just took them a long time to finally reach the conclusion that they did."

DeCourcy remembers covering a Purdue-Michigan State game in West Lafayette in February of 2010. He was in the press room and at that time it was nearing the end of Crean's second season in Bloomington.

"And in the press room there was constant discussion about whether (Crean) was going to make it," DeCourcy said. "And I was just flabbergasted by that. I remember being astonished by it. This guy had been there two years and he walked into zero scholarship players. How can anyone even be talking about that?

"And I knew at that point that he was in trouble. That it was going to be difficult to ever get Indiana back to where it needed to be."

Don Fischer had some of those same thoughts. He felt like it was in year 3 that you really started to hear it.

"If you think back to year 3, there was already starting to be grumbling because we weren't winning the way Indiana fans thought we should be winning," Fischer said. "They were all talking when he first got here that they were going to give him four or five years to get the program back on top. By year 3 they were already grumbling. So from my perspective I just think the guy did a remarkable job of rebuilding the program, doing it the right way and getting good kids to come to Indiana."

Chronic Hoosier, the Indiana super fan that I've permitted to just use his alias in the book because he's well known in the IU community, said even after Crean initially resurrected the program he never felt like the coach got completely comfortable at IU.

"I don't think he ever caught his breath," Chronic Hoosier said. "He was constantly trying to put a team together and to plug the holes that kept popping up on his roster. But his problem was it just never felt like a fit that not only the university administration ultimately felt it could accept but the broader Indiana community didn't feel it could accept.

"Look at the way he was received by the state's basketball coaches and players, and the fruits or non-fruits of those relationships. I think that may have led to his undoing more than anything. He was never able to really keep a permanent pipeline with the local basketball community."

Bob Kravitz wondered aloud if Crean's inability to have consistent success at Indiana might be just a piece of a bigger problem at IU.

"I have to wonder after it has been 30 years since they won the national title, maybe IU just isn't a blueblood program any longer," Kravitz said. "That's not to say it can't be again. UCLA fell off the map for years and they came back. You just have to wonder if there's something systemic about IU basketball that makes it difficult to win at the very highest level."

DeCourcy doesn't buy the argument that Crean was a poor in-game coach. He said he can counter that argument with several examples of when Crean pushed all the right buttons that helped Indiana win games it had no business winning.

"You look at the Michigan game in 2013 where they went on the road against a coach (John Beilein) who is universally acknowledged as a great tactician, especially on the offensive end," DeCourcy said. "And Indiana won on the road. They had to have it to win the league and they won.

"And the Michigan State game. Same year against a Hall of Fame coach in Tom Izzo. IU had to have the game on the road to win the league and they won it. You look at the Kentucky game in 2016. Same scenario. Kentucky has a Hall of Fame coach and it was a four seed against a five seed in the NCAA Tournament. And Crean finds a way to win."

DeCourcy said he just thinks it's too simplistic to say that poor in-game coaching was what doomed Crean at Indiana.

"I really believe the program was so broken when he picked it up," DeCourcy said. "It was like you walked into a friend's house and you walk in and all of sudden there's a shattered mirror on the floor and you look around and you say, 'I didn't do this'. And yet who takes the blame for it? You didn't have anything to do with it but it's broken and you're standing there. And that's kind of what happened to Tom. And he never was

Tom Crean with the microphone at Hoosier Hysteria

able to get back from it. He did some good things and he did some things that didn't work. Some of what happened in regards to their recruiting is certainly on him but I really never believed that he had a fair chance.

"If he had been hired in 2006 – and he certainly could have been a great candidate at that point – I think that the history of the program and the history of Tom Crean and the program would be much different."

One thing Crean always talked about was how proud he was of the group of assistant coaches he had assembled. The one constant on all of his nine staffs was former Ball State head coach Tim Buckley, who came with Crean from Marquette. Bennie Seltzer spent four seasons on Knight's staff and later was a head coach at Samford. Steve McClain, a former head coach at Wyoming and later the head coach at Illinois-Chicago, was on Crean's staff for five seasons. One of IU's top recruiters was Kenny Johnson, who was with Crean for two seasons before moving on to Louisville.

His final staffs included Buckley, Chuck Martin and Rob Judson, a trio that had all had Division I head coaching experience.

As good of a staff as Crean believed he had put together, though, some believed that his staff was ultimately part of Crean's demise.

Former IU player Steve Risley, who played on the 1981 national championship team, said Crean needed to surround himself with better assistants.

"If Tom Crean had surrounded himself with better people, he would still be the coach at Indiana today," Risley said. "Tom is just not a good bench coach. He recruited well. He was a great ambassador for the program. He was a little bit too rah-rah at times but I think the man generally cared about Indiana basketball, probably more so than anybody since coach Knight in his heyday. I think he wanted to do well there. He just wasn't a good bench coach.

"Rule number one in business is you always surround yourself with people who are smarter than you are. That's the first thing a great leader does is surround himself with people smarter than him. And for whatever reason, loyalty or whatever, he wouldn't do that."

Risley felt that was one of Bob Knight's strongest areas. He always had good bench coaches. Guys like Dave Bliss, John Hulls and Bob Weltlich early on, and later Bob Donewald, Jim Crews, Kohn Smith, Royce Waltman, Joby Wright, Ron Felling, Norm Ellenberger and Dan Dakich. In his final few years the assistants were Craig Hartman, Mike Davis, his son Pat Knight and John Treloar.

"Knight always had great bench coaches around him and all of them knew what was going on in a game," Risley said. "And Knight had no problem letting them talk or they would feed coach Knight information and he would bark it out. And it was always a working timeout with Knight.

"I heard stories of Crean's timeouts that prayer wasn't answered. I just think if Tom had surrounded himself with good assistants, not even great assistants, he would still be at Indiana."

6

The Mystery that was Kelvin Sampson

Over the years I have often tried to figure out just what Kelvin Sampson was thinking.

A lot of people wonder the same thing about what Indiana University was thinking, too, back in March of 2006 when it hired Sampson as its head basketball coach.

And that makes for interesting discussion, too. There's no doubt about that. It's something that I'll address as we go through this chapter. As one person put it earlier in this book, the day that Indiana hired Kelvin Sampson it did the most un-Indiana like thing that Indiana has ever done.

But I just want to focus on Sampson.

He had been branded a cheater while at Oklahoma and actually arrived at Indiana while his Sooners program was under investigation by the NCAA for illegal recruiting practices.

He told Indiana he had made some mistakes, he promised he wouldn't do them again, and IU swallowed the bait, hook, line and sinker.

And then he cheated again and two years later the Indiana basketball program was left in complete shambles directly because of his actions. Dan Dakich did an admirable job of keeping the ship righted after Sampson was dismissed but ultimately the decision was made to hire Tom Crean as the head coach.

But I still go back to Sampson and say, 'What the hell?'

What was he thinking? Why did he do it? Could he just not help himself? Did he just think it would be a minor enough of an infraction that no one would really care? Or did he just not take the whole thing very seriously and somehow believed he was above it all? Was it simply a case of someone who believed he was above the rules?

I believe there is probably a little bit of truth in all of those thoughts. I really have never felt it was just one cut and dried thing.

There are so many questions that have always pretty much been left unanswered. Sampson gave a couple of canned answers the night he resigned as the IU basketball coach in February of 2008 but there wasn't a lot of depth to it.

But it comes back to one basic question: What was Sampson thinking before he took IU basketball on an afternoon drive through the muck?

A lot of things have made sense throughout the history of Indiana University basketball.

No names on the back of jerseys made sense because you play for the name on the front and not the name on the back any way.

Candy striped warmups made sense because it has become part of the IU basketball brand not to mention everyone outside of Hoosier Nation thinks they're hideous. So why not be different?

Branch McCracken and Bob Knight made sense because they were two of the greatest college basketball coaches of all time.

Kelvin Sampson never made sense.

Something just didn't add up. A university that had always prided itself on doing things the right way climbed in bed with the devil the day it hired Kelvin Sampson. Or at the very least, IU probably took a chance it had no business taking.

Get the best guy for the job and you have to think there were dozens and dozens who were clamoring for the chance

IU athletic director Rick Greenspan (left) talks with Kelvin Sampson on the sideline of an IU football game. In the background is IU assistant coach Rob Senderoff.

to coach IU basketball. You shouldn't have had to even consider the possibility of damaged merchandise.

With all of his baggage, the hire simply didn't make sense. Just ask former IU two-time All-American Ted Kitchel. The day after Sampson was hired Kitchel told Philip B. Wilson of the *Indianapolis Star* that he wouldn't have wanted Sampson coaching his daughter's fifth grade girls team.

Kitchel turned out to be a visionary.

Another former player and teammate of Kitchel's on the 1981 national championship team, Steve Risley, shared Kitchel's sentiments.

"That was the brain fart," Risley said. "What could you say positively about him coming to Indiana? I can't find anything positive to say about that decision or even rationalize how that decision could have ever come to pass. It was just a brain fart. There was just no reason to make that decision at all.

"It's one of the things that has always amazed me about the Indiana process but just how quickly Indiana always finds another coach. They approach it like they have to get a new coach and they have to get him by tomorrow. And Sampson was another example of that. Take your time and get the right guy."

Risley said that it seems like everyone is afraid that if they wait too long and don't hire a new coach quickly that they'll lose out in recruiting.

"But I say get the right guy and we'll overcome all of that," Risley said. "But let's buckle down and find the right guy and get the perfect fit. And with Sampson, that's what comes back over and over again. How in your right mind can you check all of the boxes and do all of your homework and at the end come back and say Kelvin Sampson is the right man to coach at Indiana?"

Jake Query, the afternoon sports talk show host in Indianapolis, has always had a flair for the dramatic. He said the whole situation remains one of the three biggest mysteries in the history of the United States. (He really did say that by the way.)

"They are 'What's in Area 51? How many people were involved in the Kennedy assassination? And what in the hell did Indiana see in Kelvin Sampson?" Query said.

But Query didn't stop there. The zingers kept coming and coming.

"When Kelvin Sampson came from Oklahoma to Indiana he had to have flown on Southwest Airlines," Query said. "Because bags fly free and he had so much baggage that Indiana could not have afforded to have put him in a seat on any other airline."

But Query didn't have the market cornered on zingers.

Former *Indianapolis Star* columnist Bob Kravitz went one step further after starting to say that Sampson was the wrong guy at the wrong time.

"Actually he was the wrong guy at any time," Kravitz said. "With all of the baggage he came in with from the NCAA problems and his graduation rate which was miniscule, the reality is that Sampson was just an outlaw. He fit in to Indiana the way I would fit in to a lineup of underwear models. He just didn't belong."

Former ESPN college basketball analyst Andy Katz may have summed up the Kelvin Sampson era of Indiana basketball the best.

As I wrote at the very beginning of this chapter, Katz said when Indiana opted to hire Sampson, in essence it did the most un-Indiana like thing that Indiana had ever done.

"The Sampson era was (Indiana's) version of trying to hit a home run with a big name that they clearly did not get," Katz said. "It really is amazing to me that they hired Kelvin when the Oklahoma problems were still raw and it was still out there.

"And they got burned. Badly. And some will try to say 'Oh, it was just phone calls.' No, it was repeated abuse of the rules and a complete disregard for it. Yes, phone calls are not the most egregious thing in the world but it's still disrespecting that there is a rule of law in place with the NCAA whether you agree with it or not."

Mike DeCourcy of *The Sporting News* called the decision to bring Sampson on board a "tone deaf hire" by Indiana.

"Please make it clear, I think Kelvin is a terrific basketball coach," DeCourcy said. "I like him a lot and he's someone I've always had a good relationship with. But he was not the person for Indiana in 2006. I have no problem saying that.

"To hire someone who had an active NCAA case and whose program had an active NCAA case against it, that was just an absolutely tone deaf move by the Indiana administration at the time."

Dave Revsine of the Big Ten Network recalls that when he heard Sampson had been hired at Indiana he was absolutely stunned.

"For a place that prides itself on doing things the right way and has never been a win at all costs mentality it was unbelievable," Revsine said. "You can say what you want to say about coach Knight, and I know he has a ton of detractors, but at least as far as the rules were concerned he always did things the right way. But you follow the rules, you bring in kids that are capable of doing the work and be good student-athletes and represent themselves in the right way when they're there and basically you're going to do it a certain way.

"And with Sampson, to bring in someone who was under investigation at the time just flies in the face of all that. I just remember being absolutely stunned that they hired Kelvin. I had always respected the things Kelvin had done and I thought he had done a good job at the two places he had been, but he just wasn't the kind of guy that I thought Indiana would hire."

•••••

In doing this book, I had the opportunity to speak with former Indiana athletic director Rick Greenspan. Greenspan was the Indiana A.D. when Sampson was hired and later resigned. Shortly after Sampson left, Greenspan was out, too, choosing to resign at the end of the calendar year after the university was hit with a "failure to monitor" charge by the NCAA.

I asked Greenspan some of the questions I had posed at the beginning of the chapter. Basically, looking back on it with the benefit of 20-20 vision, 10 years later, what did Greenspan think Sampson was thinking? Why did he do it? Could he just not help himself? Did he just think it would be a minor enough of an infraction that no one would really care? Basically, questions like that.

I thought Greenspan had a most interesting perspective.

The basic point was that coaching at Oklahoma and existing under a different set of compliance expectations had simply

Drew Hoeppner, son of late IU football coach Terry Hoeppner, Pittsburgh Steelers quarterback Ben Roethlisberger and Kelvin Sampson on the sideline of an IU football game.

not prepared Sampson well enough to be the next coach at Indiana.

"In many ways, Mike Davis was both professionally and personally not prepared to take over for Bob Knight but Kelvin was unprepared on a different level," Greenspan said. "Kelvin had recruited, Kelvin had coached, Kelvin had seasons of success. He had done a lot of those things. And he had spent a lot of his time at Oklahoma. And Oklahoma was big enough to have had pretty good luck with basketball success and irrelevant enough in the eyes of the fans because nobody gave a crap."

Greenspan made the point that Oklahoma, like many predominantly football schools, was a great basketball gig.

"I think some of the best jobs may be the basketball coach at Florida, the basketball coach at Texas, the basketball coach at Alabama, those kinds of places," Greenspan said. "Places where you have all the resources, you have the big name, you have all of that stuff to be successful but if you're not successful, okay, there's next year."

Greenspan said at Oklahoma, basketball was the fourth sport in terms of importance.

"There was football, there was spring football, there was recruiting for football and then there was basketball," Greenspan said.

He said basketball was way down the list of importance at the University of Oklahoma.

"There is less fan scrutiny, there is less external scrutiny and their level quite honestly of administrative care and concern and accountability was not comparable to Indiana," Greenspan said. "When you pick up some newspaper or you look at some blog (in Indiana) and they seem to have more information about who you are recruiting than the coach does, that's scrutiny. That was not the case at Oklahoma but it was at Indiana."

And Greenspan said when Sampson came to Indiana he was quickly playing by rules that he had never experienced before.

"I think the level of compliance in my mind and this is my perspective but the level of compliance that was put in place when Kelvin was hired was unlike anything that had been put in place before," Greenspan said. "And I think that level of scrutiny was such that at a lot of other places it would have been undetected. Or it would have been viewed as a minor indiscretion and therefore it wouldn't have risen to the level of accountability that I think we had.

"That was the way I felt it needed to be coming from the phone call NCAA issues that he had brought with him from Oklahoma. Maybe that's a nice way of saying that's who he was and always was but the level of accountability caught up to him."

So Sampson had always done things a certain way and he was unable or unwilling to change the way he went about his business.

"That's my take knowing a little bit about Oklahoma and a little bit about how they run themselves administratively," Greenspan said. "I just think Indiana was a different level of scrutiny."

Greenspan has always chosen to take the high ground and not make excuses about how the Kelvin Sampson situation played out under his watch. Nearly 10 years have passed and nothing has changed on that front.

"I've tried very hard to avoid Twitter battles or whatever," Greenspan said. "The way I've always said it is that I was the athletic director at Indiana when Kelvin was hired. I was the athletic director at Indiana when he broke the rules and that was my job and my responsibility. That's not being falsely humble or anything else. It's just the way I've always viewed the chain of command."

Former IU president Adam Herbert gave an interview with the *Jacksonville Times-Union* in late February of 2008, a few days after Sampson resigned, and in his own words, explained how the hiring had come about.

Herbert claimed in the story that it was Greenspan who had initially had Sampson on a short list of potential candidates for IU's head coaching vacancy.

Herbert said Greenspan recommended hiring Sampson and that "I concurred with that."

"We had every confidence that the letter and spirit of (Sampson's contract) would be met," Herbert said. "We had to have a pretty high comfort level (to hire him).

"My view at the time, and still is, was that when you have a chance to hire someone with his track record, and whose only offense was telephone calls . . . When you look in the broader scheme of things, it was worth giving him a second chance."

Herbert said it was Greenspan who first came to him with Sampson's name.

"In this case, the AD developed the list of candidates to be considered," Herbert said. "He initiated the appropriate background checks. He hired a consultant to help us. No one knew who was on our final list of candidates. (Greenspan) went through the process of narrowing the list to three or four people, with the help of a consultant. Because of the significance of basketball in this state and the issue raised about NCAA sanctions (in Sampson's case), I asked two members of the Board of Trustees to review the process."

The two were Jeff Cohen and Stephen Ferguson.

Herbert said in the interview with the Jacksonville Times-Union that he knew it would "raise eyebrows" if Sampson were hired because of the baggage he would bring from Oklahoma.

While at Oklahoma, the university was investigated for three years by the NCAA for recruiting violations. In the end, the NCAA issued a report that cited 577 impermissible phone calls made by Sampson and his staff to 17 different recruits between April of 2000 and September of 2004.

The NCAA also alleged Sampson failed to adequately monitor his staff's telephone calls to recruits during that time and Oklahoma had inadequate monitoring procedures in place.

Still, eventually Indiana pulled the trigger and hired the coach with excess baggage.

Looking back nearly 10 years later, Greenspan remembered things a little differently than his college president but for the most part still opted to take the high road.

"Adam Herbert and I haven't talked since he left and he's entitled to his perspective on history but I think some of the folks that were intimately involved in that situation would probably have a different take on it," Greenspan said. "If that's something that makes him feel good to think he had nothing to do with it, then so be it. Maybe he thinks that's one notch in his belt that he didn't deserve, I don't know. Who knows?"

I'm not certain if it was Herbert, Greenspan, the board of trustees, or just exactly who pushed Sampson's hire through the system.

My own take is that it's hard for me to fathom that it was all Greenspan. I always think of three names: Terry Hoeppner, Kelvin Sampson and Tom Crean.

Basically, how could Greenspan haven't gotten two of three so right and one of them so terribly wrong?

You could also add Todd Berry to that list as a coach Greenspan had hired at a different institution. In this case it would be institutions. Greenspan hired Berry as his football coach at Illinois State and also at Army. He didn't have a lot of success in terms of his record at either place and the same was true later in his career at Louisiana Monroe. But he has always been considered a standup guy who was well-respected by his peers.

It's probably no surprise that Berry is the executive director of the American Football Coaches Association.

"When you think of coach Hoeppner and coach Crean and coach Berry, those were the kinds of people that I wanted to be around," Greenspan said. "Those are the people that I would always want my son to play for and I think that's an important criteria."

● ● ● ● ●

March 29, 2006.

That was the day Kelvin Sampson was named the new IU basketball coach. That was the day IU, with the benefit of that 20-20 hindsight again, climbed into bed with the grim reaper.

Many believe that Sampson's hiring was orchestrated in large part by then-IU president Adam W. Herbert. Sampson was believed to be Herbert's man from the beginning. As I talked about above, IU athletic director Rick Greenspan also was involved in the decision and would later take the fall and resign his position after the NCAA delivered a "failure to monitor" charge against the university for its inability to keep its basketball coach under control.

The night before IU introduced Sampson at a press conference in Bloomington, there was a meeting in Houston, Texas. The site was chosen because it was considered to be an out of the way place.

At that meeting was Sampson, IU president Adam Herbert, Rick Greenspan, and IU board of trustee members Jeff Cohen and Stephen Ferguson.

Ferguson said he spoke with Sampson that night for about an hour before having to leave because of a business obligation.

"My main message was, if he came to Indiana University, we have high expectations, and I said, 'I want you to understand that, and are you committed to that?' " Ferguson said in a story in the *Indianapolis Star* that also appeared in my book, *Rising From The Ashes.*

According to Ferguson, Sampson answered, "I understand what you expect."

Following that meeting, Herbert said he was confident that Sampson realized he would have no margin for error while at Indiana.

"We came away from that feeling like (Sampson) was someone who understood what he went through and wasn't likely to make that same mistake again," Herbert told the newspaper. " He cared about the young men that played for him. All his players loved him. The parents were appreciative of what he did for their children. All of us wanted to feel comfortable that (NCAA charges against him) was an aberration."

Sampson was then hired on March 29. He initially signed what was termed a "Memorandum of Understanding" offer which amounted to an agreement of terms. It was a seven-year deal with an annual base salary of $500,000 per season. There was also additional compensation on a graduated scale over the seven years of the deal.

In that initial memo of understanding, there was also a clause that said, "Notwithstanding the above paragraphs regarding compensation, it is understood that the NCAA will hold an infractions hearing in April or something thereafter, regarding certain actions by you that occurred at your current place of employment. If the NCAA imposes sanctions against you personally for those actions, or if the NCAA requires that your prior employer's sanctions against you be enforced, Indiana University shall impose those same sanctions against you. Such sanctions may have an effect on the figures set forth above, and by signing this Memorandum of Understanding you explicitly acknowledge and agree that the University may adjust the figures above to reflect the sanctions taken."

At the end of the memo, which had been written by Rick Greenspan, was this final sentence. "I have every confidence that you will lead our athletics program with integrity and pride, and I look forward to welcoming you as a member of the Indiana University family." The memo was signed by Greenspan, Sampson and President Adam W. Herbert and dated March 29, 2006.

In his introductory press conference at Indiana, Sampson had a quote that was truly staggering. He said when asked about the illegal phone calls (at Oklahoma), "I don't know that as a staff we took that rule seriously enough."

That's kind of what Greenspan alluded to in what he thought was Sampson's problem looking at it 10 years later.

Jake Query, the Indianapolis sports radio talk show host, almost fell off his chair when he heard that one. He had to go back and listen to it over and over again just to make sure he really heard what he thought he heard.

And what he heard was accurate.

"He came with violations and then broke them here," Query said. "I'll never forget his answer when he said it was a rule that he didn't take very seriously. Not 'that was a rule that we didn't understand' but it was a rule 'we didn't take very seriously.' I'm not a lawyer but I can pretty much assure you that that defense has never stood up in a court of law in the history of the United States.

"I didn't mean to kill her, I just didn't take that murder law that seriously. I mean, really? That was just ridiculous."

On April 20, Sampson signed his official contract which had plenty of language aimed at making sure he wouldn't have any similar behavior at IU.

The terms of the contract read that IU "may take further action, up to and including termination" if the NCAA imposes more significant penalties or sanctions than the University of Oklahoma's self-imposed sanctions. The contract also gave Indiana the right to fire Sampson without obligation if his assistant coaches committed serious or repeated NCAA rules violations.

Article 2.02 of the contract included the heading "Employee May be Disciplined for Violations of NCAA Rules or Regulations."

That article went on to say, "Without limiting University's rights as otherwise set forth in this Employment Agreement, if the Employee is found to be in violation of any NCAA regulations, the Employee shall be subject to disciplinary or corrective action as set forth in the provisions of the NCAA enforcement procedures, including suspension without pay or termination of employment for significant or repetitive violations."

The day after he signed the contract, Sampson and Greenspan attended an NCAA hearing along with officials from Oklahoma in Park City, Utah. The hearing focused on the impermissible phone calls from 2000-04.

On May 25, 2006, the NCAA committee on infractions issued Sampson penalties that prohibited him from making any recruiting phone calls or taking part in any off campus recruiting for a period of one-year.

The fact that Sampson had gotten into this kind of trouble while at Oklahoma was even more ironic given that at that time he was the president of the National Association of Basketball Coaches (NABC). While he was heading the association, the NABC formed an ethics committee to address many of the problems college basketball faced.

On Aug. 16, 2006, that same ethics committee sanctioned Sampson for his Oklahoma recruiting violations and gave him three years of probation.

For that one-year period, Sampson appeared to be living and existing under his new rules. On May 25, 2007, the NCAA sanctions were lifted after Sampson had completed his one-year penalty.

It only took four and a half months, however, to reveal that Sampson's problems from Oklahoma were not the "aberration" that Herbert and IU had hoped they would be. On Oct. 14, 2007, IU announced that a series of recruiting sanctions and corrective actions were being imposed on Sampson and his staff after finding further phone call violations.

The preemptive strike had been made just over a week before, when on Oct. 3, IU sent the NCAA a report conducted by Ice Miller, a law firm that was hired by the university. According to that report, Sampson had made more than 100 impermissible phone calls while at Indiana that violated the recruiting restrictions he had while at Oklahoma.

In a letter from Greenspan to Shep Cooper, the NCAA's director of the committee on infractions dated Oct. 3, 2007, the IU athletic director wrote: "As you will see in the attached report, Indiana University has identified issues with the successful fulfillment of some sanctions. Specifically, the athletics department compliance staff recently discovered a number of phone calls that the University has decided, after a careful and thorough review, are contrary to the sanctions regarding phone calls.

"Indiana University takes these transgressions very seriously and has imposed a number of additional sanctions on the basketball program and on individual coaches, as noted in the report, to address any impact caused by the lack of total compliance with the sanctions and to send a clear message that absolute compliance is expected form all of its coaches and staff."

The Ice Miller report included this passage under the heading "Chronology of the University's Investigation."

"As described above, the University conducted regular checks of phone records throughout the year. On July 10, 2007, during the course of the compliance staff's additional year-end review of recruiting logs and phone calls

Kelvin Sampson with the microphone at Hoosier Hysteria

for all sports, a compliance intern noticed that one men's basketball prospective student-athlete had been called numerous times, all permissible under NCAA rules. Upon further inspection of the phone records, the Director of Compliance noticed that on January 29, 2007, there were two calls made by assistant men's basketball coach Rob Senderoff from his cell phone to the prospect on the same day and that both involved a three-way calling pattern to a number that was ultimately determined to be the home number of the head men's basketball coach, Kelvin Sampson. The director of compliance then searched the men's basketball coaching staff's cell and office records for other three-way calls."

And the three-way calling Indiana Phone Gate controversy had been born.

Later in the Ice Miller report was the following regarding three-way calls.

"Three-way phone calls are permissible under NCAA rules and University policies, including recruiting calls when multiple coaches are on the phone. However, due to Sanction 7 of the revised sanctions, which prohibited Sampson 'from making any phone calls that relate in any way to recruiting or being present when members of his staff make such calls' from May 25, 2006 to May 24, 2007, three-way recruiting calls involving Sampson were not permissible.

"Of the 27 three-way phone calls that occurred during the period of the sanctions, approximately 10 to 18 involved an assistant men's basketball coach connecting Sampson into a phone call with a prospective student-athlete or an individual involved in the recruitment of a prospective student-athlete (e.g. relative, coach). Indiana University has determined that these calls are contrary to the intent of Sanction 7 as well as a clarification received from the committee's staff prior to June 13, 2006 regarding the impermissibility of three-way calling."

IU, in the report, however, also tried to put the infractions into perspective.

"Indiana University takes these transgressions very seriously and has imposed a number of additional sanctions, many of which are already in effect, on the basketball program and on individual coaches as detailed below, to address any impact caused by the lack of total compliance with the sanctions and to send a clear message that absolute compliance is expected from all of its coaches and staff.

"The University is disappointed and does not condone the actions of the involved coaches, but it is important to place this issue in context. The men's basketball coaching staff is involved in over a thousand recruiting calls a month and three-way calls at issue here total at most 18 over approximately eleven months, a fraction of one percent of all calls."

So basically, despite being restricted from making any recruiting phone calls, Sampson participated in approximately 10-18 three-way calls with recruits that violated the terms of the sanctions against him. Rob Senderoff also made 35 impermissible calls from his home. Senderoff subsequently resigned his position.

Any way you looked at it, it was a mess. And like Andy Katz had said, it was simply the most un-Indiana like thing that Indiana University had ever done.

Clark Kellogg, one of the chief college basketball analysts for CBS Sports, had an interesting perspective on the Sampson situation. Not only is Kellogg a successful broadcaster, but he's a former college basketball player at Ohio State and in recent years has been a member of the Ohio State University board of trustees.

He feels like that has given him perhaps more of an informed opinion and certainly has caused him to look at things different. He said the thing that really stands out is that coaching decisions like that one are not easy to make.

"Sometimes you can operate under the pressure of circumstance versus conviction," Kellogg said. "And it's hard sometimes when you're in the position where you want to re-capture or regain some of the runs of success that you've had as a program and it has slipped away. You feel like you've got to do something big and fast. It's a difficult thing to stay the course and to really stay diligent about alignment and fit. And sometimes you can be blinded by resume or stature or press conference winning and not necessarily thinking the whole thing through."

Kellogg said looking back you always have 20-20 vision, too.

"It's always easier after the fact obviously to look back," Kellogg said. "We all see pretty clearly after all of the things have unfolded. Clearly that may have been part of it in terms of stepping outside of what may have been traditionally the way of operating."

Kellogg said adding to the difficulty was that the landscape of college athletics had changed dramatically since Bob

Knight's heyday. And that brought with it a whole different set of challenging questions.

"You have to think about who are we, who do we want to be?" Kellogg said. "How committed are we to who we are and who we've been? Can we continue to go about things that way and have success in a changing landscape? Are we willing to take that chance regardless and be true to who we are? Those are all things that are hard questions for leaders and athletic directors and presidents in those situations."

Kellogg said Indiana basketball had been lulled into a false sense of security because it had one man roaming the sidelines for such a long time. And when he left, all of the challenges of finding the right coach have played into every decision that has been made on that front since then.

"It was pretty easy and at least not as challenging because you had coach Knight there for three decades, or close to it," Kellogg said. "So you have a template, you have a way of doing it, you have a powerful presence who has had success and garnered respect and admiration so despite some of the polarizing things there was a sense of loyalty and alignment. This is who we are. But then when you have to make changes it can be a little difficult.

"That's all I'm saying. This isn't an exact science and there's always a chance that mistakes can be made even when people honestly believe they are doing the right thing."

Indianapolis Star beat writer Zach Osterman said that when Sampson was hired, there were a lot of things about the hire that Indiana fans liked.

"If you're talking culturally what Kelvin Sampson wanted to do, Indiana fans loved the idea," Osterman said. "He had tough nosed teams that were built on defense. If you look back statistically at some of his teams they were winning games 56-50 and 60-56. There was always the feeling with his teams that they were greater than the sum of their parts.

"And then the success he had in recruiting with Eric Gordon and Jordan Crawford, who maybe at the time we didn't know was going to be as good as he would be but he had a pretty decent NBA career. But the reality is that Kelvin Sampson's legacy at Indiana will always be defined first, foremost and last by the cheating."

• • • • •

Former Purdue coach Gene Keady was a good friend of Sampson's when the two were both involved in the National Association of Basketball Coaches board. Keady said it really came as a surprise to him when Sampson got into trouble.

"It really surprised me when he got hung up with the phone call situation," Keady said, not intending (I don't think) to make a pun. "It kind of shocked me because I didn't think he was a guy who would have that kind of problem. I think it was surprising that Indiana would hire someone like that but I don't think they knew what they were getting into.

"I think the people that hired Kelvin really believed he could change. Sometimes coaches change in their philosophy you know. You want to have good integrity, you want to do things the right way and sometimes you take shortcuts and I think you realize pretty quickly that shortcuts don't work. And I think sometimes you get fooled by the people you hire."

Indianapolis radio talk show host Jake Query said the biggest problem with Kelvin Sampson was Kelvin Sampson.

"Kelvin Sampson's biggest problem was that Kelvin Sampson thought that Kelvin Sampson was bigger than Indiana," Query said. "Here's the biggest problem with the Kelvin Sampson hire. Kelvin Sampson was given an unbelievable opportunity at an elite historic basketball program and was convinced that Indiana had an unbelievable opportunity of hiring an elite basketball coach.

"And it was a disaster from day one."

One thing you find from former Indiana players is that by and large they want a reason to come back and support their alma mater. They want coaches who understand the tradition and want to embrace that tradition. Most will tell you that both Mike Davis and Tom Crean did a good job with that. They'll also tell you, in the early going, that they like what they see from Archie Miller.

But Sampson? That was a different story.

"Sampson was by far the worst at it," said former Indiana player Joe Hillman, a member of the 1987 national championship team. "He didn't embrace anybody from IU."

Hillman remembered the first time that he ever met Sampson. He said Sampson told him, 'There's not a single person that I'm recruiting today that was born when Bob Knight won three national championships.'

Hillman said he came right back to Sampson with "Kelvin, are you telling me that you don't think UCLA still uses John Wooden's name?"

"And he said, 'OK that's a fair point'," Hillman said. "But he wanted to create the Kelvin Sampson way at Indiana and that's a bad way to start. We're a close knit group. Indiana's alumni guys have a lot of pride in honoring the Indiana tradition. We're pretty tight. And why wouldn't you want that help?"

Todd Meier, one of the three seniors on the 1987 IU national championship team, agreed with both Query and Hillman's assessments.

"With coach Sampson, all he wanted it to be was his program and I think that turned a lot of people away," Meier said. "I don't think people like the way he coached, nor did they like the players and particularly the type of players that he brought in.

"I'm not really sure what he was brought in for but it certainly wasn't for the continued excellence of the program."

Meier said he was living in Wisconsin at the time but knowing the kind of program that Sampson was running and the kinds of players he was bringing in, getting involved in IU basketball wasn't something that was high on his list.

"I didn't even want to come down for games when Sampson was the coach," Meier said. "It just wasn't a good experience for myself or most of the former players. I still find myself scratching my head over those couple of years of Indiana basketball."

Derek Schultz, Query's sidekick on their afternoon sports talk radio show in Indianapolis, said he thought Sampson simply had the wrong approach to Indiana basketball.

"Sampson treated Indiana like it was just any other job and I think that was his biggest mistake," Schultz said. "Because people in this state don't feel like it's just any other job. He was a good coach. I don't think anybody is disputing that but when you talk about the right fit, he wasn't close."

Longtime Indiana University beat writer Ken Bikoff wasn't particularly fond of some of the players that Sampson brought in to play at Indiana.

"Sampson came in and had all of the opportunities to repair things quickly but his problems I thought were personnel related," Bikoff said. "Sampson brought in guys that he didn't need to bring in at Indiana because he didn't know better. At Oklahoma, there was a caliber of player he could bring in and nobody would have a problem with them. But at Indiana, you don't need to bring in the guys with the sketchy backgrounds or a lot of junior college guys.

"You just don't need to do that but he never understood that. I really thought that was a lot of his undoing on the court and then we saw all of the problems he had off of it."

Pat Graham, the former 1989 Indiana Mr. Basketball from Floyd Central, just shakes his head when he thinks about what Sampson did to the program he loves. "Kelvin Sampson was such an embarrassment and I'm not just saying to Indiana,"

Graham said. "It was just a bad situation. The issues that were going on in the parties and other places, we all know what it was but to run our program like Oklahoma football in 70's after what coach Knight had made the program, what a slap in the face to anyone in the state of Indiana.

"And like I said I really don't mean just Indiana. That was a slap in the face to anyone who enjoys college athletics in any sport."

Former IU All-American Brian Evans, who played for the Hoosiers from 1992-96, said the first time he met Kelvin Sampson he thought Sampson might be the guy to get it done with IU. He said he was a bit of a hotshot and had a huge ego, but Evans thought that might be exactly what Indiana needed.

"I thought he might be good. I didn't know," Evans said. "He was bringing some players in. I think it's so hard as a fan to see what kind of players they are. I think the first thing I do as a fan is just watch them play. And he had some guys who could play. He had those Chicago kids, the kids that came in and ended up being trouble makers. But I was watching them at first as basketball players and thinking these guys had some real ability.

"The question, though, was where did he get them from and what were they all about? What kind of integrity did they have and was their integrity a reflection of his integrity or lack thereof? I think it ended up being that."

Evans said his whole approach at the beginning with Sampson was the same approach he has with every coach that has followed Knight.

"I remember just thinking, 'Ok, let's see if you can win,'" Evans said. "That's the way I feel about every coach. I just want this program to have sustained success. I'm not looking for a free ticket or rose pedals when I come to town, I'm not looking for any of that. Yes, I'm a former player but I'm a fan. I have been since I was a little kid. I'm a fan of the program."

Evans still remembers one of the first times he met Sampson and as Evans walked in the room, Sampson said, "Brian Evans, the 27th pick in the NBA Draft of the Orlando Magic."

Evans admitted he was impressed that Sampson knew that. "I said 'Wow, how did you remember that?'" Evans said.

"He said he talked to this guy and that guy in Orlando and he listed off all their executives and he said they told him that they were thinking about drafting me and he told them they were crazy if they didn't draft Ryan Minor," Evans said.

Evans said he told Sampson thanks a lot.

"I told him I was glad they didn't listen to him," Evans said.

For the record, Minor was a former All-American basketball player at Oklahoma that had played for Sampson. He was ultimately a second round pick, the 32nd selection overall, in the 1996 NBA Draft by the Philadelphia 76ers.

When I asked Evans to give his initial opinion of Sampson, he just smiled.

"I don't have anything nice to say about him, if that's what you want to know," Evans said. "I'll never be OK with the way he left our program."

That's a sentiment shared by many.

Greg Rakestraw, the program director at 1070-The Fan in Indianapolis, said never before has someone taken so little time to completely blow up a program that once was held in the highest regard.

"The dude does this remarkable job of burning the place to the ground in two years," Rakestraw said. "I mean Sherman's March has nothing on Kelvin Sampson and what he did in Bloomington. Obviously he could bring in players and obviously he could coach them up but as far as doing anything that comes close to following the rules, he fails.

"And so now the program has been set even farther back than it had been in a few of the years of the Mike Davis era."

• • • • •

Don Fischer, the longtime voice of Indiana University basketball and football, had an interesting perspective on Sampson. He said if Sampson had not repeated his Oklahoma transgressions after arriving at Indiana, he believes that Sampson might still be Indiana's coach today.

Now that's kind of like saying the guy that cheats on his wife 10 times could have been a dutiful spouse if he had just not continued to cheat but Fischer saw something in Sampson that maybe some others didn't see.

Fischer said he believed that Sampson could really coach. To Fischer's way of thinking the Indiana coaching progression could have been Knight to Davis to Sampson. Period.

"I'm not going to sit and come up with alibis for Kelvin Sampson and what he did at Indiana," Fischer said, "but I will say this that Kelvin Sampson had he not dropped back into the same scenario that he did at Oklahoma, had he not repeated his previous offense, I think coach Sampson would have won big at Indiana because I think he was that good of a basketball coach."

Fischer said he believed Sampson had many of the same attributes as Bob Knight.

"I'm talking about in the sense of his ability to break down players and understanding what their strengths and their weaknesses were," Fischer said. "The other aspect of it was that he didn't take that same kind of player that Indiana was normally used to taking. He took kids that were maybe troubled in some way or had really negative backgrounds and he tried to help them become better people.

"I think if you talk to the players that played for Kelvin Sampson, and I'm talking about the good ones now, I think you'll find that they really enjoyed playing for him."

ESPN college basketball analyst Jeff Goodman said

"I think Kelvin is a helluva coach and I don't think anybody in the industry would disagree with that," Goodman said. "His problem was everything else."

Lance Stemler's two seasons at Indiana were also Sampson's two seasons. And he echoed what Fischer had to say.

"Whenever I talk to people today and they ask what coach I played for at Indiana and I tell them Sampson, I get some odd looks," Stemler said. "But when I tell them how much I liked coach Sampson and how much I enjoyed playing for him, a lot of times they are really surprised and taken back.

"What you have to know is that all of that other stuff was going on behind the scenes and what we saw was a coach who was really committed to us and committed to winning. I don't have a bad thing to say about Kelvin Sampson."

Mike DeCourcy of The Sporting News and the Big Ten Network said Sampson had a short sighted philosophy when it came to putting Indiana back together.

"Kelvin wasn't around long enough to really get a feel for what know his philosophy would have been (to rebuild the program)," DeCourcy said. "Myself, I think Kelvin is a great coach but I don't think he really understood what Indiana could do for him. He had an idea in mind and went for it. It was just let's go get whoever I can get that can play and let's go see how many games we can win. And for long term success at Indiana that is not the way to go."

Another interesting viewpoint on the Sampson situation came from Derek Schultz, an afternoon sports radio talk show host in Indianapolis. Schultz was a student at Indiana in the early 2000's during the time that Mike Davis was the coach and just prior to Sampson taking over in 2006.

Schultz said it was a tumultuous time in Indiana history in terms of it being a revolving door with multiple athletic directors and university presidents.

In terms of athletic directors, you had Clarence Doninger, Michael McNeely, Terry Clapacs, Rick Greenspan and Fred

Glass all in about an eight-year span. As for college presidents, Myles Brand was at IU until 2002, Adam Herbert was there from 2003-07 and Michael McRobbie has been at Indiana as president since 2007.

"We throw Sampson under the bus a lot and rightfully so, as he did do a lot to nuke the program, but this was a time where Indiana had like five athletic directors in seven years and three college presidents," Schultz said. "There was so much upheaval in the university at this time in the administration. There was like no organization or direction."

Schultz said the athletic administration was focusing on things that seemed trivial at the time instead of more important, pressing issues. McNeely's 16-month rein included IU trying to establish a consistent logo, a consistent crimson color across all sports and trying to choose a mascot, a practice that has been attempted at various times without success over the years. It's simply too difficult to capture the essence of what is truly a Hoosier.

"They were like wasting time on things like changing the logo and I think there was a campaign to choose the new mascot," Schultz said. "It was almost like 'What in the hell are you guys doing?' And they got Gerry DiNardo and that hire for the football program and it seemed like things were just kind of going to hell at IU around that time at IU in the mid-2000's."

This is off topic, but it reminded me of one of my favorite quotes I got back in the day from Kyle Hornsby when I asked him about the new crimson color that McNeely had chosen to be used across all brands in the IU athletic department.

Hornsby just looked at me and smiled.

"You mean cranberry and cream," he said.

Schultz's point is that in some ways Indiana University was a rudderless operation and it shouldn't be that surprised that Sampson's transgressions were a result of that time in the university's existence.

"I don't like laying everything on the feet of Sampson," Schultz said. "I think from the administration standpoint and the athletic directors and the presidents and nobody really being on the same page and nobody really having an understanding of where Indiana really wanted to go from here that comes into play, too. They were looking for kind of a quick fix. I think that led to a lot of the problems they ultimately ended up having there at that time."

Chronic Hoosier, the Indiana super fan that I've permitted to just use his alias in the book because he's well known in the IU community, said of the three permanent coaches that followed Knight he believed Sampson was the best coaching fit.

"I thought coach Sampson was probably the best coaching fit, strictly between the lines for the job," Chronic Hoosier said. "But it was everything else that wasn't a good fit. For Sampson, it was his off-the-court issues that were his undoing but I really believe in terms of which of the three was the best ball coach, I would say it was Kelvin Sampson."

Indianapolis Star beat writer Zach Osterman has a different view of Sampson, too. Osterman was a reporter for the *Indiana Daily Student* at the time that Sampson was let go by the university.

"He was cheered off the floor after he coached his last game at Indiana," Osterman said. "They lost to Wisconsin on that Brian Butch bank shot and that was a Wednesday night. The Thursday is when all the NCAA investigation stuff came out. That Saturday they beat Michigan State at home with D.J. White who got hurt and then he beats Purdue, and that was a pretty good Purdue team and he was cheered off the floor.

"And then two days later he was gone."

Osterman called it a "confusing time" for Indiana basketball.

"It was a confusing time, I certainly don't think it was a good time for Indiana basketball," Osterman said. "It was not a hire that made sense in that you knew all of the other stuff was lingering over him. And yet there were so many things about Kelvin Sampson in the profile of coach that the things he did in two years that I really feel like Indiana fans embraced.

"But ultimately Indiana just isn't the place where they're going to sacrifice that sort of virtue that they see in the program for results. Whether that's right or wrong, whether it is Pollyanna-ish or not."

7

Managing Expectations

The one thing you know when you accept the head basketball coaching position at Indiana University is that there will be plenty of expectations.

Both realistic and unrealistic, but there will be expectations. And you will hear, read and see them at every turn.

And if you get to a point where those expectations are not being met, well then the noise can get pretty loud in Bloomington.

It was enough to force one former IU coach to not want to leave the friendly confines of his own home because he didn't want to subject his family to the ridicule from people on the street. It was enough with another former coach that it actually spilled over into chants heard at a high school basketball game that his son was playing.

Coaches will often tell you that they read every word that is written about them but that would be far from therapeutic at Indiana, especially if things weren't going well. Some coaches just have to find a way to turn everything off or it can be difficult to focus on the job at hand.

No, expectations can come from all levels from the top of the university to the guy sitting in the balcony at Assembly Hall.

If anyone knows about the expectations launched by fans from the cheap seats or the privacy of their own living rooms either via Twitter or posting on a message board, it would be

Mike Pegram, the longtime publisher of the popular IU fan website Peegs.com.

Pegram admits that sometimes those opinions can be a tad bit unrealistic.

"I think it's unrealistic when they look at one or two games and draw wide conclusions from what they've seen," Pegram said. "That's a typical fan thing but it can be bad for Indiana. They'll look at one substitution pattern or one particular defense that has been played and make broad statements about it.

"It's just the way it is. I think it's a little because of coach Knight which is how they got attached to IU basketball in the first place. They loved that man-to-man defense and the motion offense and some of them can't let it go. The other thing is that back then players seemed a little less selfish in their shot selection and so if it strays from that they voice their concerns there, too."

A recent case in point was provided by IU athletic director Fred Glass on the day he fired Tom Crean. In his statement he talked about the expectations he had for the next IU basketball coach.

And remember, this happened on the day he fired Crean, a coach who had made three Sweet Sixteen appearances in the previous six seasons and won two outright Big Ten titles in the last five years. Add to that a Big Ten coach of the year honor just one season earlier and it made for a pretty solid resume.

And yet, one year later, Crean was out as the Indiana coach and Glass gave the impression it was because he wanted more.

In a statement put out by the university's media relations department on March 16, the day that Crean was fired, Glass made known his expectations.

"After deliberative thought and evaluation, including multiple meetings with Tom about the future, I have decided to make a change in the leadership of our men's basketball program," Glass said in the statement. "Tom Crean brought us through one of the most challenging periods in IU basketball history, led his players to many successes in the classroom and on the court and represented our university with class and integrity. While winning two outright Big Ten titles in five years and being named Big Ten Coach of the Year, Tom worked tirelessly to develop great young men and successful teams. However, ultimately, we seek more consistent, high levels of success, and we will not shy away from our expectations. Tom is a good man and a good coach and we owe him a great debt of gratitude for his many positive contributions to Indiana basketball. We wish him well.

"The national search for our new coach begins immediately. The Board of Trustees and the President have expressly delegated to me the responsibility and authority for this search and hire. While I will not be establishing a formal search committee or advisory committee, I will consult with basketball experts from around the country and throughout the State of Indiana, including many former Indiana University basketball players. The expectations for Indiana University basketball are to perennially contend for and win multiple Big Ten championships, regularly go deep in the NCAA tournament, and win our next national championship—and more after that. We will identify and recruit a coach who will meet these expectations."

There were a couple of key points made in that statement. One came in the first paragraph when Glass said that while recognizing the things that Crean had been able to do that ultimately it was Crean's lack of consistency that cost him his job. And that's true. Crean's highs were plenty high enough. Winning two outright Big Ten titles in a four-year span and making three Sweet Sixteen appearances in the last six years were all significant. But it was the year after IU was No. 1 in the nation for 10 weeks in 2013 and then garnered a No. 1 seed in the NCAA Tournament that IU didn't make the tournament field at all in 2014. And then in 2017, one year after winning the Big Ten title outright in 2016, Indiana struggled again and didn't make the NCAA Tournament. This time it played in the NIT but had a first round exit in a loss to Georgia Tech.

The other key point though again repeated that word "expectations" and specifically focused it toward whoever would be IU's next coach. Glass said that the expectations for IU basketball are to "perennially contend for and win multiple Big Ten championships, regularly go deep in the NCAA Tournament, and win our next national championship – and more after that."

And then he said "We will identify and recruit a coach who will meet those expectations."

Ultimately, when he hired a new coach nine days later, Glass believed he had found that coach in Archie Miller.

On the day he was introduced as Indiana's coach, Miller talked specifically about those expectations. The more he talked, the more you felt like he was a guy that was ready to embrace those expectations.

"I don't think you come to Indiana if you don't want to live in the neighborhood," Miller said in his press conference. "If you don't want to move into that neighborhood, then you shouldn't be here. If you like the neighborhood, then you come. I think I've been at a high level at a lot of different spots. I've been with great people. I think I'm very confident that what we do works, and I'd like for the opportunity to try and make it work here.

"I think the Big Ten is an excellent league with great coaches to be with, to be against, and you're going to get better. They're going to make you better, and you're going to be better for it. To me, I know where we're at, and I know what the job is. That didn't waver me. I think more than anything, this is what you want if you love the game."

Basically, it was another example of Miller saying all the right things.

144

• • • • •

Still, some believed that Glass might have gone a little too far though with his thoughts on his expectations for Indiana basketball. Perhaps the word "goal" would have been a better word choice rather than "expectations" which seems to swing a silver hammer that pounds that thought home.

Former *Indianapolis Star* columnist and current WTHR-Channel 13 columnist Bob Kravitz said he thought Glass went too far.

"For (Miller) I just think that Fred Glass has raised the bar so ridiculously high that the only way that this guy can be viewed as a success is if they win multiple Big Ten championships, they go deep in the NCAA's virtually every year, put up a banner – at least one – and that he's the new Bob Knight without the baggage," Kravitz said.

"That he's here for the next 30 years and I think that's probably the only way that you look at this guy and say, 'Yep, it has been a total success. I just think the bar is incredibly high for this guy."

Kravitz said he felt like in some ways Glass had done Archie Miller a bit of an injustice.

"No question," Kravitz said. "When you come out and say that two outright Big Ten championships in five years and three Sweet Sixteens in six years isn't enough, then whoa. Now what I like about Archie is that he isn't afraid. He thinks like Fred thinks. He thinks there could be a return to greatness. I like that about the guy. He's not shying away from the expectations but I do think they are extraordinarily high and good luck reaching them because it's a very competitive world out there. There are a lot of good programs, a lot of good head coaches and he's got his work cut out for him."

I read that quote about Glass's expectations to former Purdue coach Gene Keady when I interviewed him for this book. Keady just laughed.

"I'm glad nobody said that here at Purdue when I took the job," Keady said. "That would have scared the heck out of me. That's not a good way to introduce someone especially when you've been struggling."

Jon Crispin, the former Penn State and UCLA basketball player who as of 2017 was an analyst with the Big Ten Network, called Glass's remarks "appalling."

"It shows a lack of vision in my opinion," Crispin said, taking Glass's remarks on face value. "The vision is not just what we want. Vision is 'I know what I want and here are the steps I have to take to get there.' And when you just go out there and talk about hanging banners, to me it just shows a true lack of vision. Basically you're sitting there saying, 'I know what we want. I don't know how we're going to get it but I know what we want.'"

Crispin said if he were Archie Miller that would be his biggest concern as he takes over as the latest coach attempting to return Indiana basketball to a sustained level of winning.

"And if I were Archie Miller I would look at this and say, 'OK, what's going on? How much time do I really have?'" Crispin said. "Because in three years if he doesn't win a Big Ten championship and Indiana doesn't go to the Elite Eight at least, what's happening? Are people starting to call for his head because Fred Glass said Indiana is going to hang banners?"

Crispin just said it's an unrealistic expectation to put the end game as the priority.

"If you sell yourself as an administration and you get behind the process and you get behind Archie Miller and you say 'We have a plan with Archie to restore this program,' I think that's what is most important," Crispin said. "Not just to win championships but to be the type of program that has great student athletes that go on to contribute in the basketball arena and beyond. And we're going to have a culture that is a winning culture one way or another."

Crispin said he thinks that approach would be more appealing to the fan base and in the end be more fair to a new coach like Miller.

"If that was the focus, I think the fan base is more easy to deal with," Crispin said. "I think the fan base can say, 'You know what? I like that. We're going to win, yes, but we're going to do things the right way.' I think the fan base would get behind that. But when your leadership says we're going to hang banners and that's what we are and that's what we're all about that is naturally what fans are going to want. If they don't get that, they're going to look around and say 'What's going on? We're not hanging banners.'"

Again, Crispin said if he was Archie Miller he probably would have addressed that on Day One.

"I would have said, 'Look, of course we want to hang banners but what you need to understand is to get to a point where we can hang banners we have to develop a solid winning culture," Crispin said, "and somewhere along the way we have to focus on the process of developing that culture as opposed to just the end game which is hanging the banner at Assembly Hall."

When I talked to Fred Glass a few months later in an interview for this book, he believed that people were in a way missing his point.

"I think there's understandable confusion about this," Glass said in an interview in August of 2017. "First of all, while Tom (Crean) was here I had said for several years that my expectations for Indiana basketball are to perennially contend for the Big Ten championship and go deep into the NCAA Tournament and ultimately get a sixth banner. I've never made any bones about that. I think that is what our expectations should be."

Glass went on to repeat what he had said the day he let Crean go in that he honestly believed that Crean had made several great contributions to Indiana basketball.

147

"I'm literally not sure that anybody but him with his doggedness and focus, energy and commitment could have pulled us out of where we were when he got here," Glass said. "He got us to where we were nationally relevant again. I think he did a great job with that and I think we owe him a great debt of gratitude.

"The confusion I think and something that I know I struggled with is how can you take a guy who won two outright Big Ten championships in four years and was the Big Ten coach of the year the year before and fire him?" Glass said. "That just seems incongruous. And that was part of the reason I really struggled with the decision. In part because I think Tom had done great things for IU at some personal and professional cost to himself and second that he had such great accomplishments in a really narrow window in winning two outright Big Ten championships, getting to the Sweet Sixteen three times and winning the Big Ten coach of the year."

Glass said people look at that and can't understand how he could have reached the conclusion in March of 2017 that he needed new leadership at the head of the Indiana University basketball program and ultimately would turn to Archie Miller to take over the reins of the program.

"People look at that and either because they're confused or because they want to state their own case say 'Glass is crazy,' he said. "They say Indiana should be satisfied with two outright Big Ten championships in four or five years. And I think under certain circumstances I would be thrilled with two outright Big Ten championships in four years. And I was thrilled with that.

"But for me the issue was about the future. And given the number of years that Tom had on his contract I felt like the decision I had to make was about the future. Tom had a lot of great accomplishments but there were a lot of other years that weren't as good. And I had the benefit of working closely with him for nine years and I just believed that if you took that all

148

together, and didn't comment on any two or three year period, I just didn't think he was the right person going forward and in the future to have us meet our goals which I've clearly stated."

Glass said for him his statement about expectations wasn't a commentary on the two outright Big Ten championships not being good enough.

"The calculus I'm required to make because of the job I hold is what did it look like for the future and ultimately I didn't see it," Glass said. "So reasonable people can disagree about that, I get that, but that was really my thinking."

Glass said he saw, particularly from the national media, a perspective that he was crazy. I used this quote in an earlier chapter but felt it was worth repeating.

"One of the guys literally said that I should have a Members Only jacket on because I'm still living in the 80's," Glass said. "And that my ambition to go deep in the tournament and win a sixth championship and be thought of in the same breath as Kentucky and Duke and North Carolina was crazy and I just reject that.

"There is no reason why we can't be there and should be there. And I don't apologize for that."

CBS Sports college basketball analyst Clark Kellogg said ultimately though it will still come back to the expectations and how Miller is able to live within them. If you want to take Miller's own neighborhood analogy, it will come back to how he fits in that neighborhood.

Will he be able to blend in with his neighbors or will he be the guy with a car or two on blocks sitting in his front yard?

As Kellogg put it though, the higher the level of the conference, the more scrutiny someone like Miller will be under. At Indiana, it simply comes with the territory. Mike Davis experienced it and didn't handle it particularly well at times. Davis got to where he wasn't comfortable going into the neighborhood – literally – and became a hermit of sorts because he both wasn't comfortable with the criticism and truthfully didn't understand why people who he felt knew very little about him were his loudest critics.

Kelvin Sampson dealt with the scrutiny but mostly after the first wave of NCAA infractions became known at Indiana. And even then, as Sampson continued to win in that second season when Eric Gordon played his lone campaign with the Hoosiers, some in the fan base chose to look the other way because Indiana was still winning basketball games. A few people were outspoken about his hire from the beginning – the Ted Kitchel's of the world – but a lot of the pushback came after he had gotten in trouble again.

And with Tom Crean, a lot of the scrutiny, fair or unfair, went back to that Syracuse game in the Sweet Sixteen in 2013. After that, things were much more difficult for the Indiana coach. As one person said in an interview for this book, to be able to be successful at a place like Indiana you have to be able to outcoach the fan base. Some can pull it off, some can't.

"The noise is so much greater now," Kellogg said. "There's nothing you can do in isolation. Everything today is front and center with the social media platforms. You have to be well aligned with the athletic director, the university and your staff and then you've got to be able to do the job of bringing in players, developing them and getting them to perform at the highest level."

Kellogg was quick to point out that it's not rocket science either.

"It's not easy but it's not complicated," Kellogg said. "It's challenging. The nuts and bolts of a solid program are the same. Players, leadership, alignment and sustaining that by being true to who you are and getting kids that fit that and are able to embrace and run with that. You've just got to be able to stiff arm the noise the best you can and hopefully you have enough success that keeps the real cage of rattlers quiet."

Do that, Kellogg said, and Archie Miller will have a real good chance of being successful at Indiana.

"There are a lot of positives at Indiana," Kellogg said. "The resources are there, the support from the administration is there and you have a talent-rich area to recruit from. It really though has so much to do with managing expectations and I really believe that will be a big key."

When you talk about Indiana football one of the things people have said for many years is that the biggest key to turn that program around is to get the Hoosiers playing annually in the postseason. When IU football was at its best during the Bill Mallory years, it was because Indiana was annually going to bowl games. Six times in eight seasons to be exact. It doesn't matter what the names of the bowl games are but in order to attract more quality kids to your program you need to be able to say that most every season they will have the opportunity to play in the postseason.

Basketball is the same way. One of the reasons Bob Knight is considered one of the greatest coaches of all time is that his teams were nearly always in the post season. Knight's teams at Indiana made either the NIT or NCAA Tournament his final 23 seasons at the school. Obviously, making the Big Dance is the more important of the two primary postseason tournaments and Indiana qualified for the NCAA Tournament in Knight's final 15 seasons and 19 of the last 20.

Jarrad Odle, who played for both Knight and Davis during his IU career that spanned from 1999-2002, said one thing that would really endear Miller to Indiana fans would be if he could find a way to make the NCAA Tournament a given once again. In Crean's nine seasons at Indiana, the Hoosiers made four NCAA Tournament appearances and one NIT stop.

"From a success standpoint making the NCAA Tournament has to be a given," Odle said. "Even in the years when I was there with coach Knight we weren't great but we never once

IU athletic director Fred Glass (left) looks in as Tom Crean talks during a press conference

worried about not making the NCAA Tournament. I just think that goes back to that level of excellence that everybody expects.

"The other thing is finding a way to be near the top of the Big Ten every year. If you have a team that is competing for a Big Ten championship year in and year out, there's a real good chance that you'll be somewhere in the NCAA Tournament, too."

In the Tom Crean era, not taking into account his first three years where Indiana basketball was in a state of disarray, Indiana's teams were all over the place in the final Big Ten standings. IU was fifth in 2012 and Big Ten champs in 2013. That was followed by finishes of ninth, seventh, first again and then 10th.

In both of Kelvin Sampson's seasons at IU, the Hoosiers finished third. But Sampson's issues weren't on-the-court problems, they were off the court.

In six seasons under Mike Davis, IU was fourth, tied for first in 2002, sixth, ninth, fourth and fourth.

Add those 17 seasons up, including the first three with Crean, and Indiana has had eight seasons since Knight left in September of 2000 where the Hoosiers finished seventh or worse in the Big Ten. That's 47 percent of the time that Indiana finished seventh or worse in the Big Ten under Davis, Sampson or Crean. On the more positive side, five times in those 17 seasons Indiana finished third or better in the conference standings. That's 29 percent of the time.

So how were things different in Knight's 29 seasons at Indiana? Knight's worst finish in conference at Indiana was seventh. That happened in 1985 and again in 1990. So that means Knight's Indiana teams finished seventh twice in 29 seasons. That's roughly 7 percent of the time.

And on the positive side, Indiana under Bob Knight finished in the top three in the Big Ten 21 out of 29 seasons, or 72 percent of the time. Eleven times Indiana either won or shared the Big Ten title in those 29 years.

Derek Schultz, an Indianapolis sports radio talk show co-host, doesn't dispute the job that Crean did in getting IU back from the ashes. At the same time he was never overly excited about having Crean lead the IU program in the first place.

"I think Crean had a clearly defined ceiling," Schultz said. "With Indiana's situation (post Kelvin Sampson), they really couldn't have the pick of the litter from a coaching standpoint at that time because not very many people would have undertaken the task of building them back up again.

"And Crean deserves all the credit in the world for being like 'Yeah, sign me up, I'm not afraid.' But at the same time, and I felt this way about his Marquette teams, yeah they had the Final Four run with Dwyane Wade but the rest of his teams were kind of just all right. They were like a lot of Knight's teams at Indiana in the latter part of his career. They would win 19 or 20 games and finish fifth or sixth in their conference and they'd make the tournament and they'd have a quiet exit. I don't think any of his Marquette teams even made the second weekend outside of the Wade team that made the Final Four.

Schultz said that even when Crean took the IU job, he was a little bit underwhelmed by IU's new coach.

"This is going to sound like 20-20 hindsight but I was never really enamored with Tom Crean in terms of being a coach," Schultz said. "In year 3, I was really disappointed because by then I thought Indiana maybe shouldn't be a tournament team but I thought they should at least be competent and competitive. And I think they were 3-15 in the Big Ten that year."

The bottom line: The consistency simply wasn't there.

Indianapolis Star beat writer Zach Osterman said it was all about inconsistency.

"Whenever people ask me the question if two Big Ten titles in five years is not enough or some variation of that question, I always say the same thing," Osterman said. "And that's that two Big Ten titles in five years is absolutely enough. What wasn't good enough was 31 Big Ten losses in the other three years and average a losing record in the other three years."

Former Indiana player Pat Graham said Crean could just never gain any momentum.

"I just felt like coach Crean was always running in quicksand,"Graham said. "It was almost like he could never catch traction. He had a couple of good years and then a couple of bad ones. He'd have a nice recruit and then not so much."

Longtime Indiana radio play-by-play announcer Don Fischer said he thought a lot of things went into why Crean was unable to have a consistent level of winning.

"Why it was not able to be sustainable at that point is anybody's guess," Fischer said. "Part of it had to do with that class that departed after 2013. Losing Cody (Zeller) and Victor (Oladipo) a year and two years earlier than expected and the fact they graduated a few other players at that juncture, that really hurt that next team. After they got beat by Syracuse in 2013, that next year was tough.

"That was already going to be a tough year because the experience level was not going to be there and they were basically using a lot of players who had not played at the college level before. When you lose those veterans like that and that leadership it tells you what the problem is right away."

Fischer said he felt the same way following Crean's Big Ten championship team in 2016.

"I think that proved to be the case (in the 2016-17 season) when they lost key guys like Yogi (Ferrell) and Troy Williams who were veterans and leaders," Fischer said. "And the two guys that came in, Nick Zeisloft and Max Bielfeldt, were terrific leaders in their own right and were able to contribute that way. Maybe some other coaches could have dealt with it better than Tom, I don't know. I can't answer that question.

"All I know is that in the situation that they were in and then having had some of the off the court issues they had with players and how guys had to leave or did leave, all those things played in to why Tom's success level wasn't to the level that people thought it should be."

On the rollercoaster ride that was Indiana basketball, here is a look at how Crean's teams fared in the Big Ten. Out of fairness, the first three years have been omitted but Crean's final six seasons show plenty of peaks and valleys.

Indiana's Big Ten finishes in that span were fifth, first, ninth, tied for seventh, first and 10th.

More specifically, it looked like this.

In the 2011-12 season, the 'Wat Shot' by Christian Watford, a 3-pointer that lifted IU to a 73-72 victory over Kentucky, signaled the return of Indiana basketball. At that time the Hoosiers were 9-0 in the non-conference portion of the schedule and would improve to 12-0 before losing the Big Ten opener at Michigan State. IU would go on to finish 27-9 including 11-7 in Big Ten play. IU beat New Mexico State and Virginia

155

Commonwealth in the first two games of the NCAA Tournament in Portland, Oregon to advance to the Sweet Sixteen in Atlanta and a rematch with Kentucky. There, IU's season came to an end with a 102-90 loss to the Wildcats.

Following the NCAA Tournament, however, in the early preseason rankings, several outlets listed Indiana as the No. 1 team in the nation for the following season. And when the official rankings came out in the fall, sure enough the Hoosiers were listed as the No. 1 team in the land. Immediately, expectations for IU soared.

In the 2012-13 season, Indiana finished as outright Big Ten champions, spent 10 weeks as the No. 1 team in the nation, and was the No. 1 overall seed in the NCAA Tournament. Indiana got past James Madison and Temple in the first two rounds of the NCAA Tournament in Dayton, Ohio (IU beat Temple 58-52 to move on) and headed to a second consecutive Sweet Sixteen. There, IU ran into a difficult Syracuse zone defense, however, and dropped a 60-51 decision. Still, the Hoosiers finished 29-7 overall and 14-4 in conference.

But in an offseason when IU lost players like Jordan Hulls and Christian Watford to graduation and Cody Zeller and Victor Oladipo to lottery picks in the NBA Draft, the Hoosiers were unable to maintain the level of consistency that Glass had addressed. IU would go 17-15 overall and 7-11 in Big Ten play in 2013-2014 and not only miss out on the NCAA Tournament but on the NIT, too. That season IU lost to Northwestern, Penn State and Nebraska – all at Assembly Hall.

The 2014-15 season saw IU drop a non-conference game to Eastern Washington at Assembly Hall but seemed to right the ship in conference play. IU was 8-5 through 13 Big Ten games but went on to lose four of its final five games including three at home to Purdue, Iowa and Michigan State. IU would drop its final three conference games to finish 9-9 in the Big Ten. Indiana would sneak into the NCAA Tournament before dropping a first round game to Wichita State.

The next year, in 2015-16, Indiana was back on top. Crean was named the Big Ten coach of the year after guiding IU to a 15-3 record and another outright Big Ten title. Again, the Hoosiers made it to the Sweet Sixteen where they ran into a tough North Carolina team that would ultimately make it to the national championship game. IU was 27-8 overall.

Again, Indiana lost the bulk of its leadership from that team with Yogi Ferrell graduating and Troy Williams going pro. Fifth-year transfers Max Bielfeldt and Nick Zeisloft also graduated. Add in the fact that Collin Hartman, one of the team's most experienced players tore his ACL in September and missed the season and OG Anunoby suffered a knee injury against Penn State in February that cost him the year and Indiana simply didn't have a team that could compete consistently at a high level.

IU opened the 2016-17 season with a win over Kansas and later beat North Carolina in the ACC-Big Ten Challenge. Indiana was ranked as high as No. 3 in the nation in the Associated Press poll.

And then IU fell flat on its face.

It started with a road loss to Fort Wayne (formerly IPFW) and it went downhill from there.

Indiana would finish with an 18-16 overall record, miss the NCAA Tournament again, and bow out in the first game of the NIT against Georgia Tech. A few days after the Georgia Tech loss, Crean was fired as Indiana's coach.

How did other IU coaches in the post-Knight era handle all of the scrutiny?

Kelvin Sampson seemed to go with the flow. But that doesn't mean he never had any times when he was mad about either what people thought was an expectation or something that had been written about him.

I remember I was out in California one summer visiting my mom and I got a telephone call from Sampson. And he was irate. This, by the way, is a somewhat normal occurrence for a beat writer whenever you write something that someone isn't happy with. I had it happen more times in the Tom Crean era than anywhere else but this time it was an angry Kelvin Sampson on the other line.

But for a change, the coach (whoever it might be) wasn't mad at me.

Sampson told me he had a dilemma. He said the *Herald-Times* in Bloomington had written a story where they gave Joey Shaw's father a soapbox to rip Sampson up and down for the way his son had been treated at IU. If I'm remembering this correctly this would have been the summer of 2007, in between Sampson's two seasons at the school. Shaw had decided to transfer and the Bloomington paper had gotten ahold of Shaw's dad and the man went off.

What Sampson didn't like was that the newspaper hadn't offered him a chance to give his side of the story. They just went with Shaw's father and Sampson had no opportunity to rebut the criticism. And frankly, I get that. As a journalist the one thing I've always tried to do in cases like that where someone is being critical of other people or of the school, I make a call and ask if the party wants to defend themselves. Probably eight times out of 10, they say no but I think it's the right way to do business to give them the opportunity to face their accusers.

So anyway, Sampson is on the line and I remember he had this to say.

"I just don't get it," he said. "I've been in this business a long, long time and I've never been in the situation before where a newspaper hasn't given me the opportunity to respond to something critical. Isn't there something in your business where you at least attempt to be fair or something?"

And then he asked me the question, I've remembered over the years.

"You and I have a good relationship and I value your opinion and that's why I'm calling you," Sampson went on to

Kelvin Sampson does a sideline interview with ESPN during an IU football game

say. "If you were in my situation, what would you do?"

Now I tend to be a tad sarcastic or flip at times, and the first thing I thought of when he said that was, "You call their editor and complain but I'm not sure how much that's going to help you," I said."I think if I were you, though, I would just give me all the scoops on the IU beat for a while which might get their attention."

I could almost see Sampson smiling through the phone.

"I like that," I remember him saying.

And for the next few months, the *Indianapolis Star* got any breaking IU story a few days ahead of time. Now, in the dog days of summer and before the season begins, there aren't a lot of great stories to be getting but the few that were out there, whether it be a staff change or someone new that would appear on the IU schedule, I got it first.

But again, most of the time with Sampson things were pretty quiet. But there wasn't a lot to complain about until all the rules infractions stuff started hitting late in the fall of 2007. His first season, Sampson's Hoosiers went 21-11 and 10-6 in the Big Ten and made it to the second round of the NCAA Tournament where they lost to No. 7 UCLA in Sacramento, Calif.

The next year would be Sampson's second and final year and IU was 22-4 when Sampson was replaced by Dan Dakich on an interim basis. That team eventually lost in the first round of the NCAA Tournment to Arkansas in Raleigh, N.C.

But the most basic of expectations on Sampson were to get IU back in the NCAA Tournament on a regular basis again and he accomplished that in both of his two seasons.

He simply cheated along the way.

• • • • •

The one I really felt for was Mike Davis, a really good guy who as I have said in previous chapters was simply in a little over his head at Indiana. And again, he is the first to admit that.

But Davis faced challenges that the other coaches didn't, too. Not having the right resume for such a position was certainly one of them. But it wasn't limited to that.

One expectation Davis faced and myself I think it was unfair is that with the 2002 Indiana team that reached the national title game, the second-year IU coach (at that time) was in an absolute lose-lose situation.

In its most basic terms, if Davis doesn't have a great year with that team people will say he underachieved with a talented group that included future NBA player Jared Jeffries. But if by some chance the team goes on a deep NCAA Tournament run, a large majority of the fan base has the opinion that he was just doing it with Bob Knight's players.

Now I've talked to several players on that team for other books I've written who have said that notion is ridiculous. Kyle Hornsby for example, in my book that I co-wrote with Tom

Brew called *Missing Banners*, said he has never been able to understand why people think Knight would have automatically had great success with that team.

"You can take it the other way and say that coach Knight had good players for the last five to seven years and wasn't able to take anyone even to the Sweet Sixteen," Hornsby said. "So why do you think all of a sudden that he was going to be able to take a team to the Final Four?"

Former IU athletic director Rick Greenspan, who was the athletic director when Davis resigned in February of 2006, said when Davis had his good years the fan base simply wasn't accepting that somehow it could be to his credit.

"When Mike had success a large portion of the fan base didn't give him his due," Greenspan said. "You take a team to the national championship and it's not your players. He wasn't going to win a thing and he was a bridge to the next guy. I'm not a Mike Davis apologist but I think he accepted a phenomenally difficult position."

But as the Indiana University beat writer for the *Indianapolis Star* at that time, I wrote a story on April 3, 2004 that chronicled much of what Davis was experiencing at that time. The headline read, "IU coach waits out fans' fury."

And remember this when you read these words: This was almost two years to the day (two days more to be exact) since Indiana had played Maryland for the 2002 national championship in Atlanta.

Here's the text of that story which pretty much sums up what Davis was experiencing at Indiana in his personal attempt to 'Follow the General.'

BLOOMINGTON, Ind. — It has been 22 days since the Indiana University basketball team ended its first losing season in more than 30 years.

Mike Davis says he has been outside his home only five times since then.

161

Mike Davis and his players on Senior Night following the 2000-01 season, his first attempt at following the General.

A doctor's appointment. A visit to the dentist. Two trips to meet with his boss at Assembly Hall. A Thursday flight to San Antonio for the Final Four.

That's it. No trips to the mall or local restaurants. No time in his office on campus. Not even a visit to church. You know things are bad when Davis is not spending his Sunday mornings at Second Baptist in Bloomington.

It might sound extreme, but it's the way Davis is dealing with the pressure that comes with coaching a storied basketball program that took a step backward this season. He's following a legendary coach, Bob Knight, and dealing with a fanatical fan base where the expectation is an annual run deep into the National Collegiate Athletic Association tournament.

It's when it becomes personal, when the fourth-year IU coach feels he has to shield his mother, wife and young son from the onslaught of criticism, that Davis chooses to avoid interaction at all costs.

"I worry about Mike all the time, and he's constantly in my prayers," said the Rev. Bruce Rose, pastor at Second Baptist, Davis' church for the past year. "He's been on my heart a lot lately because of all of the negative publicity and all the stuff that surrounds trying to follow a legend."

In many ways, Davis is living almost like a hermit because he would rather do that than deal with strangers he thinks might be critical of him and his program.

"When you're out on the street, people come up and ask questions, and they talk to you like you're their best friend," Davis said. "But they ask you questions that you only talk to your best friend about.

"I'm not the type of guy who would be rude to anyone, so I choose just to avoid the situation altogether. Maybe someone else would do things a different way, but that's the way I choose to handle the situation."

The heat has been on Davis since IU closed the nonconference season with a 6-5 record. Forget that three of those losses were to teams that made the Sweet Sixteen: Kentucky, Wake Forest and Vanderbilt.

It continued when IU went 7-9 in the Big Ten Conference and eventually finished 14-15 overall. Indiana hadn't had a sub-.500 season since 1969-70.

The heat has been supplied by angry IU fans and delivered in Internet chat rooms and local radio talk shows. Greg Rakestraw, host of a sports talk show on WXLW-AM (950), said the IU fans who call were about 60-40 against Davis.

"They all say the same thing," Rakestraw said. "They say, 'Mike Davis is a real nice guy, but he can't coach,' or 'He can't do this' or 'He can't do that.' I hear it all the time."

There's even a Web site, firemikedavis. com, run by an anonymous group of basketball fans, which provides the opportunity to voice frustration in a public forum.

Among the Web site's features is a merchandising area that includes T-shirts that ask for Davis' removal. One reads: "WWJD? (What Would Jesus Do?) He would fire Mike Davis."

"Things like that are really troubling to me," IU Athletic Director Terry Clapacs said. "Everyone is entitled to their opinion, but when it gets personal, I think it crosses the line. I know this was a tough season for IU fans everywhere, but this is the time we need to bind together and support our coach."

Davis has brought some of the heat upon himself. Considered a possible candidate for the vacant Auburn coaching position for the past two weeks, he has chosen not to say definitively that Indiana is the place he wants to be.

"Every year, I hear the rumors, and I'm just tired of responding to them," Davis said. "This is the fourth year in a row I've been rumored to be going somewhere, but every time I'm always back at Indiana. I think that says everything that needs to be said."

'Down' time

Davis said he's always down when a season comes to an end. He said that once the Final Four is over, however, he usually gets revitalized by going on the recruiting trail.

But he also admitted the past three weeks have been more difficult than ever.

Davis can't get past the boos he heard at Assembly Hall in February, or the memories of someone coming out of the stands after a home loss to Ohio State to confront him as he made his way to the locker room. Security prevented a further incident.

He said he also hurts when he thinks about his wife, mother and 5-year-old son sitting in the stands amid IU fans yelling obscenities.

"I love my family more than anything," Davis said. "I love my boys, and my wife, and my mom is here with me. And I don't think people realize sometimes what you go through when your family goes through things. People think this just

164

all comes with the territory, and maybe they think that way, but it's a whole different ballgame when it's you.

"I wonder how many people would be able to just look the other way if someone came into their home, in front of their family, and said things that have been said about me in front of the people I love this year. That's what I don't think people understand."

Web sites, such as firemikedavis.com, fan the flames. Similar sites have been around for at least the past five years, emerging when a coach finds himself on the hot seat.

At Iowa, there's firestevealford.com, which has merchandise such as wall clocks, lunch boxes, teddy bears and tote bags. There's even infant wear and bibs that include the "Fire Steve Alford" slogan.

Some feel it comes with the territory at big-time college programs.

Steve Lavin experienced it at UCLA, where he had a 145-78 record in seven seasons and took the Bruins to six NCAA tournaments, including five Sweet Sixteen appearances. But it was never good enough for a program that expected national championships.

When the Bruins went 10-19 in 2003, their first losing season in more than 50 years, it turned into almost a daily Steve Lavin Watch among UCLA fans wondering when he would be fired. It happened at the end of the season.

Two seasons removed from playing in the national championship, Davis' Hoosiers did the unimaginable this season — not making the NCAA tournament for the first time in 19 years. Davis said he can handle the criticism — up to a point.

"The thing I liked about being here the first couple of years was that no matter if we were doing good or bad, no matter what the people said, it never got personal," Davis said. "The thing with this last team is that we knew going in that we were going to struggle, but it's hard for anyone to accept that.

"They want us to look like the IU teams did 20 years ago, and we need better personnel for that to take place. I know people get tired of me saying that, but I don't know any other way to put it."

And so, rather than take a chance at hearing those negative comments in public places, Davis has chosen not to face the music.

He spends a lot of time on the phone with friends and colleagues. He doesn't watch basketball (he says it's too painful), but finds other programming to pass the time. He said he's become the sitcom king.

"I hate to lose," Davis said. "Every year after we lose since I've been in high school, it has taken me a while to get over it. And that's every year. But this year was different because we just couldn't match the right buttons with this group. We were so close in games that we should have won, and it was a tough year.

"Everybody I talk to tells me, 'Well, you had a tough year.' Well, I know we had a tough year, but I don't want to hear it 10,000 times. That's frustrating for me. I'm the first one to admit it: this was a tough year. All I can think about is recruiting better players to come to Indiana so we can challenge for the Big Ten title and get back in the NCAA tournament again."

Tamilya Davis looks forward to when her husband can again have a spring in his step.

"I've told a few people I wish they would come over and take him out somewhere," she said. "But he would rather stay in. He just doesn't want to get in a situation where he has to answer question after question."

• • • • •

Bob Kravitz, the former *Indianapolis Star* columnist, said it was a story like that one that made him realize just how bad things were for Davis at IU.

"I think the outside noise and the madness that comes with coaching at Indiana is what ultimately doomed Mike Davis at IU," Kravitz said.

Another aspect of managing expectations at Indiana has to do with playing basketball the way Indiana fans hope you will play. This doesn't mean they want the motion offense (or at least you would hope they wouldn't in the current decade) but it means they want fluidity. They want organization. They don't want one guy playing one-on-one while the other four just stand around, but they don't want an offense that just throws up 30 3-point shots per game either.

No, Indiana basketball fans want a semblance of a plan. They want to see screens being set and players properly running off of those screens. They're fine with you playing fast but not so fast that you're turning the ball over at an alarming rate. They want to work inside/out when you have a big man that can take up space inside and then utilize his services around the basket. And they don't want their guards just dribbling the ball 35 feet from the basket and getting deep into the shot clock.

As former IU football coach Terry Hoeppner was known for saying: Have a plan, work the plan and plan for the unexpected.

Indiana fans simply want their team to play Indiana basketball.

Style of play was a problem early on with the Mike Davis era of Indiana basketball.

It started when Davis deployed more of a pro-style offense rather than the motion offense that had become a staple at Indiana under Knight. Forget about doing things a different way. Indiana fans were of the 'if-it-ain't-broke-don't-fix-it' mentality and didn't see any reason to do things differently. And again this was 2000 and not 2017 so it wouldn't have been completely far-fetched to see the Hoosiers playing basketball the old way.

Dave Furst, the sports anchor for WRTV-Channel 6 in Indianapolis, said growing up in the state every kid either was on a team that ran the motion offense or at the very least knew how to run the motion offense. That's how powerful Knight's influence had been with Indiana basketball.

Furst said after Knight was let go by Indiana he distinctly remembered having a conversation with Mike Davis and asking him what he thought about the motion offense? He said Davis looked back at him like he had three heads.

"He looked at me stunned that I would even ask that question," Furst said. "And then he said, 'You know what, I don't know the first thing about the motion offense.' That was the moment I could tell we had a wholesale set of changes coming here at Indiana."

With Kelvin Sampson, style of play wasn't a big factor. But that's because he had athletes and they were relatively efficient in what they tried to do. He had D.J. White in the middle and then talent around him like Lance Stemler, Armon Bassett, Rod Wilmont, Earl Calloway and A.J. Ratliff early on.

His second year, a kid named Eric Gordon came to town and Indiana fans were happy to just to watch whatever he could do in an IU uniform. He averaged nearly 21 points.

But the point was that Indiana was winning, making it to the NCAA Tournament every year, and they were running enough of an offense and playing good defense that Hoosier fans were content with the style of play.

The Tom Crean era was a little different story. Some good, some bad but you would get lots of opinions on the topic. When it comes to Indiana basketball and specifically Indiana basketball fans, you always get lots of opinions on pertinent topics.

When you talk to different people and ask what they thought was the ultimate variable that ended Crean's tenure after nine years in Bloomington, you would get several different answers.

Some point to not being able to defend the state's borders in recruiting and keep the top Indiana kids at home at the state school. Some will point to style of play that was often predicated on a run-and-gun up tempo offense that scored a lot of points and made a lot of 3-pointers. But when those 3-point shots weren't falling it was much more difficult to be successful.

Some will say that Crean's players were not completely bought in on the defensive end. Others will say that IU simply didn't value the basketball either. The number of unforced turnovers the last few seasons of Crean's nine-year run in Bloomington were at times mind-boggling.

Todd Meier, one of three seniors at IU that played on the 1987 national championship team, said Indiana, under Crean, may have put too much of an emphasis on playing at the fastest pace possible. When you're playing fast there's a natural tendency to make unforced errors. And Indiana at times would make them in record numbers.

"His style was offense focused," Meier said. "In my opinion it was all about going fast, going fast, going fast. Execution didn't seem to be a key thing. Tough fundamental defense didn't seem to be at the core of what he did. His was all about the offense and the pace of go fast, go fast, and then go even faster."

Meier compared Crean to Knight, mostly because that was his own point of reference having played for the General.

"One of coach Knight's things was always to say don't hurry just to hurry," Meier said. "Go with a purpose. Under Crean, having five guys involved in the flow of the offense was not there anymore. There was a lot of 2 on 2, 3 on 3 playing and that's a lot of the style of play in college basketball in general. You don't have five guys involved in the offense. You have two or three guys creating. And I think that's one of the biggest philosophical differences between coach Crean and coach Knight."

Another former player, Jarrad Odle, who played for both Bob Knight and Mike Davis, thought in-game adjustments were a big area where Crean was unable to be successful.

"I think one of the gripes a lot of fans had with coach Crean was that he couldn't make the adjustments as the game went on to be any better than they had been at the beginning of the game," Odle said. "You kind of have to have all aspects of it. That why I think guys like coach K (Mike Krzykewski) and coach Knight they just all had or have a little bit of everything."

Odle said another issue was at the end of the day if you don't have the players that when things aren't going well can step up and make something happen, it's going to be a long game.

"I think we had those guys when I played there and we had them back in 70's, 80's and 90's with coach Knight's teams," Odle said. "But I don't think coach Crean had those types of players that could just go out and take over a game with true grit and toughness. And I think that was a problem for his teams, too."

Mike Miller, the IU beat writer for *The Herald Times* in Bloomington, said style of play was a big issue for Crean.

"I just think Crean's style of play was a bad fit for Indiana," Miller said. "When you look at how loose they played, which is something that really became obvious with how many turnovers they had and also their lack of a defensive identity, those are two components right there that I just think are inherently important to Indiana basketball fans. IU fans want those two aspects of the game to be a constant. They want to know that you're not going to turn the ball over carelessly and they want to see a high level of defensive intensity.

"And it just wasn't there. Style of play was just a bad fit. And it was probably a bad fit from the very beginning."

Dave Revsine of the Big Ten Network also pointed to Crean's style of play as being part of his downfall with the Hoosiers.

"I think his style of play just drove people crazy, too," Revsine said. "And it goes back to Knight and kind of the notion that he hangs over everything when it has come to Indiana basketball moving forward. Knight wouldn't have tolerated the turnovers, he wouldn't have tolerated the lack of defense, he wouldn't have tolerated that lack of precision that they played with."

Revsine said it's another example of how it has been difficult for all three of these coaches to completely escape Knight's shadow at IU.

"You're kind of at a point where you're so far removed from (Knight) and yet no one can get past him," Revsine said. "I feel like there is that kind of notion that Bob Knight looms over everything. It's not just that there's an expectation that Indiana wins, there's an expectation that they win playing a certain way.

"And that every kid from Indiana kind of rolls out of the cradle knowing how to throw an accurate chest pass and an accurate bounce pass. And so when the ball goes flying out of bounds at an alarming rate, then no one is willing to cut you any slack for that."

Revsine said what Indiana fans had come to expect over the years was that you didn't lose games because of an inability to value the basketball or a lack of playing good, hard-nosed defense.

"That's not how you lose at Indiana," Revsine said. "You lose because you execute well but you just don't make shots. Or if you play really hard and you grind it out on the defensive end, but they just make more shots than you then OK. But it just felt like the way that they played year in and year out just didn't jive with the way Indiana fans envision their team playing."

Conversely, Revsine said that stylistically, Archie Miller's teams will play a style that is more to the liking of Indiana basketball fans.

"Archie's teams, from what we saw at Dayton, will play good, hard-nosed defense and they'll take care of the basketball," Revsine said. "I don't think there are many true Indiana basketball fans out there that will object to a style of play that includes those two elements."

Mike Miller, the IU beat writer for the Herald-Times in Bloomington, said there's no question in his mind that style of play is something that will be important for Archie Miller to help win over the IU fan base.

"Valuing the ball and playing some defense are important and also kind of embracing the expectations which I think he has done already," Mike Miller said. "He seems to understand that this is a tough place to play. Some of the expectations are almost impossible sometimes. It's a lot to ask to try and follow in the footsteps of what has come before you. So I think it to degree to just have to embrace that degree of difficulty. It seems early on that's what he has done.

"You have to understand that there's some tough criticism that comes with this job and you kind of have to own it and you kind of have to wear it."

Pat Graham also agreed that something else that will help Archie Miller at Indiana will be his style of play. Basically, Graham's point was that Miller will need to stay true to himself.

"I think style of play is important and not using John Wooden's or Mike Krzykewski's book on basketball," Graham said. "You have to do your own thing. And I think that's one thing that coach Miller is very good at. He's from a basketball family. He has a chip on his shoulder. He had a chip on his shoulder when he played. How can you be 5-10 and play point guard at North Carolina State and not have a chip on your shoulder?

"I think where he'll be successful is that he has his own way of doing things. And sure he has taken a lot of things from different people but it's not like 'I'm going to do this because I read this book.' Have your own idea or you shouldn't be coaching at that level. You should have your own idea of your style of offense and your style of defense and what makes for a successful program."

8

Recruiting the
State of Indiana

Talk to Indiana basketball fans about the No. 1 problem they have had with the coaches that have followed Bob Knight at Indiana and one of the first topics with everyone has been IU's inability to keep the best players in the state of Indiana at home and playing for the Hoosiers.

There are a couple of givens when it comes to Indiana's home grown players:

- Indiana is annually one of the most talent rich basketball states per capita in the country.
- Indiana fans like to see Indiana kids on the roster.
- Indiana fans don't want to see Indiana kids on other Big Ten rosters or at rival schools of IU.

One of the biggest problems is that it's difficult to compare the success that Bob Knight had recruiting the best players from Indiana compared to what has transpired under Mike Davis, Kelvin Sampson and Tom Crean, and what may or may not happen under new Indiana basketball coach Archie Miller.

Why is it so hard to compare? As we discussed in an earlier chapter, the game of college basketball is so different.

Back when Knight was coaching at IU, if he wanted one of the better kids in the state he simply would extend an offer and often times players would come running to play for Knight and the Hoosiers. Players talk about how it was an honor to play basketball for Knight and Indiana.

"He could secure commitments from freshmen and sophomores and lock it up and go fishing," said Mike Pegram, publisher of the popular peegs.com IU fan site. "Outside of the little footprint that Purdue had in the northwest corner of the state, he would get those commitments most of the time. Unless a party was involved that would steer a kid a certain way for all the wrong reasons.

"For a long time under Bob Knight, Indiana really did own the state in terms of recruiting."

If you want a comparison, forgetting all the differences for a moment, here is a very basic one when you look at in-state recruiting.

Let's start with the best of the best. In the state of Indiana, the highest prestige is to be honored as the state's Mr. Basketball recipient. In Knight's 29 seasons at IU, he had 12 Indiana Mr. Basketball's on his roster.

For an apples and apples comparison, let's just look at his final 17 years compared to the 17 years after he left. In Knight's final 17 seasons, he had nine Indiana Mr. Basketball's come play for the Hoosiers. That list included Steve Alford (1983), Delray Brooks (1984), Jay Edwards and Lyndon Jones (1987), Pat Graham (1989), Damon Bailey (1990), Luke Recker (1997), Tom Coverdale (1998) and Jared Jeffries (2000).

In the 17 years since Knight was dismissed as the Indiana coach, the three coaches who have followed the General on a permanent basis have attracted a total of four Indiana Mr. Basketball's to stay and play in the state. Mike Davis had A.J. Ratliff (2004), Kelvin Sampson had Eric Gordon (2007) and Tom Crean had Jordan Hulls (2009) and Cody Zeller (2011).

But again, the list of the recent misses is what is particularly difficult for Indiana basketball fans to swallow. That's because in many of those cases, the players went either to Big Ten schools or rival programs or most recently a school that is coached by a former IU All-American.

Kelvin Sampson

That list includes Gary Harris (2012) who went to Michigan State, Zak Irvin (2013) who went to Michigan, former IU commit Trey Lyles (2014) who later de-committed and played one season at Kentucky, Caleb Swanigan (2015) who went to Purdue, Kyle Guy (2016) who went to Virginia and Kris Wilkes (2017) who went to UCLA.

And those are just the best of the best.

Also, as for the Knight days of being able to simply wave his hand and kids would want to automatically play basketball at IU, those days are gone.

• • • • •

When Knight was at Indiana the world was a smaller place in terms of recruiting. Kids didn't go as far away from home and there was more of a loyalty factor. Kids weren't nearly so NBA-centric to where everything was geared toward creating their own brand and finding the best program that gave them the best opportunity to play at the next level.

Television exposure was much different, too. When Knight was in his hey-day, only a handful of programs had their games televised nationally. Indiana was one of them. Today, nearly every team is on TV all the time. The world is a bigger place. And the recruiting reach is coming not only from the Midwest but from everywhere nationally.

There's also the AAU piece and how that has changed the game and recruiting, too. And within that world is the competition between the three major shoe companies and how players get aligned with certain shoe companies, too.

Another big difference was where the priorities were in terms of relationships. Alex Bozich, the publisher of Inside the Hall, said that's an area that has completely changed over the two time periods of recruiting.

"I think the emergence of AAU has been the biggest piece," Bozich said. "Obviously with social media and recruiting rankings and all of that stuff it creates a way for how kids can brand themselves and they can pretty much go anywhere. It used to be if you grew up in Indiana and you were a great player the expectation was that you were going to Indiana. Today you can really go anywhere and I think AAU has been a big part of that.

"But really I just think high school has been de-emphasized and I think these kids realize kind of with the AAU stuff that they're going to go play with whoever gives them quote unquote the best deal and then that kind of trickles over to their mindset in terms of picking a school."

Bob Lovell, who coached at IUPUI from 1982-93, believes there is still an important element in play with maintaining relationships with high school coaches.

"If you're going to be successful as a coach at Indiana you've got to develop relationships with the Indiana high school basketball coaches in the state," Lovell said. "Indiana has the largest coaches association in the country. We're not a big state, everybody knows that, but you're going to have trouble if you don't have a good relationship with the coaches."

Some will say that's an old school way of thinking. But back when Knight was the Indiana coach, it was also the correct way of thinking.

"I think the basketball coaches in the state respected what Knight was as a basketball mind," Pegram said. "And so they would really want their kids to play for coach Knight so they could see what those kids could do in that system that they loved to watch."

Another coach with what may perhaps be that old school way of thinking was Knight's biggest rival when the former was the head coach of the Hoosiers – Gene Keady at Purdue.

In fact, Keady said the best advice he could give Archie Miller is that he needs to spend time getting to know the high school coaches in the state. He said if you're ultimately going to be successful at a place like Indiana or Purdue, you have to have the coaches in the state in your corner.

"Most of the high school coaches in Indiana really wanted the jobs at Purdue and Indiana," Keady said. "So the first thing you're dealing with is they think they ought to have your job so you need to get close to them. They think that you think you're better than they are and you need to go out and sell your program and let them know that you want to help them get better, too.

"You want to do things for them and be around them. If any Indiana coaches didn't do that in the past, that was a huge mistake. Because Indiana high school coaches are some of the best high school coaches in the nation."

Pegram said he thought the relationship with coaches slipped initially during the Mike Davis era of Indiana basketball from 2000-06.

"I thought things tailed a little bit under Mike Davis and then coach Sampson kind of got it going there for a little bit when he got guys like Eric Gordon, Armon Bassett and Derek Elston," Pegram said. "He had some good relationships already built with some of the high school coaches. I think that's one of the reasons they landed Eric Gordon was because of the relationship he had with Doug Mitchell.

"And I thought in the first part of Tom Crean's run, maybe the first half of his tenure, he did pretty well with the coaches. They had the camps and brought down teams and he did clinics and things. But I'd say in the last few years, they stopped doing some of those things and that was hurting the relationship, too, with those high school coaches who would talk to each other."

Pegram said there just wasn't that same attachment between the coaches and Crean as there had been with Knight so many years before.

"There was just never an attachment to a system or wanting their kids to go there because they loved watching Indiana like they did with coach but maybe they'll never have that again," Pegram said. "But I do think that was one of the first things that Archie Miller saw was that he was going to have to repair some of those relationships with Indiana high school coaches and then maybe with a couple of AAU programs, too."

But similar to what Alex Bozich's point was regarding the changing climate of those relationships with coaches, Brian Snow, the national college basketball recruiting analyst for Scout.com, agreed that things are different in that regard.

"It's just not the same anymore," Snow said. "When you look around all of this colleges do coach's clinics. So what do high school coach's do, they'll go to Tom Izzo's coaching clinic, they'll go to Chris Mack's coaching clinic and you build relationships that way. I don't think that stuff was as prevalent back in Knight's day for colleges to do that. So now high school coaches are going to be exposed to so much more.

"On top of that you have parents, you have AAU coaches, you have whoever it may be who now for the most part handle the recruiting process. Indiana generally is a very parent driven state, extraordinarily so on the recruiting trail. Now that's not every kid because that wouldn't be accurate but it's the vast majority of kids and with them it's the parents running that show."

And when it comes to listening to those who matter, most parents, No. 1, are simply going to have their kids' best interests at heart.

"A parent might listen to a high school or they might listen to an AAU coach, but at the end of the day it's their kid," Snow said. "So I don't think the relationship factor is nearly as important as it once was."

Take the recruitment of Gary Harris, the 2012 Indiana Mr. Basketball from Hamilton Southeastern High School in Fishers, Indiana. Harris was heavily recruited by Tom Crean and his staff along with top schools nationally, too. His list of schools had a distinct Midwestern flavor though. Most believed his final four schools included Indiana, Purdue, Michigan State and Kentucky. He went through the process, took four official visits and gathered all the information.

His first official visit was to Purdue on Oct. 1, 2011. His second was to IU for Hoosier Hysteria on Oct. 15. Then came an Oct. 22 official to Kentucky and finally a Nov. 5 visit to Michigan State. On Nov. 9, he committed to the Spartans.

And Snow's point regarding that recruitment was that you could have all the relationships that you wanted but there were only three people that really mattered.

"Your ability to recruit a kid like Gary Harris was not impacted one iota positively or negatively by talking to his high school coach or his AAU coach," Snow said. "Not one bit. All you had to do was talk to three people. Joy Harris, Gary Harris Sr. and Gary Harris Jr. You didn't have to talk to anybody else.

"So that relationship with the high school coach, while you'd rather have it than not, at the end of the day, a lot of times it really makes no difference."

•••••

Another challenge for a school like Indiana is that it doesn't hold the same name recognition at it once did the players of today. A high school senior in 2017 was likely born in that 1999-2000 time frame. Given that, they barely would have known that Bob Knight even coached at Indiana. They definitely wouldn't know, unless perhaps they grew up in the state, that Indiana won its last national championship in 1987. And even then it probably seems like a long, long time ago.

I remember former IU player Todd Leary telling me in the last few years that one of his high school aged sons knew of Steve Alford but that was only because he was the coach at UCLA. And obviously he knew that Alford played at IU because his dad had told him stories. But that wouldn't have necessarily been the case for many of his buddies at school.

181

Tom Crean at a Tailgate Tour stop at Lucas Oil Stadium in Indianapolis

Ask most kids today what they know about Isiah Thomas and they would probably tell you that he played point guard at the University of Washington and was now a young, hot shot player for the Boston Celtics.

Snow said he thinks the Indiana name still has value but don't expect kids today to be able to recite IU basketball history like their elders may.

"I think Indiana still has cache and I think Indiana as a brand still means something but do I think these kids know a darn thing about Scott May or Quinn Buckner or Isiah Thomas? No," Snow said. "For them, Michael Jordan is an old timer. That's just the reality and he's the most famous basketball player ever to live. So I don't think they're as familiar with what Indiana was but at the same time Indiana still has a brand and still has facilities and it has a national following.

"So it's still a program to be reckoned with in that regard."

Snow said he doesn't think there's the same sense of pride with kids today of wanting to stay in-state and play for the state school.

"I think kids look at it and parents look at it like let's find the best school for us," Snow said. "And if that's a state school that's great. But let's find the best situation for us. And if we find the right situation, then our life is going to be more successful down the line."

Jon Crispin, an analyst with the Big Ten Network, said there was obviously a time in the state of Indiana when that was different. But he quickly pointed out that that time is in the past.

"There used to be a pride in that," Crispin said. "There used to be a pride in that 'I'm an Indiana kid and I want to go to IU and I win a national championship.' There are no more Damon Bailey's. It just doesn't exist anymore. Kids are going to go to where they feel they have the best opportunity where they can be superstars not great college basketball players.

"And in a lot of ways that's a shame."

There's nothing easy about it for an Indiana coach trying to keep Indiana talent in the state. And then beyond that, the cruel reality is that Indiana coaches have not done a particularly good job of keeping the talent within the Indiana borders.

Here is another recent set of numbers to chew on.

In the last four years of the Tom Crean era of Indiana basketball, there were 20 players from the state of Indiana that were ranked in the Rivals top 150. Want to guess how many of them chose to attend Indiana?

That answer would be one: James Blackmon Jr. in 2015.

Again though, making matters worse is that a total of six of those 20 went to other Big Ten schools and a seventh went to Butler. Two of the six Big Ten players went to Purdue.

Snow said from an Indiana perspective there's no getting past some of the bigger misses. And some of them, because they went to rival schools, just keep haunting you over and over every year when those players come through Assembly Hall on an opponent's bench.

"All you have to do is look and see a guy like Caleb Swaningan, who was a national player of the year candidate this year," Snow said. "If you put him on Indiana last year, Tom Crean still has a job. That's just reality. If they had another guard like Kyle Guy, Tom Crean still has a job. And no, you're not going to get everybody and contrary to popular belief Bob Knight didn't get everybody either but Indiana, per capita, is one of the best talent producing states in the country and more importantly it produces high end talent. A state like Georgia may have more depth, but Indiana consistently produces more McDonald's All-Americans."

And as Snow went on to point out, while not every kid is going to work out, if you're able to land a high percentage of top-rated and highly recruited kids, you're going to be successful as a coach.

• • • • •

So what has been the problem in recent years? Has it been a case of the coaches at Indiana not doing a good enough job establishing the right relationships and making the proper inroads with kids in the state, or is it a bigger issue with the fact that kids today just have so many more options and the world is bigger place when it comes to where they ultimately want to go play? Or is it something else entirely like the influence of shoe companies in today's recruiting game?

Snow said in the state of Indiana shoe company influence is extremely low.

"I'm not going to say it doesn't happen but it's an extraordinarily small percentage of the time," Snow said. "I just think it's a culture change. It's easier to get places now. There is more awareness of the recruiting process now both for parents and coaches. Everyone just has so much more information that it just becomes tougher to be the one school with the most information on a kid or this kid has this innate tie to."

Pegram said he thinks the shoe companies do have an effect at some level though, too.

"The three major shoe companies that kind of control a lot of things now," Pegram said. "Most coaches that run those things maybe have relationships with other colleges that have been good to them and because Indiana was kind of fair game for a while (after the recruiting violations with Kelvin Sampson) all of those colleges have kind of gained a foothold in some of those relationships.

"That just makes it harder today to lock down kids and get those early commitments and so forth. I think there was definitely a disconnect that existed but I feel like Archie Miller and his staff have done a good job in the first few months on the job of repairing those disconnects."

Bozich said he thinks it's a little bit of both in terms of whether it's an IU coaching problem or a difference in players today. Bozich's time covering Indiana began in 2007 right at the end of the Kelvin Sampson era and so his primary focus has been on the way Tom Crean has recruited Indiana. He said he feels like there were a couple of instances in particular where Crean went astray in terms of recruiting in the state.

One he said had to do with the 2012 class where Indiana signed the players dubbed "The Movement". Just the mention of that term is like fingernails on a chalkboard to a lot of Indiana fans still today. It was a five player class that included Indiana kids like Yogi Ferrell, Jeremy Hollowell and Ron Patterson. Add in Hanner Mosquera-Perea and Peter Jurkin and it looked like a class that had big potential for the Hoosiers.

As it would turn out, one would never suit up for the Hoosiers, three would leave and complete their eligibility elsewhere and one, Ferrell, would end his career as the sixth leading scorer in IU history with nearly 2,000 points and as the school's all-time assist leader.

"With that class everybody thought that especially with those in-state kids it was going to be this next big thing and really the only one that turned out to be anything was Yogi," Bozich said. "And then obviously there were just so many guys that he missed on for various reasons.

"I think the consistency was really the problem. People like to point to the fact that he got Blackmon Jr. and Zeller and Yogi and I understand that you can't get them all but there were just so many misses, too."

Indianapolis sports radio talk show host Kent Sterling believes the disconnect with 'The Movement' was also a turning point for Crean in his ability to recruit the state of Indiana.

"I think there's a difference in the way the state of Indiana has been recruited," Sterling said. "I think part of it was that Tom just went for the wrong guys. Just look at 2012. A kid like Jeremy Hollowell? You knew what he was. Ron Patterson? You kind of knew what he was, too. Hanner Mosquera-Perea scored four points down at Bloomington South for God's sakes. Peter Jurkin was another one that didn't work out in that class.

"I think if you're going to recruit Indiana you have to recruit Indiana. You have to survive the ebbs and flows of the talent level. Or you're going to lose the brand that that's where Indiana kids want to go. I just think after 2012 there was a disconnect between Crean and the rest of the state."

In Crean's defense, the kids he thought he was ending up with in the class of 2012 from the state of Indiana were all highly ranked players. And you can't get all the kids out of the state, especially in a talent rich year like 2012. But it does go to show that when you miss on players, even if the recruiting services believe they're the ones you should be going after, it can definitely put you in a hole.

Just consider this about 2012:

There were 10 kids that season from the state of Indiana ranked in the top 131 by Rivals.com.

Glenn Robinson III, who went to Michigan, was ranked No. 11. Yogi Ferrell was No. 19. Gary Harris was No. 25 and chose Michigan State. Jeremy Hollowell and Hanner Mosquera-Perea were ranked No. 41 and No. 43 respectively.

Three kids who ended up at Purdue were in that class, too. A.J. Hammons ranked No. 77, Ronnie Johnson was No. 94 and Rapheal Davis was No. 96. And Ron Patterson was No. 131.

Another name that was high on Alex Bozich's miss list in 2012 was Kellen Dunham from Pendleton Heights who went to Butler. Dunham was ranked No. 93 in the class and according to Rivals.com he had IU interest but no offer. In fact, Rivals showed that his only offer was from Butler.

"He was a kid that I think a lot of people would have said was a perfect kid for Indiana and instead you take somebody like Ron Patterson who never even suited up," Bozich said. "Then there were just so many instances where he took kids that just weren't good enough and they transferred after a year or two. Myself, I think if you're not going to get one and done's consistently you've got to keep kids in your program three or four years so they can have experienced leadership guys that know your system.

"It seemed like every year we would hear the same message that 'Hey, we're young' and there was no really retaining any guys that were going to stay in the program for four years."

Bozich also mentioned not getting Kyle Guy out of Lawrence Central in 2015. Guy ended up at the University of Virginia.

"You've got Kyle Guy in your backyard and I'm pretty sure his great uncle was on the IU Board of Trustees," Bozich said. "He's 45 minutes up the road, he's a McDonald's All-American and he goes to Virginia. He's a McDonald's All-American from Indianapolis and you think you have a pretty good shot at him and gets away, too."

And all of that considered, Bozich said he thought the class that was truly "the back breaker" for Tom Crean was the class of 2017.

"You've got four kids who are in the top 40 or top 50 from the state of Indiana and you recruit all of them for a decent amount of time and you don't get any of them," Bozich said. "I know for sure that Williams, Scruggs and Wilkes were all recruited for three plus years.

"If you just get 25 percent of the guys I just talked about then maybe you're not even talking about a coaching change here," Bozich said. "A few of those guys would have been difference makers and it could have completely changed the outlook of the last couple of years."

Snow said he doesn't think there's a simple answer to the problem with Crean and his lack of productivity with in-state talent over the latter half of his Indiana career.

"I think it's a complex issue," Snow said. "I think part of it is personality driven. Part of it is when you're just at one place, and Thad Matta saw this at the end at Ohio State as well, when you're just at once place for so long you begin to make enemies. And sometimes it's your fault and sometimes it's not. But if you're going to recruit guys that come from the same areas and come from the same high schools and come from the same AAU programs, the reality is a few of those kids are going to have bad experiences and that's going to create enemies in that community."

Snow said he believes that all of it just snowballed on Crean.

"And he didn't know quite how to get out of it," Snow said. "And he didn't know how to adjust to get out of it and in the end it ended up really hurting him."

Others have opinions on the topic, too.

Mike Miller, the IU beat writer for the *Herald Times* in Bloomington, said when in-state recruiting seemed to dry up for Crean is when his problems really escalated.

"Clearly things had dried up inside the state and when you're Indiana and you're not getting the best players out of Indianapolis, or the top players in state, I thought that was a huge issue for this program Crean's last few seasons," Miller said.

"I think for me it always started with recruiting and I just could never figure out how some doors that had once been open and allowed him to get players like Cody Zeller and Yogi Ferrell earlier in his career had suddenly become closed later in Crean's career."

Miller said he isn't sure if Crean was responsible for the closed doors but something clearly happened.

"For whatever reason it just seemed some relationships soured," Miller said. "Maybe there were some people in the state who didn't feel this was a good fit and heading in the right direction."

Pat Graham, the former IU Mr. Basketball from Floyd Central, said he hates to say this but the player he blames is the success that Victor Oladipo had under Crean. Oladipo came out of high school barely ranked in the top 150 by the recruiting services. Then after three seasons at Indiana he had blossomed so much that he was the No. 2 pick in the NBA Draft by Orlando in 2013.

"Tom Crean hit this huge home run on Oladipo and then he never got an Oladipo again," Graham said. "You need a guy like Oladipo in your sixth, seventh or eighth year. He almost got him too early and then he could just never catch any traction."

When Graham talked about Crean not being able to "catch any traction" he also was referring to Crean's inability to get the best of the best out of the state of Indiana.

• • • • •

Early in his tenure, Crean found in-state recruiting success. In his first recruiting class, he signed Jordan Hulls from Bloomington South and Derek Elston from Tipton. In his third class, he signed mega-recruit Cody Zeller from Washington, Ind. and Austin Etherington from Hamilton Heights.

189

Later would come players like Yogi Ferrell and James Blackmon Jr. In fact from 2009-2014, Crean signed 12 players from the state of Indiana.

But that in-state success took a nose dive in his final three recruiting classes. In that span, he signed just one in-state recruit – Crown Point point guard Grant Gelon, who spent one season at Indiana and transferred just after Archie Miller was named head coach.

Crean did just fine outside of the state getting players from the east coast like Noah Vonleh, Thomas Bryant, Troy Williams, Robert Johnson and Victor Oladipo. But Indiana fans have an affinity for players from the state of Indiana on their roster. And that's where Crean lost some traction, according to Graham.

"When you start losing kids to Purdue and Butler I just think that's a bad sign for Indiana University basketball," Graham said. "I really think the state of Indiana, the state of Illinois, the state of Ohio, you could even say Michigan. If you can't recruit state of Indiana basketball players it's kind of like football players in the state of Florida. If there's not enough football players in the state of Florida for Florida and Florida State and Miami to go after that they have to go to New Jersey or the east coast to find them, wow.

"The thing about Indiana, Illinois, Ohio and states like that, there are enough good basketball players and you've got to go get them. And that's where I think coach Crean fell short. He just couldn't get the players he needed to get. That's where I kind of think he was running in quicksand."

Brian Snow, the national college basketball recruiting analyst from Scout.com, said there are a lot of factors in place but in the end it comes down to closing the deal and getting the best players.

"If you get good players the rest will take care of itself," Snow said. "Had Kelvin Sampson stayed at Indiana, my guess is that he wins a national title. Now, IU fans probably don't want to hear that. But I really believe if Kelvin Sampson is the coach at Indiana for six, eight, 10 years he's going to win a national title because he's getting good players and he can really coach.

"Tom's problem at the end of the day was that he got good players but he didn't get enough of them. And I think there were some communication issues and some roster management issues, too. I can't say I really have a great feel for the Mike Davis era but he seemed to struggle with Indiana kids and he was replacing Knight directly."

Former *Indianapolis Star* columnist Bob Kravitz said that Crean told him once that people just don't realize how difficult it is to keep Indiana's best players in the state. He said you need to take them on a case by case basis but that there are some extenuating circumstances, too.

"I think part of what made it challenging for Tom was that Indiana, especially when he was in charge, would not cut corners in recruiting," Kravitz said. "Crean would talk all the time about how they wanted him to get every kid in Indiana. He told me, 'You know what I'd have to do to get all the kids in Indiana?' Not stuff that they want me to do.'"

Derek Schultz, the Indianapolis sports radio talk show co-host along with Jake Query, said he has a problem with people who say that Crean's biggest failing was that he didn't recruit Indiana well enough.

"I think some of that is overrated," Schultz said. "I think you just need to get guys who get it. You need guys that understand the program and understand the culture. I mean Victor Oladipo was a city kid from Washington D.C. He wasn't a Hoosier but he came here and he got it. Christian Watford was from Alabama. A.J. Moye I believe exemplified what it was to be an Indiana University basketball player and he came from Atlanta. So I think some of that is over-rated. I think people want Indiana to have 20 Bryant McIntosh's but myself I think some of that is a little bit of wishful thinking.

191

"Plus he brought in a lot of Indiana guys like Ron Patterson, Jeremy Hollowell and Devin Davis. Hey, Indiana guys right? But for one reason or another they flamed out."

Schultz said he's not advocating that you don't need to recruit the state of Indiana. It's not that. But there's more to it than having to have every Indiana kid on your roster.

"I think there are some people who are trapped within this ideal of Indiana basketball that you need to need to have everybody who shot hoops on their barn or knows how to execute a great bounce pass," Schultz said. "I just don't think that's realistic anymore to have just Indiana guys on your roster and compete at a national level."

Chronic Hoosier, the Indiana super fan that I've permitted to just use his alias in the book because he's well known in the IU community, said not landing the Indiana Mr. Basketball players and other top level talent can definitely come back to bite you.

"It's a double-edged sword," he said. "Where it hurts is not just losing those players but when they go to key opponents and play and now all of a sudden they're wearing Michigan State colors or Ohio State colors or Michigan colors and now a couple of times every season you're reminded of the fact that this was a good Indiana player that you allowed to get away."

Chronic Hoosier said he thought Crean's time at IU could be broken up neatly into three phases – the pre Cody Zeller era, the time with Cody Zeller, and the post Cody Zeller era.

"Looking back at what proved to be his most successful teams during the Cody years, those teams were largely assembled on promises," Chronic Hoosier said. "There was not tape to sell those guys on what would happen one day when he was assembling that group that would ultimately be the backbone of his most successful teams. Maybe you could make the case that Cody had enough that he could see what was happening at IU to make a decision on but that wasn't the case for the earliest people that he recruited."

And he's right. In the early going, after Crean was brought on in April of 2008 and basically asked to put an entire team together, a lot of the players that committed to IU were late bloomers or players who had waited until past the second signing period for some reason to make their college decisions.

Guys like Devan Dumes, Verdell Jones III, Tom Pritchard, Nick Williams, Matt Roth and Malik Story. Crean's second class had a few bigger names that would add to that backbone, guys like Jordan Hulls, Christian Watford, Derek Elston and Maurice Creek.

"Those guys really committed on a prayer and to a coach who promised what he was going to build here," Chronic Hoosier said.

His third class was a two-man class that featured a pair of players that had flown under the radar. Both Will Sheehey and Victor Oladipo had ranked over No. 140 in the nation in rankings of the best players coming out of high school. Before they would leave IU, however, Sheehey and Oladipo would both score more than 1,000 points in their IU careers and combine for 2,237 points.

In 2011 is when Zeller, Austin Etherington and Remy Abell were added to the mix.

But after 2013, when Zeller, Oladipo, Watford and Hulls were gone, that's when things got quite a bit more challenging for Crean. And that's when the rollercoaster existences of Crean's tenure began to show its face.

"Once the promising players were gone, it fell completely on coach's shoulders to keep it together and make something happen," Chronic said. "And it proved too much in the end for him there."

• • • • •

But this hasn't just been a Tom Crean problem at Indiana by any stretch. Some will argue that Davis didn't do enough in terms of recruiting the best in-state talent to Indiana.

Mike DeCourcy, the longtime college basketball analyst for *The Sporting News*, said Davis was at a bit of a disadvantage recruiting the state because he was a first time head coach.

"Mike came in and hadn't had any time really to build those connections," DeCourcy said. "And the nature of his accepting that position, the nature of it was not conducive to him building those relationships. He took that spot in such a tumultuous circumstance that him coming in and saying 'OK, forget about coach Knight, it's all me now', that was just not going to work. He had to rely on the people he knew and the people that believed in him and that's the recruits he went after."

Bob Lovell, who was the head coach at IUPUI from 1982-93 back when they called themselves the Metros, said it's all part of the challenge of recruiting the state of Indiana.

"I think coaches who have been there since Knight left have not done as good of a job recruiting the state of Indiana as they probably should have," Lovell said. "But if you're hoping to be one of the top teams in the country, I think you have to do a few things. One, you have to protect your border. You have to recruit your state as hard as you can again with no guarantees that you're going to get those guys but you have to be there.

"And secondly you have to have a national profile. You just look at the teams that are competing for championships year in and year out. Kentucky, Michigan State, Kansas, Louisville, right down the line. Those programs recruit at a high level nationally but they also usually are able to keep the local kids in their program, too. I think you have to do both."

Bill Murphy, the IU historian who wrote the book *Branch* about former IU basketball legend as a coach and a player Branch McCracken,

"I think what happened with Davis was that in his first three recruiting years that he recruited not the years that he first took over because those were Knight's recruits, is that he only recruited three kids from Indiana," Murphy said. "And that's totally. And I was coaching at the time and there were a couple of state coaches meetings that he was supposed to show up for that he didn't.

"So he didn't endear himself to the Indiana high school coaches. And so that became a problem, too."

The next big question is whether Archie Miller can have more success than his predecessors who have followed Knight. Specifically, can the momentum he built up at the University of Dayton translate to Indiana?

"I guess we're about to find out," Snow said. "Sometimes it does and sometimes it doesn't. I think Archie Miller is a tremendous basketball coach and I think he's a proven recruiter. He has a great pedigree. But none of that means it's going to work out. Now if you're making me guess, do I think Archie Miller is going to have a tremendous tenure at Indiana, I would say yes.

"But I never saw some guys failing at places the way they did and so that's just the reality. You really just don't know until you have a sample size to compare it to."

Ask people what Archie Miller needs to do to be successful at Indiana and you're going to get a lot of different answers. But just about everyone is going to point out the importance of recruiting the state of Indiana.

Miller heard it in the interview process with athletic director Fred Glass. He heard it in his introductory press conference when members of the media asked him about that very point. And he has heard it every step of the way, every speaking engagement, every visit with IU alumni.

Indiana fans want to root for players from the state of Indiana. It's truly that simple.

Indianapolis Star columnist Gregg Doyel said it's vital. He said IU fans want to see kids they've been reading about for three or four years in high school play at IU. He said it's a whole different level of affection that Indiana fans have for players in their state.

Mike Davis during the magical NCAA Tournament run in 2002.

When Bob Knight was the coach, rosters were loaded with Indiana kids. In recent seasons, with a few exceptions, that hasn't been the case.

"There's a reason that guys like Tom Coverdale will forever be revered in this state," Doyel said. "And he was good, I'm not saying that. But he wasn't like all-American good, but he will always hold a special place in their hearts because he was an Indiana kid that played at Indiana. Yogi Ferrell was good but he'll be remembered forever. This state continues to produce big time, huge recruits that with the exception of Yogi, they all went somewhere else.

"The quickest way to turn your program around, especially in a state like this, is to put a wall around the state borders and get who you want or at least compete with Purdue, Notre Dame and Butler and get who you want. And don't let Kentucky and Louisville and UCLA and Duke come and take them. No coach has been able to do that since Knight was here."

•••••

Dave Revsine of the Big Ten Network said keeping Indiana kids at home has to be a big priority for Miller at IU.

"You're going to have to get some in-state kids, I don't think there's any question about that," Revsine said. "You have to make some in-roads within the state of Indiana to where if you've got three kids who are all top 50 players and they're playing in the state of Indiana, you need to get one or two of them at IU. So I think part of it is going to have to be taking on this identity of the state a little bit again.

"At its core to real Hoosier fans, Indiana basketball is about the state. It's about kind of a way of life and basketball is synonymous with Indiana. And so I just think it's really important that that identity is created again."

Revsine said it's not going to be easy. This isn't going to be Miller snapping his fingers and all of a sudden the borders are going to close and kids are going to grow up wanting to play at Indiana, much like they did when Bob Knight was the coach.

No, it's going to take time and as Revsine said, it's going to take developing relationships with the state's high school coaches and getting them on his side.

"It's a tougher environment to do it in," Revsine said. "Purdue has always been right there. They had a certain way of playing with coach Keady and obviously he had more success than anyone against Knight. And so Purdue is always going to be there. But now that Notre Dame has it kind of rocking and rolling a bit with Mike Brey and Butler has clearly had a great run, it's a more challenge environment to recruit in than it was when it was just Bob against Gene. Maybe Digger (Phelps) would get a guy or two but it was a lot more about Indiana and Purdue."

Mike Marot, the Indianapolis-based Associated Press reporter who has covered IU basketball for more than two decades, said there's something missing about the way kids in the state are being recruited today by school's like Indiana.

"I don't know if it's something where they didn't recruit kids from Indiana as hard or didn't put that sort of panache to come here, but it's something," Marot said. "It used to be 'Come and represent the state and wear the crimson and cream' and that's what it was all about. Almost a cheerleading kind of approach. That has disappeared. I think they can get it back but right now it doesn't exist."

Mike Miller, the Indiana University beat writer for *The Herald-Times* in Bloomington, said Archie Miller needs to reverse a recent trend where the best kids in the state are not attending IU.

"I don't think in this day and age that you necessarily have to have a team full of guys from Indiana, but there were certainly some guys in recent years that got away," Mike Miller said. "You need to get the higher ranked guys in the state. There's no question about it. And for a few years here Indiana has not done that. They have not gotten the guys they needed, but instead seemingly prioritized other areas of the country.

"Instead of getting guys in Indiana, IU has been plucking guys out of New York or the Washington D.C. area. I don't think there's anything wrong with that but at the same time I think you need to show a willingness and the ability to recruit the state."

Mike Marot said there's too much talent in the state of Indiana not to have the Hoosiers capitalizing on it.

"I really think if Archie can recruit Indiana he can get this program back up and going," Marot said. "But I think he's a patient enough of a guy, and a low key of enough of a guy to be able to do things that maybe Tom (Crean) wasn't able to do. I think Tom felt in some ways that he needed to play up to the fans and I don't see that in Archie at least not yet."

Greg Rakestraw, the program director of 1070-The Fan in Indianapolis, said that the single thing that will allow Miller to return Indiana basketball to a more lofty national status is recruiting. He said all of the other building blocks are firmly in place.

"You're not coming off of NCAA sanctions, you're not coming off completely having to gut the roster, and you're now on level footing as far as facilities," Rakestraw said. "Now the important thing for someone like Archie Miller is to repair some bridges with in-state high school basketball coaches. I do think relationships with high school coaches in the state still matter. A lot of the recruiting is done during AAU season and I get that but this is still a state where being close to the high school coaches is important. And for whatever reason, that importance with Tom (Crean) seemed to shrink over the course of the last four years."

When media members were polled in the previous chapter they weighed in on the importance of Indiana being able to own the state once again in recruiting. It's not just about getting those players to come to IU but to keep them from going to play for other schools in the Big Ten or neighboring programs that may be a rival.

Former players feel the same way. Close the borders, improve relationships with high school coaches and find a way to keep the best of Indiana basketball playing in the fall and winter at the Simon Skjodt Assembly Hall.

Pat Graham was on vacation for spring break in Florida at the time Archie Miller was hired at Indiana. The Monday after he returned home, he drove north to Bloomington to talk to Miller.

"One thing I mentioned to (Miller) and he's a smart guy, in fact all of these coaches are smart guys," Graham said. "But it was one of those things where I didn't want to feel after the fact that I didn't say something that I felt was important and I told him, 'You've got to own the state of Indiana.' And he looked at me and said 'Absolutely.'

"And I think that's the No. 1 thing that Archie Miller has to do at Indiana. He has to own the state. He has to get the Midwest style player which is what I think Indiana fans want."

Graham said there's a trust factor there, too.

"I never felt that Indiana basketball fans ever held Davis, Sampson or Crean tight to the vest," Graham said. "I get the first one and maybe even the second one. It was kind of like, 'You're not Bob Knight so we don't like you.' But there has to be a level of trust between the fan base and the head coach at IU. Let's face it, you have to have the fans to succeed. Assembly Hall cannot be half full or three quarters full and have it be the way that we used to be. It can't happen."

Kirk Haston, an IU All-American in 2001 who played both for Bob Knight and Mike Davis, is now a high school head basketball coach himself in his hometown in Tennessee. He said a big key for Miller will be reversing that trend of state of Indiana kids going elsewhere.

"I think that one of the big things for him will be getting all the in-state kids to buy into wanting to make Indiana one of the best programs in the nation again," Haston said. "Sure there have been some exceptions to that rule in the past 15-20 years but there has just been a pretty large exodus of top talent in the state of Indiana that have gone somewhere other than Indiana University.

"If you could just get high school kids excited about being a part of their in-state program it can kind of gain its own momentum. Do that and you can just tap into the pipeline and you can be really consistent."

Jarrad Odle said everything he has heard about Miller is that he's going about recruiting in state the right way.

"I just know he's spending a lot of time in high school gyms in the state of Indiana," Odle said. "Hopefully that turns the tide of Indiana high school coaches wanting to get their kids better so that they have a chance to play at Indiana University versus going to North Carolina or Duke or Kentucky and leaving the state. If Archie is doing those things, he's giving every effort to make the program great again."

9

You Have to Be Able to Outcoach the Fan Base

Of all the points that people made along the way as I was doing research for this book, I thought this was one of the most interesting.

The basic point was this: If you're going to be a successful basketball coach at Indiana University, you had better be able to outcoach the fan base.

And that's not an easy task.

Former *Indianapolis Star* columnist Bob Kravitz, who now writes for WTHR-TV in Indianapolis, said that everyone in the fan base believes they can outcoach you.

"Whether they can or can't it doesn't matter because they all think that they can," Kravitz said. "It's like being a hockey coach in Montreal or a baseball manager in St. Louis. It's the same thing. Everybody in the fan base thinks they can outcoach you. And sometimes they're right."

On one hand, Indiana basketball fans deserve credit because they are an extremely knowledgeable group. They know the game. They know what looks right and they know what doesn't. And if what is happening on the floor isn't in line with what they think is the correct way, the coach is going to hear it.

On another hand though, they may be all wet, too. It's just part of the fan thing but at Indiana it seems to be something that is amplified to a larger scale. If the fans think that they know more than you do, well, let's just say the level of noise is going to reach near a high decibel volume.

Fans may hide behind their Twitter handles to voice their opinion or make an opinion known on one of the various sports talk radio shows in the Indianapolis area or around the state. They may pen an opinion on one of the countless number of IU basketball fan sites from Mike Pegram's site Peegs.com to the current Rivals site TheHoosier.com to Alex Bozich's popular Inside the Hall forum.

They may write comments at the end of stories on Indiana beat writers' websites. Sometimes they'll get a little daring and call into the coach's radio show that is hosted every week by the voice of Indiana Basketball, Don Fischer.

And sometimes, as has been the case many times over the 20 years I've covered Indiana basketball, you may just have some guy in the 20th row of the East Main at Assembly Hall stand up and scream something in the direction of the current IU coach. I can remember that happening with Mike Davis and Tom Crean both over the years. I can still picture Davis on one knee in front of the scorer's table, hearing one of those comments and just shaking his head, slowly from side to side.

I can also remember Crean's reactions, too, which often times would be very different. And it usually always seemed like the person would yell something at that one moment where things got really quiet. Somebody would yell something and the crowd would react in their own way either to boo or to nod in an agreement. But with Crean there would often times be a reaction. Sometimes, he might turn around and glare at the person making the noise, and then many times an Assembly Hall security person or usher would be dispatched to have a conversation with the opinionated person.

But the whole idea of trying to outcoach the fan base at Indiana is very real. I have spoken to very few people with that concept who didn't think it was accurate. Most feel like it's spot on. And I have to agree.

If you're an Indiana fan, think about it. It makes way too much sense. Think about how bad things got for Mike Davis

Tom Crean (top) and Mike Davis (below) combined to coach IU basketball for 15 seasons.

at Indiana because the fan base never really thought he was the right guy for the job. And over time, that fan base looked for every possible negative thing that Davis did and then trumpeted it for all to hear.

Kelvin Sampson? It was different because for the most part Sampson had enough success in nearly two seasons at IU that you didn't hear the noise. He only lost a total of 15 games in two seasons and he didn't have the real bad losses that made you scratch your head.

Dan Dakich? Same thing. He only coached seven games in his interim tenure as the Indiana coach, filling in for Sampson after he was let go. And at that point a good segment of the fan base had tuned out because they were so disappointed in what had transpired under Sampson with the rules violations and they couldn't believe what had been done to THEIR program. Many took it personally, which is understandable considering the affinity that Hoosier Nation has for its basketball program.

But it was definitely a problem for Tom Crean. There was the infamous Syracuse debacle in the 2013 Sweet Sixteen that I'll delve deeply into later in this chapter. But there were other games over time that left people scratching their heads as to how a team like Indiana could lose to THAT opponent.

I usually don't count those teams in the first three seasons because Crean was playing with a non-Big Ten caliber group himself for the most part. All you have to know about that three-year stretch is that Indiana went 8-46 in three seasons in conference play. In other words, IU was not a competitive bunch.

And so losses to teams like Northeastern and Lipscomb that first year can be explained. Or to Boston University or Loyola of Maryland in year two. But the bad losses later in his career were red flags to the IU fan base that thought they knew better how things should be done. That Eastern Washington loss in the 2014-15 season jumps out. So does Wake Forest in

Maui in the 2015-16 campaign and no one will soon forget the lost to Fort Wayne in Crean's final season, 2016-17.

So you have a situation where Indiana fans simply think they know better. Sometimes you feel like you're sitting in Assembly Hall with 17,000 plus people who think they are qualified to be calling the shots.

Mike Miller, the talented young beat writer for *The Herald Times* in Bloomington, said Indiana basketball fans are a special breed.

"It starts in the state with high school basketball at the grassroots level," he said. "You can be sitting in the stands next to, for the lack of a better term, a little old lady who probably knows more about the game than anyone on the court. It's just such a part of the fabric of the state.

"And what that leads to is a certain level where you're always kind of coaching against the people who are there supporting you. The second guessing is always going to happen especially on Twitter. That's always going to be a unique challenge about a place like Indiana, especially since (Bob) Knight taught the people about the way he thought the game should be played."

And that is definitely part of it. Indiana fans were educated by Bob Knight in his 29 seasons at Indiana. They understand the fundamentals. They know about the difference between going over and going under a screen. They think they have a pretty good idea on what should be correct substitution patterns. And of course they know the motion offense.

What some may or may not be willing to admit, however, is that there are a lot of IU basketball fans out there still today, educated by Knight, that can't understand why Indiana doesn't still run the motion offense? I kind of say that in jest but at the same time it's not completely farfetched to think that some people out there really think that way.

And again, this can all be a part of the IU fan base believing they are smarter than they really are.

Former IU player Todd Leary, who played for Bob Knight and the Hoosiers from 1989-94, said it's just the nature of the beast when it comes to Hoosier Nation.

"A lot of those fans grew up watching who they feel was the best coach of all time and you're not going to change their opinion of that whether it's true or not true," Leary said.

Mike Pegram, the publisher of the popular IU fan site Peegs.com which is now under the Scout.com umbrella, said the Indiana fan base is different than what you find at a lot of major programs.

"Kentucky and North Carolina fans for example obsess a lot more about recruiting than Indiana fans do," Pegram said. "And Indiana fans obsess more about game management and coaching decisions within a game than any fan base I've seen.

I asked Indiana athletic director Fred Glass to comment on that premise of coaches needing to outcoach the fan base when I interviewed him for this book. At first he chuckled when presented with that notion, but it resonated with him, too.

"I totally agree," Glass said. "One of the real strengths of this place is that the fan base is so incredibly knowledgeable. They've played the game. They've coached the game. They know good coaching when they see it and they know bad coaching when they see it, too. And that's great because if you're good that will be appreciated and if you have some flaws it will be laid bare.

"I think that's a pretty insightful comment actually."

Another Indiana athletic director interviewed for this book was Rick Greenspan. He was Fred Glass's predecessor at IU. He couldn't disagree either.

"The fan base at Indiana, in general, is a very educated group about college basketball," Greenspan said. "They notice things about substitution patterns and little things like when you call timeouts and all the fundamental things like defensive stances and blocking out. Basically, you can't B.S. them.

"You have to be able to say, 'Yeah, we screwed up' and then work on it as opposed to saying 'That's irrelevant. That's not the way I see things.'"

• • • • •

Bob Lovell, who was the head basketball coach at IUPUI from 1982-93 and is now the host of Network Indiana's popular syndicated Indiana Sports Talk program, agreed with the premise. He also questioned how often it is true.

"I'm not really sure that the fan base is as astute as some would think they are to be honest," Lovell said, breaking into a grin.

"But I think you do have to outcoach the fans for sure. You have to be able to articulate to your kids, and to the media and everybody around just exactly what you are."

Lovell said every year that he coached he would ask his players before each season a couple of simple questions. One was 'What are we about? and another was 'What are we? He would tell his players that if they had to describe that current team to someone as a group, what would that description entail?

"If you think about it and you asked that question when coach Knight was coaching I think you had an easy answer," Lovell said. "What was IU about as a basketball team when coach Knight was there? I don't think you'd hesitate to give the same answer.

"But I don't think you get those same kind of answers today. I think you have to articulate what you are and then stay true to what you are. I think outcoaching the fan base is being able to tell them what your expectations are and how you're going to do it. And then go out and do it."

Local Indianapolis sports radio talk show host Kent Sterling said that over time Knight taught IU fans the basic nuances of basketball. And because of that, IU fans believe there's really only one way to do things – the Knight way.

"I think Bob Knight's greatest legacy as the head coach at Indiana is that he taught this entire state for 29 years how the game of basketball works at the highest level and how basketball needs to be coached," Sterling said. "And he shared information generously with the fan base in a way that I don't think a lot of other guys have done. Certainly, Tom (Crean) never did.

"Because of that it was really, really difficult for a guy like Tom to outcoach the Indiana fans. And I'll tell you this, if you're going to be successful at IU you had better be able to outcoach the fan base."

• • • • •

Some point to one game in the NCAA Tournament in 2013 when top-seed IU fell to No. 4 seed Syracuse as perhaps being the performance that Crean could never rise above. It was almost as if in the minds of Indiana basketball fans, IU's inability to have success against the Syracuse zone forced them to completely lose confidence in their head coach. Whenever you would talk to IU fans in the four years after that game, a common theme that would always come up was the loss to Syracuse in the Sweet Sixteen.

In 2015, I wrote a book called *Missing Banners* along with my co-author Tom Brew where we looked at all the seasons in Indiana basketball history where the Hoosiers came close to hanging a national championship banner but didn't.

2013 was one of those seasons we focused on and pretty much an entire chapter was focused on the game against Syracuse. I talked to a lot of IU players from that team about that game in the aftermath of a crushing defeat that sent the No. 1 seeded Hoosiers home and eventually got Syracuse to the Final Four.

I thought I would share a quick excerpt here so that you can get a flavor for what IU's players felt went wrong when they faced the Orange in Washington, D.C.

"They were just long and active," Victor Oladipo said in the postgame press conference. "We just didn't take care of the ball like we should have. In the first half we got a little too anxious, catching the ball, moving out the ball, not having the ball secure in our hands, and our shots weren't falling at the same time. So that's pretty much it."

The beef from Hoosier Nation in the days, weeks, months and even years after that game was that IU coach Tom Crean had a week to prepare for Syracuse and yet the Hoosiers looked completely befuddled and unprepared.

Christian Watford said Indiana's struggles in the Sweet Sixteen had nothing to do with being unprepared to face Syracuse's vaunted zone. He said if anything he thinks, looking back, that IU spent too much time in preparation worrying about the zone.

"Now that I look back on it, I think we were so worried about their zone and what they were going to do that we weren't that much about our ourselves and the things that we needed to do," Watford said. "I think we put too much of an emphasis on it. We made it too much of a big deal. Instead of just going out and doing what we do. We had a group of guys with great basketball IQ and I just wonder if maybe we were just a little too robotic when it came to attacking that zone.

"We were all caught up in the fact that the ball had to go here, here and here instead of trusting our instincts and just doing what had got us to that point that season."

Jordan Hulls said anyone that says that IU wasn't prepared for the Syracuse zone simply wasn't paying attention. He said that wasn't the case at all. Looking back in the spring of 2015, Hulls said Indiana had a good game plan, it simply didn't execute that night against Syracuse.

"We just didn't play how we needed to in order to win," Hulls said. "We didn't make shots, didn't attack the zone as well as we needed to, never got in a rhythm and didn't defend them like we had to. It's so easy for us to look back now and analyze the film to see other ways to attack it but it's what we thought was the best at the time and that's all that matters. Our coaches prepared us with a gameplan they thought was best for us to win the game and we believed in them, just as we had all year long.

"You need a little break every now and then to win it all and we just didn't have it that game. We could've hit more shots, got more stops, got to the free throw line more. There are so many things that go through my mind but what's done is done and we have to live with it."

Derek Elston agreed wholeheartedly with Hulls that Indiana had a perfect gameplan for Syracuse. It just didn't make shots. And when you don't make shots, on the biggest stage under the brightest lights, it's going to be very difficult to win deep in the NCAA Tournament.

"We watched that Louisville vs. Syracuse Big East Championship game so many times we could have literally told you what play was next after every situation," Elston said. "It was the perfect example of how to defeat the zone and we ran it to perfection all week in practice. It's just very hard to emulate the length they have. Honestly we were running our zone plays perfectly but you still have to make shots."

When Elston thinks about that game, that's what comes to mind. IU was 16-of-48 from the field, 33 percent. It was IU's lowest shooting percentage of the season. Next lowest was 37 percent against Wisconsin. In 36 games, IU only had five games where it didn't shoot better than 40 percent. For the season, the Hoosiers hit 48.2 percent from the field.

And then here's a little bit more from the book toward the end of that chapter when I went back two years later and talked to IU's players about their memories of that night and how long it had taken them to get over it.

Two years later, in the spring of 2015, a few players on that team were asked to reflect on the way it had ended. Specifically, how long had it taken to get past the feeling that in losing to

Syracuse and not advancing further in the NCAA Tournament the Hoosiers had potentially let a great opportunity get away.

All of the answers were extremely insightful. Of course, the seniors ached the most.

"For as long as I live, I will never get over that game," Hulls said. "I hate losing more than anything, even more than winning. All I remember from after the game is frustration and sadness, saying to myself, 'It's really over. I'll never play for Indiana University again. I'll never wear the candy stripes and run out of the tunnel in Assembly Hall in front of a sold out crowd. I missed every shot in the final game of my career. Why did I have to hurt my shooting shoulder against Temple? What could I have done better? I let my team down.'

Hulls said his mind was filled with those kinds of thoughts and emotions. He said he then had to speak to the media in the locker room at the Verizon Center for one last time and that didn't help at all.

From there, the team headed back to the hotel.

"Going back to the hotel, I was in shock still," Hulls said. "I roomed with Cody Zeller on the road and we had become real close. We just kept talking about the 'coulda, shoulda, woulda's' and how we couldn't believe it was all over. We all truly believed this was our year to win it all, we had all the pieces, but it just wasn't meant to be. It was one of the longest nights of my life."

Hulls was asked if he has ever gone back and watched the Syracuse game. He answer was quick and to the point.

"I have not gone back to watch the game," Hulls said, "and I never will."

Elston said it was difficult to get over that game. He said he heard from Indiana fans who wished that the 2012-13 Hoosiers could just stay and play moving forward at Indiana because of how much people appreciated the way that team played.

"It's crazy when I get random messages from fans saying they would love nothing more than to just watch our group of guys come back year after year and play," Elston said. "We had an exciting run and a very exciting group of guys to play with, but to have fans say they don't need to see any other players come through IU they just want to watch that 2013 group again means a lot."

Elston said he remembers the next morning at the hotel when the team ate together before they boarded the bus to head for the airport. He said it was an interesting scene.

"For some, NBA workouts were in the near future and for others I think they were happy that it was over because the pressure was starting to get to a few of the players and it wasn't the same group of guys like we all knew," Elston said.

As for watching the game again, Elston said it's also difficult for different reasons. Elston's knee was really bothering him and so he didn't get in the game until the final minute. And that was more of a curtain call. All of that makes the thought of watching the game again almost unbearable.

"I never have (watched it) and probably never will," Elston said. "Maybe my kids will want to see it one day, I'm not sure, but for me not being able to go out and be a part of it like I wanted to be, it was a very depressing time in my life so I try not to relive those bad memories."

Yogi Ferrell was in a little bit of a different situation because he still had three years of eligibility remaining. But even he said it was really difficult to get past that loss to the Orange.

It took a while. It definitely took all summer," Ferrell said. "That offseason was one of my hardest working ones and I wanted to come back with a chip on my shoulder. I think what hurt the most was knowing I would never play with those particular guys again and we just missed out on something that could have been really special."

Watford said he still isn't over the Syracuse loss. He then said he was kidding but it didn't sound like he was.

213

"We still talk about it," Watford said. "Every time we're together we all know that we should have hung a national championship banner in Assembly Hall and we talk about it. I don't feel like our season was a failure because we did do some great things and had a lot of high moments.

"But at the same time, we do feel like we let one slip away."

•••••

Some think it's unfair to judge Crean's legacy on that one game. Dave Revsine, of the Big Ten Network, however, would not be counted in that company.

"I don't think it's unfair to judge him on that game," Revsine said. "Yes, it was a bad matchup but they just looked so befuddled. I think they clearly had prepared for the Syracuse zone and it's unfair to say they weren't prepared for it, but they didn't execute anything offensively against that zone. There was nothing that led you to believe that even with a great set of players out there that they had in any way figured out a way to make Syracuse uncomfortable.

"Obviously (Jordan) Hulls had a terrible shooting night but it was a mess. To me it wasn't so much that they lost, it was how they lost. They just looked so inept offensively with as much talent as they had. That is what bothered me. Had they lost a one point game where someone hits a shot at the buzzer I think you look at it differently then but they were just so befuddled throughout the game that's what really bothered me."

Alex Bozich, publisher of Inside the Hall, agreed.

"I do go back to Syracuse and a game where you had three or four days to prepare for a 2-3 zone," Bozich said. "And you've got two guys who were picked in the top four in the (NBA) draft and you had two other seniors playing heavy minutes and you come out and score 50 points as the No. 1 seed.

"It's a tough loss to defend."

Bozich was correct about that, too. The 50 points scored by Indiana that night were a season-low and more than 28 points under IU's season scoring average.

Revsine called the Syracuse game "the pivot point" of Crean's tenure at Indiana.

"Had that team as the No. 1 seed made it to the Final Four, I still think (Crean) would be the coach of Indiana today," Revsine said. "Is it fair or unfair? I think it's fair. You're in a business where there are expectations and you're being paid a lot of money and you take a job like Indiana and obviously the place was decimated and you do get a certain grace period. But when you look at getting to the point where you had Cody Zeller and Christian Watford and Victor Oladipo, I think it's fair to say that that team should have been a Final Four team."

Former ESPN college basketball analyst Andy Katz was in attendance in Washington D.C. on March 28, 2013 when the Hoosiers squared off against Syracuse. He said Indiana had better talent but it was a terrible matchup for the Hoosiers.

"Indiana was the better team but they didn't win the game," Katz said. "Indiana had better players. But that's happened countless times. UConn in 2011 and 2014 was not the best team and yet they won two titles. I firmly believe that with Wisconsin if that shot hadn't gone down by Aaron Harrison of Kentucky in 2014, I think for sure Wisconsin beats Connecticut that year.

"My point is matchups. It was just a bad matchup for Indiana that year and if they beat Syracuse they go to the Elite Eight and maybe they get to the Final Four. That's the year that Louisville beat Michigan for the national championship. Who knows? First of all they're in the Final Four and who knows what happens in that Final Four?"

Katz said it could have been the kind of game that served as a springboard for Crean in his IU career. Instead, it almost had the opposite result.

"If Indiana wins that game, I think IU fans would always look at Crean differently than they do today," Katz said. "He would have gotten past the Sweet Sixteen wall and gotten closer to a Final Four. And I think in terms of public perception that would have been huge for Tom."

Former *Indianapolis Star* columnist Bob Kravitz also blamed the Syracuse loss on a case of bad matchups.

"It was a really bad matchup," Kravitz said. "Indiana's backcourt was so small. It had Yogi Ferrell as a freshman and Jordan Hulls as a senior. They couldn't really see the basket much less make one. I realize they were the No. 1 seed but if that performance is Tom Crean's legacy then holy smokes."

Mike Miller, the IU beat writer for *The Herald Times* in Bloomington, said the Syracuse game was the beginning of the end for Tom Crean.

"It really was," Miller said. "You almost saw it coming, too. That was a team that at the end of the year just looked tired. It was a team that for two years was kind of carrying those expectations of being the group that brought it all back and when it all came crashing down that night, the frustration and the anger that that season ended the way it did, I just don't think it ever died.

"It carried through to the next season which was tough to stomach. Then came all the off the court stuff that got in the papers and it just sort of all flowed together. You almost always pointed back to that night against Syracuse and wondered if anything was really salvageable after that."

Miller said you can say what you want but that was the night that Crean's credibility with the Indiana fan base came to an end.

"Granted that staff stuck around for four more years but you got the sense that all of the frustration and all of the criticism, all the nit-picking kind of went back to that as far as the coaching," Miller said. "Basically, how can you go against the vaunted Syracuse 2-3 zone and look like that? There were times in that game when it looked like you were doing what you should probably do against that zone. They were flashing to the middle in the high post but they just didn't follow through from that point. The consistent execution on that night just wasn't there and that team, looking like that on that night, I don't think they every got past it."

Indianapolis Star beat writer Zach Osterman said the way the 2013 season ended was just so difficult on Crean.

"I remember Bob Ryan of the Boston Globe saying later that the 2013 IU team was one of the best college basketball teams he had ever seen that didn't make a Final Four," Osterman said. "And so there was a general perception with that team that anything less than making a Final Four was basically unacceptable."

Another Big Ten Network guy, Jon Crispin, who played collegiately at both Penn State and UCLA, was on the other side of the fence with respect to how much Crean should be blamed for the Syracuse game.

"I look at that and say that he's not the only coach or the only team to look befuddled against the Syracuse zone," Crispin said. "If you haven't seen that defense, you don't know how to attack it. And you better have a gameplan but the gameplan is not based on just your personnel. The gameplan is based on what has worked in the past against that team. I know Tom Crean and I've considered him a friend for a long time. And I know that in his mind he felt like he knew how to attack that defense. And if it doesn't work out it's not just his fault. Maybe it's players not adhering to the gameplan. There's a lot that goes into it. So I don't just look at that and say Tom Crean didn't do his job. I look at it and say 'So that didn't work but so what?'"

Derek Schultz said that he has a hard time being too critical of Crean for the Syracuse game.

"The NCAA Tournament is random and there are a lot of times when you have a bad night and you're out," Schultz said. "Ask Kansas about that. They get eliminated by lesser teams all the time and that doesn't make them any less great."

But Schultz said the Syracuse game and getting to the level that Indiana got to in 2013 was ultimately a major piece of the puzzle that didn't fit for Crean.

"He got them to that level and then it was almost like Indiana and Crean and everybody else, all they wanted to talk about was where they had come from and I wanted to know where were they going?" Schultz said. "It's great that he built Indiana back up and yes, that's wonderful. But where are you going? So we're here and we've climbed out of the crater left by Sampson and company, now where are we going from here and it just seemed like they kind of plateaued after that."

Gregg Doyel, the columnist from the *Indianapolis Star*, maintains that Crean and the IU fan base never really connected. And he said he thinks the Syracuse game was a memory that Crean could never get beyond.

"Tom and the fan base never really connected, in part because that team in 2013 got to the Sweet Sixteen and lost to Syracuse," Doyel said. "I just think IU fans have never forgotten that. Whenever anything went wrong and the fan base wanted to vent, my Twitter feed would be full of Syracuse mentions. I don't think he ever really connected with the fans and frankly I really believe the last four years they were just waiting for him to get fired.

"He never caught their fancy and at Indiana that's simply something you have to be able to do."

Doyel said there are always moments that fans can look back and point at where they think you've done something that shows that they are smarter than you. He puts Syracuse in that company.

"I was only there for three full seasons with coach Crean but with IU fans there were a handful of those infamous moments where something would be happening on the floor and fans would say 'What are you doing?'" Doyel said. "Once the IU fan base starts to think that way it's difficult to change their minds. That's just who they are. Kentucky fans are the same way. But that's something you're always up against at Indiana when the fans start asking 'What are you doing?'"

Kent Sterling said when Indiana fans start asking that question enough times, that's when it becomes too difficult to change their minds in the future.

"When you do that enough times and Indiana fans scratch their heads enough times, they come to realize that you don't know basketball well enough to coach at Indiana," Sterling said.

And what is probably most unfair about that is that once you lose the fans, it is basically over in the court of public opinion. It's hard to get them back. Some people think that it's just a vocal minority but that doesn't ever seem to really be true with Indiana fans. When fans start voicing their opinions, it seems like you hear it everywhere. You hear it from the guy in line at the grocery store or someone walking out of your Sunday church service. You hear it from good friends and casual acquaintances. Basically, if someone knows that you are either a big IU basketball fan or in my case a member of the media that covers Indiana, chances are they're going to bend your ear about their opinions on the coach.

Alex Bozich, the publisher of *Inside the Hall*, said once the proverbial snow ball would get rolling it was hard to stop it.

"It just seemed like to me that any time you had any small incident, anything that was said or done that people didn't like it was turned into some big ordeal," Bozich said. "It was just like people were waiting for anything so that they could pounce. You'd have the memes on social media or it might just be criticizing a move that was made."

Bozich agreed that the Syracuse game in 2013 was the one that everyone would always go back to. It was like it was the one thing that had happened in Crean's tenure that they felt they could always win the ultimate argument with when they tried to make the claim that he wasn't the right guy for the job.

My own opinion of Crean after the Syracuse game is that I'm not really sure if there was anything he could have ever done from that point on to win back the trust of the fan base. Win the national championship and hang that sixth banner? Yeah, that probably would have done it.

But I'm not sure that's completely a given either.

What if Mike Davis and Indiana had won the national championship in 2002 and then everything else that followed remained the same? He still would have had a 14-15 season followed by a 15-14 season and Indiana basketball fans would have still lost their collective minds. And my opinion is that even though he had just put up the sixth banner a few years ago, IU fans would have had a short memory and still wanted him gone. That whole faction of the fan base that always believed that Davis had reached the championship game with Knight's players would have had a field day once again.

And again, when you really stop to think about it, it's completely unfair.

Let's use the Syracuse example one more time. So based on one game, which by the way as a few people have pointed out was a terrible matchup for an Indiana team that had two short guards in Yogi Ferrell and Jordan Hulls facing a zone with great length, you're going to decide that your coach is not "the guy" to lead your program?

It's probably a good thing that Indiana basketball fans didn't make that decision in the 1986 NCAA Tournament when the No. 3 seeded Hoosiers dropped an 83-79 decision in the first round to No. 14 seed Cleveland State in Syracuse, N.Y.

What would have transpired if that had happened in today's game with today's social media presence? How would Bob Knight have handled all of that criticism? I'm guessing not well but he may have been deep enough into his tenure not to worry about it, too. He probably would have gone fishing.

You could make the same claim about Jim Boeheim in the 1987 national championship game. After Smart's shot goes in, a few stunned Syracuse players stand around and 3 or 4 seconds tick off the clock. That left the Orange just a tick or two to try to run a play after they finally did call a timeout.

So should Syracuse fans have been up in arms with Boeheim and how he handled that late game situation? You can bet if that happened at Indiana in the post Bob Knight-era, it would have been analyzed and re-analyzed and left people shaking their heads as to how that could have possibly happened.

But we'll never really know because this was long before Twitter and sports talk shows for the most point and social media wasn't anything like it is today. And so people may have grumbled but you didn't hear the noise like you hear it being yelled through a megaphone today. Today, it's like that opinion is blasted over an intercom with morning announcements.

Also, in the case of the Cleveland State example, all Indiana did the following year was come back and win the national championship. .

Chronic Hoosier, the Indiana super fan that I've permitted to use his pen name for my books, said he thinks you could expand that way of thinking beyond the fan base to the high school coaches and youth coaches in the state of Indiana, too.

"I think that's perhaps even more important because I think that ultimately it is going to give you your access to the state's talent pipeline," Chronic Hoosier said. "The coaches have to feel as though they're sending their players to someone who is going to take care of them and develop their games and make them better basketball players. And when people talk about Bob Knight's legacy at Indiana I think that's probably the most understated legacy of all is his impact on the state's youth basketball. I think that's something that still exists to this day and will for some time."

221

And Chronic Hoosier said it comes back to the most basic principles that made Bob Knight successful: man-to-man defense and the motion offense.

"Those concepts permeate every youth coach I've ever had and those concepts continue to permeate every youth coach I've encountered with my children," he said. "To this day they're still learning the importance of setting the proper screen and how it's an orchestration, it's not just a one person job. It's orchestrated like ballet. Two people have to be in the same space at the same time in order to make it work.

"And it's paramount to coach here that you're able to impress upon the state's coaches what you stand for. They don't absolutely determine a coach's success at a place like Indiana but they absolutely have a whole lot to do with it."

Jon Crispin of the Big Ten Network feels like a lot of times fans just have no idea about what really goes into the job as a collegiate head coach.

"I think a lot of fans hang on to one or two games as to their justification for having frustration," Crispin said. "And that's fine. That's what fans do. But the truth is fans have no idea of what it takes to coach at this level. Fans have no idea of what goes into game planning and scheming and getting a team ready to play at this level. They don't. And that's just the way it's always going to be."

Crispin brought up the Syracuse game again and the fact he knows that fans continued to be critical of Crean's coaching effort in that game right up to the time he was dismissed by the university.

"But I look at that and you can't define his job on just one game," Crispin said. "Especially against a team that you will never see anything like what they do. You just won't. It's just the nature of that defense. It causes problems, it causes frustrations and it's the worst defense for Indiana because Tom Crean's offense and defense were all about finding rhythm within the game. When you go against a zone like that there's no rhythm whatsoever. You have to find a way to create your own rhythm and I think that was the biggest struggle."

Bob Lovell, the host of Network Indiana's Indiana Sports Talk and a former college basketball head coach himself in the state at IUPUI, agreed with the premise that Knight taught the fan base to appreciate good, solid fundamental basketball. But he was also quick to point out that the game today is much different than when Knight was roaming the sidelines in Bloomington.

"Back in the day, if you set a ball screen in motion offense coach Knight would have grabbed you and tossed you off the court," Lovell said. "Because it was always pass and screen away, pass and screen away. On ball screens, oh my gosh, you never did it."

But Lovell said a lot has changed. He said with screens for example most everything is on ball. And he said with the advent of the 3-point shot in college basketball that focuses within the coaching ranks have changed, too.

"Most coaches in today's game believe that every time you have the basketball you want to score three points," Lovell said. "You want to penetrate, dish and make a 3, or you want to penetrate, get the ball inside, get fouled and go to the free throw line. There is no midrange game in college basketball today. And I think people, especially in our state, they don't understand that. They have not come to grips with this is how the game is played."

Malcom Moran, the former lead college basketball writer for *USA Today* who also worked at the *Chicago Tribune*, the *New York Times* and *Newsday*, says that you may indeed need to aspire to outcoach the fan base at Indiana but in his opinion it's something that cannot be done.

"It's not possible," Moran said. "I think the sense of entitlement has become so much a part of the fabric of the place that to me it's very similar to Notre Dame football."

Moran said you don't want to make it seem like you're making concessions because you're not.

"But I think the only way you could try to cope with it is to have as much communication between coach and fan base as possible and you need help from the university leadership," Moran said. "There has to be a consistent voice that somehow gently explains that you're not going to be 39-0 every year."

10
Recruiting Philosophies

Todd Leary played at Indiana from 1989-94 and later was a member of the IU radio broadcast team for several years. He said whether or not Archie Miller is successful at Indiana will come down to one thing.

It comes down to the type of player you recruit. Or even more to the point, what is your recruiting philosophy?

In the cases of guys like Mike Davis and Tom Crean, both could have been accused of shooting for the moon too many times while good potential three or four-year players slipped through the cracks.

"Who you recruit is what will determine if you are successful at Indiana and are able to have that sustained level of winning or if you're not successful," Leary said. "I had a real nice meeting with Archie Miller the week after he got hired and he wasn't necessarily asking my opinion about things but I was giving it to him."

Leary told a story that really hit home to me as an interesting recruiting tidbit.

"And what I said was, 'This is the thing that I'd like you to think about and that's would you have recruited you?," Leary said. "You played at North Carolina State but if you were at Indiana would you have recruited you? A 5-10, not so athletic point guard. Would you have recruited you?'

"Because I know the three coaches that have been here since Coach Knight would not have recruited him."

And that's at the essence, Leary believes, of where Indiana has fallen short in terms of recruiting. It has focused so much on the best of the best that a lot of really good players have slipped through the cracks.

"Yes, they would have recruited Brian Evans because he was 6-foot-9 and he could shoot it like crazy," Leary said. "Yes they would have recruited Calbert Cheaney and probably Pat Graham and Greg Graham and those guys. Would they have recruited Tom Coverdale? I doubt it. Would they have recruited Dane Fife? I doubt it. Indiana basketball over the last several years has become a program that focuses on a different kind of kid and that's too bad."

Alex Bozich always thinks about a player like Bryant McIntosh. He said Indiana spent a great deal of time recruiting JaQuan Lyle (who went to Ohio State but off-the court trouble cut short his career) and didn't recruit McIntosh, who ended up in the Big Ten at Northwestern.

McIntosh was a second team all-Big Ten selection as a junior for the Wildcats in the 2016-17 season.

"Is that the kind of kid that Indiana fans would have liked to have had in Bloomington, there's no question about it," Bozich said. "He's a kid that grew up following the program and wanted to come here. But Indiana didn't ever really recruit him and (as of 2017) he's probably now one of the better players in the Big Ten.

"But he is the perfect example of the kind of guy that Indiana needs in its program. You need guys that you can develop over three or four years."

McIntosh's situation was an interesting one. He went to New Castle (Ind.) High School as a freshman and later transferred to Greensburg (Ind.) High School where he helped lead his team to class 3A state championships in both his junior and senior season.

He initially committed to Indiana State but when his stock started to rise he started getting a lot of offers. Indiana was not

226

among them. He did get offers, however, from Purdue, Northwestern, Vanderbilt, Xavier and Dayton (coached by Archie Miller). Ultimately, he chose Northwestern and was a big reason why the Wildcats qualified for their first NCAA Tournament berth in 2017.

In Crean's defense, he had had some success over the years with players who were considered, like McIntosh, to be under the radar. Just look at Victor Oladipo and Will Sheehey for two quick names. You could say the same about OG Anunoby and Juwan Morgan, too.

But there were just as many under-the-radar players that he brought in who didn't pan out, too.

Still, Bozich came back to one simple question.

"How can you explain giving a scholarship to Grant Gelon and not making an offer to Bryant McIntosh?," Bozich said. "It just doesn't make any sense."

Leary said that in his opinion how Indiana recruits under Archie Miller will determine where the program goes from here.

"To me, if Indiana basketball wants to get back to where it was, Archie Miller needs to recruit an Archie Miller," Leary said. "He can't have a roster of 13 of them. He has to have some athletes. But they have to recruit some guys who are willing to buy into the system. AAU basketball is not going to win in college basketball."

Clark Kellogg, the college basketball analyst for CBS Sports, said ultimately though, just how successful Miller is able to be at Indiana will come down to his ability to recruit.

"It will come down to the ability to be able to recruit the folks that you need to have a chance to succeed at that level," Kellogg said. "You need to get quality kids and really good players, players who are eventually going to play in the NBA. You don't have to build your full roster with them but you have to get some of those who are in your neighborhood, whatever your sense of your neighborhood is.

"It could be the state of Indiana or a four-hour radius for the most part and occasionally maybe you step out of that to zero in on one of those big time players that have interest in Indiana."

Greg Rakestraw, the program director at 1070-AM radio The Fan in Indianapolis, said you simply cannot put enough emphasis on recruiting and getting the players that both fit your system and fit what Indiana fans believe their teams should look like.

"The answer these days in college basketball is all about players and all about recruiting," Rakestraw said. "So the simple answer is that when you're getting to the level where you're competing for Final Fours on a regular basis – not just making a Sweet Sixteen – but being a No. 1 or a No. 2 seed in the NCAA Tournament and then doing something with it all comes back to recruiting.

"The short answer here is very simple. Go get players. Everything else at Indiana is in place and now you just need to go get the right players."

The problem, though, becomes what happens when you spend a great deal of timing recruiting certain kids and they still for whatever reason ultimately decide to go somewhere else. That happened a lot to Tom Crean, particularly in the second half of his IU career.

Alex Bozich, the publisher of the popular fan site Inside the Hall, said Crean's problems were never about not trying. He tried to lock down the state and he tried to get some of the top national guys but for whatever reason he just lost momentum toward the end of his tenure.

"He recruited a lot of these kids since they were freshmen but some of them might have gotten fatigued from being recruited by Indiana for that long or for whatever reason just ultimately decided it wasn't a good fit," Bozich said. "Maybe some of them didn't have confidence that Crean was going to be there long term. Toward the end there was a lot of negative recruiting because he kept popping up on the hot-seat lists. Coaches would be spreading the message that Crean wasn't going to be there much longer.

"I don't think it was a lack of trying, I think it was a lack of converting."

Bozich said by the end, when he had so many misses in the class of 2017, he believes recruits and their parents were convinced that Crean was not long for Indiana. It didn't help that situation that after IU won the outright Big Ten title in 2016 and Crean only had two years left on his contract that IU athletic director Fred Glass opted to not extend his contract.

Talk about an opportunity for negative recruiting. Opposing coaches had to have had a field day.

"There were a variety of reasons why different guys didn't come but I just think by the end that a lot of people felt that the writing was on the wall that he was probably going to be done soon," Bozich said. "And people chose to go elsewhere."

Brian Snow, a national college basketball recruiting analyst for Scout.com who formerly worked at Rivals.com, said it's fairly common for coaches at some programs to get caught up in his words, star-gazing so to speak.

The biggest problem is with the one and done's and how much production you're really going to get out of them. He said he frequently has discussions with college coaches, not necessarily specific to Indiana but in general, asking about a top 10 player.

"And I'll say, 'Listen coach, I don't think he's going to be a very good college player because he's only going to be with you for one year,'" Snow said "He's going to average 8 points and 8.5 rebounds and then he's going to go to the NBA and when he's 22, I think he's going to be a monster. When he's 19 I don't think he is going to be very good and you're only going to have him when he's 19."

Snow said it's easy for coaches take the bait and want the elite player when the better option is to go the safer route. It's

Tom Crean at practice in the open fan event at the NCAA Tournament

like the difference between laying up on a golf shot or going for the 200-yard fairway shot that has to clear the water all the way. A lot of times it makes a lot more sense to knock it to with 100 yards and give yourself a better chance to ultimately score on the hole.

"So sometimes coaches get caught up in that instead of recruiting the kid that isn't quite as talented, and may not even be as good as a freshman but all of sudden you get him as a sophomore, junior and senior and by the time he's a senior he's an all-conference player," Snow said. "And now he has a lot invested in the program. Those kids can be really dangerous in college basketball."

Snow said he wasn't really certain that the whole star-gazing situation was really a problem for Tom Crean.

"With Tom I just don't think he had a real good plan for how he wanted his roster to be constructed," Snow said. "It was like all of a sudden we know we can get a kid from this camp so let's go get him. And then it was, let's go get this kid and let's go get that kid. And there wasn't this specific far-reaching plan that this is going to work well with this and this is going to fit well with that. And that would create a cohesive roster he could have built from year to year."

Snow said the ones that always got him were the late additions in the fall. He said he preferred not to throw any IU kids under the bus but it was a head scratcher at times.

"You'd see a late addition in the fall and you'd think 'Where did this kid come from?' and why did they even take him?," Snow said. "I think that was Tom's biggest problem. It wasn't necessarily swinging for the fences but rather the planning stages of building a cohesive roster."

Leary believed that one of the reasons Bob Knight was so successful at Indiana was because of the type of players he would recruit, too.

"Indiana's rosters were not made up of all McDonald's All-Americans," Leary said. "They weren't like Duke and they weren't like North Carolina and Kentucky. I think people kind of endeared themselves to that."

Leary qualified this point by saying that he never saw Knight play in college at Ohio State but his own belief is that the Indiana coaching legend was an average college player, who was very much a role player. And the statistics are clear on that point, too. Jerry Lucas averaged 26 points and 16 rebounds, Larry Siegfried averaged 13.2 points and John Havlicek added 12 points per game on the Buckeyes' team that won the 1960 national championship.

Bob Knight averaged 3.7 points and 2.1 rebounds.

"I've seen the stats and I know he wasn't Havlicek and I know he wasn't like the star of the team but I also feel like he thought he was a pretty big part of that team in different ways," Leary said. "Whether that was stuff he did mentally or in preparation or stuff he did when he came in the game or whatever that was.

231

"And this is totally my opinion, and he might laugh it off and say it's the dumbest thing he has ever heard but I always felt like he tried to have some guys on his team who were like him. So he was not necessarily the most highly recruited."

Leary said he was definitely in that same mode of player when he was recruited to Indiana in the vaunted class of 1989 that also included Calbert Cheaney, Pat Graham, Greg Graham, Chris Reynolds, Chris Lawson and Lawrence Funderburke.

"I was definitely not a program changing recruit but I think he felt like he could win games with guys like me," Leary said. "And that's because I definitely bought in to what he said and what he was teaching and I understood it."

Ken Bikoff, the longtime Indiana University beat writer for Inside Indiana and peegs.com, agreed with that point. He said he thought Knight was successful because he was so good at recruiting to his system.

"The recruits that he got were not necessarily the cream of the crop," Bikoff said. "He got guys that fit what he wanted to do. I think there were times later in his career when he started to wander a little bit from that formula where he would bring in a guy who was talented but maybe not the best fit for him and I think that's when you saw that he didn't have the same level of success as he had previously."

Bob Lovell, who was the head basketball coach at IUPUI from 1982-93 said there has to be a plan for how you put your roster together. It's not as easy as just going out and filling up your scholarships with 13 really high level players.

"A lot of people don't understand that you have 13 scholarships and that you're not going to play 13 guys a game," Lovell said. "We know that. But part of the magic of being able to recruit and recruit well is who are taking the spots of 10, 11, 12 and 13? I mean who are those kids?"

Lovell said that some think in a perfect world that you would want all five-star kids but that's not going to be successful either. The ones that aren't getting in the game will join the long list of kids who transfer out of Division I basketball programs at the end of every season.

According to verbalcommits.com, the number of players who have transferred from Division I programs from 2013-17 was a staggering number. In 2013 it was 672 … and that was the low mark of the five seasons tabulated. The number was 753 in 2014, 834 in 2015, 805 in 2016 and 792 as of August of 2017.

So in other words if five-star Johnny was riding the pine someplace chances are he would be out the door very quickly.

"You have to find guys that have a skill that will match what you're trying to find," Lovell said. "But more importantly, those guys are really great teammates and can contribute in more ways that you can necessarily see on a stat sheet. It's a hard sell to go to a kid and say I want you to come here but I'm not sure if you're going to start or even play but I still want you to come.

"But that's the hard thing about trying to put together a roster."

Lovell pointed to Collin Hartman as the kind of player that Indiana basketball needs. But Lovell is also the first to admit that he thought Indiana had made a mistake when they recruited him. He said that's why recruiting is an inexact science.

"You need two or three difference makers on your team," Lovell said. "Because when defenses break down or offenses break down you need guys that can go and make plays. It's all about making plays. I'm not sure x's and o's are that big of a deal when you get to that level. It's all about guys making plays."

Most people admit that you also need to develop players in your program to be successful. If you can have some three or four year players it can help bridge some gaps from year to year. If you find that you never have any seniors on your roster then there's a good chance the kids you're recruiting are either

233

going to the NBA or transferring before they get the chance to develop more and shine in your system.

Jon Crispin, a college basketball analyst at the Big Ten Network and a former player at Penn State and UCLA, isn't sure Indiana fans have been real patient with allowing the coaching staff to truly develop its players.

Crispin's point was that programs have to make a choice as to what their ultimate recruiting philosophies are in that regard.

"If you're the type of team that grows and develops players and wants to compete at a high level but is not all about one and done's, you're not going to attract the top talent," Crispin said. "And that means that you're really going to have to live through the development of players and that doesn't seem to be something that Indiana fans have really been patient with.

"They've really been impatient with the development of players and I think that's a tough one for a coach because then coaches now look at it and say, 'Maybe I have to do it the way that John Calipari does it'. Where he just tries to bring in the best of the best and that's what kids look at today."

Crispin posed the question of why is it that so many top 50 players in the country want to play at Kentucky?

"It's because John Calipari has created a system where everyone in the media is looking at Kentucky," Crispin said. "Whether it be for good reasons or bad reasons, they're all looking at Kentucky. And those kids coming out of high school these days it's all about what kind of attention can I get? What type of opportunity can I get to go to the next level? It's not about can I serve my local institution well? Can I serve my state well? It's not about that anymore."

Crispin said it's a choice that programs have to make.

"I think Indiana has to take a long, hard look and decide if you want to put out very good college basketball players and kids who graduate or one and doner's who may give you a chance every few years?," Crispin said. "I think Tom Crean did something that he didn't get enough credit for. He really developed players. He took the time and the heat for doing it. He was patient with players."

Leary said he thinks a big problem that Indiana has had in the recruiting realm has been being focused too heavily on the elite players. There's nothing wrong with getting a few but when you start having a lot of years where you're losing players after one or two seasons, it's just that much more difficult to reload instead of constantly rebuilding.

And Leary believes it's just the polar opposite of what Bob Knight used to think in terms of recruiting. And while he admits he knows that recruiting has changed dramatically, he's not always sure that the IU philosophy on who it recruits is the correct one.

"I think the problem is that Indiana considers themselves a top 10 program and I think they try to recruit out of that top 50 in the country and I don't think coach Knight ever cared about what that top 50 country looked like," Leary said. "Yeah, you have to have the Calbert Cheaney's of the world. You're not going to win with five me's (Leary's) on the floor. But I think you need to have a mixture of it and that mixture is getting smaller and smaller and smaller."

Leary said he knows recruiting today is different with all the different shoe company (Nike, Adidas and Under Armour) events and the different ways that coaches can see kids play. But he just wishes IU would tweak its philosophy a little bit in recruiting. He said perhaps Archie Miller is the guy to make that tweak.

"It's just that recruiting today is just going more toward athletes and how fast and big and strong you are," Leary said. "There's nothing wrong with that but again I go back to coach Knight and I don't think that was the No. 1 think that was the deciding factor whether coach Knight recruited a kid or not."

IU basketball historian Bill Murphy said he thought Crean's problem was in the players he often recruited.

235

"I didn't think coach Crean managed recruiting well and he did not manage setting up a team well," Murphy said. "I'll give him the benefit of the doubt that people come and go. It's not like you can hang on to kids for three or four years any more. But Crean went trying to get national athletes but sometimes they weren't very good basketball players.

"He brought in some kids who were phenomenal athletes but they couldn't shoot or they didn't play basketball well. I think Butler has shown that you don't have to have the most talented athletes but go get some good basketball players."

• • • • •

We've spent a lot of time in this recruiting philosophies chapter talking Tom Crean specific. But that makes sense in a lot of ways. He was the most recent Indiana coach and he spent nine years on the IU sideline. A lot of people are going to want to debate the things he was able to do well or not so well because it's still fresh in their minds.

And frankly, as a lot of people have pointed out either in this chapter or in the chapter on recruiting the state of Indiana, if Crean had been able to land even 25 percent of some of the misses he had in the second half of his IU coaching career, he would very well still be the Indiana coach today.

But again, it just pounds home the point of how important recruiting is the grand scheme of things – both in who you recruit and your ability to land the recruits you go after.

The other IU coach in the post-Knight era that there always seems to be a lot of recruiting dialogue about was Mike Davis. And if you think Tom Crean was guilty of targeting too many elite level players, you should take a look at Davis's list sometime. Davis aimed high a lot of the time and had a great share of misses, too.

Indianapolis sports talk radio host Derek Schultz, half of the popular Query & Schultz Show, had a unique perspective when it came to Davis. Davis was the head coach at IU from

2000-06. Schultz was a student at IU from 2001-05 and remained in Bloomington through 2006.

Schultz believed that Davis's biggest problems at IU came because he was trying to recruit the highest level talent to come to Indiana and simply was unable to close the deal.

"I think after they went to the title game he felt like, 'OK, I've got Bracey Wright and Marshall Strickland coming in and I'm swinging for the fences and batting a thousand here and I'm going to keep swinging for the fences'," Schultz said. "And he goes after like Dwight Howard and Charlie Villanueva and Luol Deng and that's all well and good. I'm not saying don't pursue those guys but you can't just keep swinging for home runs and just hope that you're going to connect.

"The connections stopped happening and then you end with recruiting classes that have Jessan Gray-Ashley and Patrick Ewing Jr. and Cem Dinc and people like that. That roster talent wise really dried up and by about 2003-04 you're looking at that roster and thinking this just isn't what you expect from a talent standpoint from a school like Indiana."

Ken Bikoff, the longtime sportswriter covering IU, said that a big part of Davis's early success was that he had it with players that were in the system to play for Knight. He's not of the opinion that Davis made it to the title game with Knight's personnel because Bikoff believes that the personnel Davis inherited simply played better in his system than it did in his predecessor's.

But he's also quick to point out that where Davis began to struggle was when he became the lead man in terms of recruiting the types of players that ultimately would wear the cream and crimson.

"I think Davis fell into the same trap as both Kelvin Sampson would and Tom Crean eventually in that they went for talent over guys that may have fit their system," Bikoff said.

237

Todd Leary, the former IU guard who was the radio color commentator beside Don Fischer during the Davis years, said that the kind of player Davis recruited was clearly part of the problem.

"I think Mike Davis felt like Bracey Wright could come in and be his savior," Leary said. "He thought that Bracey Wright would be the new Indiana style of player. And I think we all know that he was way off base with that one."

Leary said he remembers having a lot of interesting conversations during that time with Davis when the former coach would talk about players he was recruiting and comparing them to Indiana greats of the past.

"I remember him saying that Bracey Wright was a better shooter than Steve Alford and how his range was ridiculous," Leary said. "I remember him saying how excited he was to have Bracey Wright. He's also the one who said that Deron Williams couldn't play in the Big Ten. I'm not ripping Mike Davis but I'm saying with that mentality of recruiting that's what happens. I think that happens when you only recruit the top 50 players in the country.

"It was like anyone else they would take them to fill a roster spot if they had to but they weren't that excited about them."

Perhaps the biggest recruit that Davis was unable to close the deal on was Sean May. And that may have been the strangest scenario of all. May was expected to be part of the recruiting class that included Bracey Wright and Marshall Strickland. In fact, if you talk to those guys both of them will tell you that it was May that had called them and tried to get them to go to IU so that the three could all play together at the next level. But in the end May got cold feet. His dad, former IU All-American Scott May who starred on the 1976 unbeaten national championship team, wanted his son to talk with Bob Knight before ultimately making his college decision. May flew to Lubbock, Texas and spoke with Knight and shortly after made the announcement that he would attend North Carolina.

Mike Davis in the NCAA Tournament

It was a tremendous blow to Indiana recruiting and the Hoosiers were left to regroup without him. May went on to lead North Carolina to the NCAA title in 2005, played three years in college, and later was a first round pick of Charlotte in the 2005 NBA Draft.

But it was still a marquee recruiting miss for Indiana and Davis, and Schultz maintains that there were just too many of those high level recruits that Davis missed on and in some ways simply spent too much time in the recruiting process on rather than building a program with enough high level individuals.

Schultz pointed to the recruitment of Josh Smith as the perfect example. Smith played AAU ball with an Atlanta Celtics team that featured future NBA players Randolph Morris and Dwight Howard. He played at Oak Hill Academy his senior season and was teammates with Rajon Rondo. Rivals.com had him ranked as the third best player in the nation and the No. 1 small forward. Davis believed he could convince Smith to play at IU and put a lot of time into that recruitment.

And in Davis's defense, Smith did ultimately commit to play for the Hoosiers. The problem was that no one really believed that Smith would ever play college basketball. Instead, most thought he would go straight to the NBA. As it turned out, he was drafted in the first round of the 2004 NBA Draft by the Atlanta Hawks, the 17th pick overall. He played nine seasons in Atlanta and later played for Detroit, Houston and the Los Angeles Clippers.

The point, though, that Schultz made was that while it was great to get a commit from a player like that, the reality is that Indiana got very little out of that commitment when Smith chose to go straight to the NBA.

"I think most people knew that Josh Smith wasn't going to play college basketball and yet Davis chose to dedicate so much time to his recruitment," Schultz said. "And that was kind of a theme in his recruiting. He would swing for the fences and when he missed it just ultimately cost Indiana a great deal."

11

What Does Archie Miller Have to do Differently?

The fourth permanent head coach to follow Bob Knight at Indiana was introduced as the 29th head coach in Indiana history on March 27, 2017.

Archie Miller, considered one of the best up and coming coaches in the country, had spent the previous six seasons at the University of Dayton where he had a high level of success. He earned a school-record four consecutive NCAA Tournament bids and won 24 games in each of those seasons. He also claimed the last two Atlantic 10 regular season titles.

Will that be enough so that someday Miller will be remembered as the coach that finally got Indiana basketball back to a sustained level of winning? That's hard to say. As of the writing of this book, Miller had an 0-0 record as Indiana's basketball coach.

But so many people interviewed for this book seemed to think that if anyone had a chance to turn Indiana basketball back to its glory days, it could be someone just like Archie Miller.

Indiana athletic director Fred Glass said when the news first broke on March 25 that Miller had been hired that the 38-year-old coach was someone he had identified very quickly in the process.

"Archie Miller was on my short list from the very beginning," Glass said in a statement. "The more I learned about him, the more convinced I became that he is the coach we need to meet our high expectations for many years to come."

Chronic Hoosier, the IU superfan who I've permitted not to use his real name for this book, said he wondered when Miller was hired if Indiana was doing the right thing in going after the up and coming coach. But the more he thought about it the more the idea seemed like a good one.

"Coach Miller obviously has a lot of impressive points on his resume but maybe not the absolute proven ability to succeed," Chronic Hoosier said. "He has never won a major conference championship. He hasn't won a national championship or made it to a Final Four. But you think back and Bob Knight had never even made the NCAA Tournament when IU hired him. They just went out and hired what they thought was going to be a solid, young coach. And that decision panned out for them.

"But it seemed for a while that Indiana was incapable of making that hire. We've gotten so full of ourselves that we had to have a name with proven results. And I think in the search for that, that process maybe led them away from the kind of coach that could not only achieve but sustain that level of success here. And now with the hire of coach Miller, I find myself wondering if maybe they didn't just reverse that and fix it all somehow."

Indiana athletic director Fred Glass said in an interview for this book that there were several things about Miller that he thought gave him a chance to be the coach who could get Indiana basketball back to that sustained level of success.

"He's a proven winner," Glass said. "Even at a comparatively young age of 38 he has won and that's really important. He has demonstrated that he can recruit and he has demonstrated that he can develop players skill wise."

Glass called Miller's pedigree "incredible."

"When you look at the various coaches in the top level conferences for whom he has worked at a young age, he has a lot of very strong experience," Glass said. "But I do like his comparative youth. I don't think there's any question that he could come here and be a 20-year guy. And he'll be our guy.

"He knows what the job is about. He embraces the expectations. He's not looking to lower expectations. He's all in. He's a tough guy that knows how to win, is very, very competitive and he communicates extraordinarily well with his players."

Glass said that was something that really hit home with him.

"He says that he's going to talk to his players and treat his players the way I would want to be treated," Glass said. "I think that's very powerful. I think the kids really react to that in a strong way."

• • • • •

In his introductory press conference, Miller spent a lot of time talking about what he needed to do with his current players. He was well aware of what had to be done in recruiting and making in-roads in the state with future classes but at the same time he felt like one of the most important things he needed to do was get his own players to the point where they were comfortable with him as their new coach, too.

"It's going to take time," Miller said in his introductory press conference. "There's only one of me right now, but as these guys know, I've already had a lot of conversations on the way. We're going to start having a lot of conversations as we keep moving forward. I have to invest in their families. I have to invest in the important people in their lives, and like I told them, I didn't recruit you, but you're mine, so at that point, if you're mine, then I have to do everything in my power to make sure that you understand there's great belief and value in you here.

"There's a clean slate. It's going to take time. I think every coach goes through that when they show up at a place. It's an awkward moment not only for them but for me, as well, but I think we're off to a good start."

Glass said that Miller is also strong in many off the court areas, too.

"He's committed to academics, he's never had a compliance issue and he's all about playing but the rules," Glass said. "He's got all the baseline stuff. But I think he's got that something extra where he can connect with these kids in a way, maybe not unlike Knight, in that it makes them believe that he knows what he is doing and they feel even more comfortable when it comes to doing what he tells them to do."

Jake Query, the Indianapolis sports radio talk show host, said the key for Archie Miller to be successful at Indiana comes down to one word.

Unlike what a lot of people have said that word is not "recruit." Query's word is simply "win."

"Who's the most popular player that Indiana has had in the last 10 years? Victor Oladipo? Where's he from?" Query said. "He's not from Indiana. Who hit the greatest, most celebrated shot that people act like it should be a state holiday and that was IU-Kentucky and Christian Watford. And where is he from? He's not from Indiana.

"What Archie Miller is going to have to do is this. He has to win and win deep. And by that I mean he has to go to a Final Four. And then recycle it again with another group of players to show that it was not a one recruiting class anomaly."

But again Query said it all comes down to winning.

"Mike Davis took his team to the national championship game and people were terrified that he was going to leave Indiana," Query said. "The same people five years later were willing to drive down with a Mayflower van to help him move out of town. But they were terrified in 2002 that he was going to leave because he had won.

"And all people want at Indiana is to win. It's really that simple."

The next to follow – Archie Miller

Gene Keady agreed that the bottom line was that if you were at Indiana or Purdue you simply had to win.

"And it's a tough job," Keady said. "It's 24/7 and you have to understand that when you take the job. Now that's the way I had always worked so that was pretty natural for me but you have to know what you're getting yourself into.

"And after everything else is all said and done, you have to find a way to win basketball games. If you can do that, everything else will take care of itself."

Ken Bikoff, the longtime Indiana writer from Inside Indiana magazine, said he thinks it's pretty simple what Archie Miller needs to do to be more successful than Mike Davis, Kelvin Sampson and Tom Crean in terms of a sustained level of winning.

He said he thinks Miller needs to be able to learn the lessons of the past.

"He's coming over from Dayton and he knows how to build a program but now the key is to connect with the high school coaches, make sure that you take advantage of the talent in the state of Indiana and never lose sight of building the roster and bringing in the kind of players that fit your culture," Bikoff said.

"That's the key to everything. And that's the ultimate key to sustainability. You need to bring in guys that fit what you're trying to do and fit your culture. And they're not going to do anything that will create problems."

Bikoff said there are plenty of programs around that fit the bill when it comes to creating a culture of success.

"It's just something that you have to do," Bikoff said. "When you look at Duke, they can pick up just about any player that they want. You look at Kentucky and it's a different culture and they have more talent than they know what to do with. But even Kentucky has guys that have to be there to show people what the Kentucky Way is.

"It's the same at Louisville. It's the same at Duke. Indiana hasn't had that because of so much roster turnover over the years that if Archie Miller wants to be successful and have sustainable success he needs to have guys who are interested in the program and he has to recruit accordingly to have guys that are going to be around for a while."

Clark Kellogg, the national college basketball analyst for CBS, said in some ways Dayton and Indiana are two completely different animals. But in other ways, he was quick to point out, there are some similarities, too, that Miller should be able to draw upon.

In its most basic form, however, the step up from Dayton to IU is significant.

"It's challenging because the dynamics are different," Kellogg said. "The stakes are a little higher. The resources are greater. The expectations are greater. The scrutiny is greater.

Everything ramps whatever number you want to put on it two or three times."

At the same time though Kellogg was quick to point out that while Dayton may not be a power five conference school it's still a program that wears big boy pants, too.

"Archie has had success at a basketball program," Kellogg said. "I know it's not the Big Ten or one of the power five conferences but Dayton, in terms of understanding, commitment to basketball, expectations for success and the academic mission, it's high up there when you look at college basketball programs.

"Again, I know it's not the Big Ten but there are some elements from his experience there that are going to serve him well in terms of the rabid following and the passion for basketball."

•••••

Kellogg said there are a few things that will be important for Miller right away at Indiana. He said the coaching staff that Miller hired will be really important and he also mentioned the importance of being aligned with the athletic administration at Indiana and others at the university level to make sure that everyone is moving in the same direction.

"Staff is important," Kellogg said. "Obviously having relationships with those stake holders at the university and around the state that can be aligned with what you're trying to build and your culture. All of those things are important. But make no mistake about it, the entire process is extremely challenging."

Mike Marot, of the Associated Press in Indianapolis, said the more distance there has been between coaches and the departure of Bob Knight, the more different the feel.

"I don't see Archie Miller having to follow Knight like (Mike) Davis did," Marot said. "I don't see him feeling like, 'Hey, I've got to get this team to the Final Four to be successful,' like Kelvin (Sampson) did. I think he wants to get there but I don't think he feels that kind of pressure right now.

"And I think for the first time in a while they've got a guy in here that looks like he's comfortable in his own skin in this job and he's going to just be himself."

Indianapolis Star columnist Gregg Doyel was asked what he thought it would take to get Indiana basketball back to a sustained level of winning again. He didn't hesitate with his response. He said, in his opinion, Indiana had already accomplished what it needed to do.

"I think IU simply had to hire somebody like Archie Miller," Doyel said. "The hard part has been done by making the right hire. Because as IU as proven for the past 20 years, the hard part is picking the right guy. They hadn't done it to this point and now they have."

Doyel said the Miller hire for Indiana was a slam dunk. He said he feels 100 percent certain that Miller will be the guy that turns Indiana basketball around.

"What he has to do is just be who he is," Doyel said. "This book is going to come out and I could be dead wrong about this in four years but I mean this. I've been paying attention to college hoops for twenty something years and I've never been more sure of a guy being the right fit at the right school than I am with Archie Miller at IU. I've never seen a hire that I thought was a home run like that one. Never. He's just that good."

Doyel said Miller has a lot going for him.

"He's that prepared," Doyel said. "He's the son of a coach. The younger brother of a coach. He was raised to be a coach. He works so hard. He's got it all figured out. He's no nonsense. He's just the real deal. He's the whole package. I don't see anything wrong with him. Not one thing wrong with him."

Mike DeCourcy of *The Sporting News* and an in-studio analyst on the Big Ten Network said one thing that will be working in Miller's favor from Day 1, which is vastly different than what Tom Crean walked into at Indiana, is that he's stepping a good situation.

In his first season with Indiana basketball in 2017-18, Miller has some good pieces to build around. Guys like Robert Johnson, Josh Newkirk, De'Ron Davis, Juwan Morgan and Collin Hartman. He has a couple of young guards in Devonte Green and Curtis Jones. So at the most basic point, he at least has some advantages that the previous coaching staff did not when they arrived at Indiana to find Kyle Taber and Brett Finkelmeier as IU's only two returning players – and Taber was the lone scholarship player.

"Indiana didn't have a great year in Tom Crean's final season but Archie Miller certainly didn't step into a situation that was broken," DeCourcy said. "Sure, they lost a lot of talent in guys like Thomas Bryant, OG Anunoby and James Blackmon Jr. who made themselves eligible for the NBA Draft but they have some decent guys and some promising guys.

"I think that gives Archie Miller a much better chance to be successful from the beginning than Tom Crean had at Indiana."

ESPN college basketball analyst Jeff Goodman believes that Archie Miller will be successful at Indiana because he is strong in areas where previous coaches who have followed Knight were not.

"Each guy that you mention out of those three had their strengths but they had their weaknesses, too," Goodman said. "Archie Miller to me has very few weaknesses. I don't even know what they are. I think Archie Miller is one of the elite coaches in the country because he's adaptable and he's versatile. And a lot of coaches these days are not."

Goodman said that Miller will be able to connect with everyone from players, to university staff to the fan base. He said in his opinion that was an area where Tom Crean wasn't as successful.

"To me, Crean lacked the ability to connect with all sorts of people," Goodman said. "Socially, I just don't think he connected with everybody. I think that hurt Crean. But he had the work ethic. I think Archie Miller has the same work ethic as Tom Crean."

Goodman said he also believes that Miller is right there with his coaching ability, too.

"I think he's as good of a coach as Kelvin Sampson or Crean," Goodman said. "And I think he has the resume that Mike Davis didn't have. I think Archie has everything. He's the most well rounded out of all of them."

Goodman rattled off a laundry list of things that Miller has going for him.

"He's likeable, he can coach, he can connect with players, he can connect with people overall," Goodman said. "He'll really get after it and recruit and develop players. I think Crean did a great job of that, too. I thought he did a really good job of developing players and evaluating players. Look at some of the guys he got like (Victor) Oladipo and OG (Anunoby), guys that a lot of people really didn't want. I think Archie has some of that, too."

Indianapolis Star columnist Gregg Doyel said he thinks Miller's no nonsense approach is just what Indiana basketball needs. It certainly didn't get that under Tom Crean as Doyel points out. But it's just a difference in philosophies. Crean had a specific way of doing things and Miller likely won't do things the same way.

Doyel said that the no nonsense approach to coaching is rare in today's game.

"A lot of coaches think they need that," Doyel said. "I know that Tom Crean, and not out of weakness of character, but he really believed that these players needed kind of another father figure because college is tough. It's hard. I've got two college kids. It's not easy. So he tried to be the second dad and he really loved them. He wanted to get the best from them and he was going to get it by loving them."

Doyel said he's certain that Miller will "support his players nonstop" but he'll do it in a different way.

"It's hard to pull off gruff, no nonsense and still maintain loyalty," Doyel said. "Bob Knight pulled that off. And Miller is not Knight but he's got some of the same characteristics. He's going to pull it off. He does pull it off."

Indianapolis sports talk radio show host Kent Sterling said he thinks Miller will be able to pull off the no nonsense approach, too.

"I don't think Archie Miller is the kind of guy who walks into the room and tries to put people in an environment where they like him," Sterling said. "I think Archie Miller is just going to be Archie Miller and be the best coach he can be and to hell with the rest of the other stuff. And I think IU fans vibe with that really well.

"He is in no way shape or form a politician. He's just who he is and I think that kind of separates him from Tom (Crean). He's not a cheat and that separates him from Kelvin (Sampson) and he's ready for the job and that separates him from Mike (Davis)."

Dave Revsine of the Big Ten Network likes Miller's approach. He likes his demeanor and he's looking forward to seeing how it plays in Bloomington.

"I've worked with Archie a little bit and I did one of his games (in 2017) at Dayton and where he's similar to Crean is that he's really intense," Revsine said. "Say what you will about Crean but I watched a couple of his practices and they work hard. There's no doubt that it's all out effort and there's passion that comes from the coach and you're going to see that with Archie as well. He's a really passionate guy.

"Obviously the difference is that defensively they're really going to lock in."

Jake Query, the Indianapolis afternoon sports radio talk show host, liked the fact that Archie Miller had had a lot of other opportunities to go other places but always had said he wasn't interested. But when Indiana came calling it proved that IU is still a destination job.

"The perception that Indiana is a destination job comes true for him because coming from a mid-major, he was in a program that when he came to Indiana it felt like he had held off on other things and other opportunities and then finally he couldn't turn down Indiana," Query said. "Whereas with Tom Crean, whether it's fair or not, you kind of got the impression that he came to Indiana because he himself knew that he couldn't believe that he got the opportunity. And he couldn't pass it up.

"Whereas with Archie Miller he had bypassed other opportunities and you felt like he knew that chance was going to come and therefore he was holding out for it. As opposed to taking it because 'Oh my God, I have to take this now because I realize I'm not qualified for it.' But it just has that feeling."

Sterling said he really feels like Fred Glass got the right man when he hired Archie Miller.

"The key thing above everything else here is that Fred hired somebody who knows what he's doing," Sterling said. "I don't think Archie is going to have the same issues that Tom (Crean) had as far as outcoaching the fan base. I think his defense is what is going to set him apart and I think Indiana fans are going to vibe with it."

Sterling called it a "simplification of ideology" when it comes to Miller and his approach to the game.

"He's a guy whose dad is kind of a Knight disciple, who worshipped Knight and ultimately taught his kids the same type of basketball principles as Knight taught his teams at Indiana," Sterling said. "And I just think that kind of approach is going to go over really well with Indiana basketball fans.

"I think Archie will quickly show that he's a really good fit for Indiana."

Another important piece anytime a new coach is hired at Indiana is making sure that former players still feel like they are connected to the program.

One thing that you have with former Indiana players is an investment. Long after their playing careers are over, Indiana players – especially but not limited to those from the state – remain involved in a variety of ways.

Former players like to feel like their four years at Indiana were worth something. All of that blood, sweat and tears that they poured out playing for a coach like Bob Knight makes them feel entitled in some ways when it comes to staying connected with the program in the future. And it's not a negative entitlement but one where former IU players have formed a fraternity of sorts.

It's not just with the players that they may have played with at IU but with players that came before and after them, too. For many seasons, IU has had reunion weekends for former players to get together, play some golf, share some stories and remain connected.

And so with Archie Miller coming on board, having the approval of that fraternity of players is important, too.

Some Indiana coaches have embraced it. Mike Davis for the most part was happy to have former players be a part of his program. With one of them in particular – Scott May – he had hoped that he would not only be a part of the program but have his son – Sean May – play at Indiana, too. Unfortunately for Davis and ultimately Indiana, Sean May chose to play at North Carolina. But again, Davis was one of those Indiana coaches post Bob Knight that seemed happy to have former players involved.

Kelvin Sampson – not so much. Sampson gave a vibe to many former players that he saw them as more of a nuisance than a benefit. That said, Sampson did have a former player in Dan Dakich as a member of his staff for one season and Dakich later became the interim coach for seven games after Sampson tendered his resignation. But the general feeling amongst former players when it came to Sampson was not one that was particularly welcoming.

Tom Crean was good at involving former players and embraced that aspect of the Indiana past. During Crean's nine seasons at Indiana it wasn't that players didn't feel welcome but toward the end many started saying that they didn't enjoy watching the product on the floor because of the lack of defense and the propensity toward turnovers. That's one thing about former Indiana players is that you find that most are students of the game.

In Archie Miller's introductory press conference he made sure to talk about his thoughts on involving former IU players in his program.

He said in his opening remarks that Indiana would embrace the past, present and the future.

"The first level is obviously our past," Miller said. "Every player, every former coach, every former manager that laid the groundwork for this place to be what it is today, we owe them a lot, and our effort level and our give-back has to be really unmatched, and they have to feel that they're a part of everything that we do, and our players have to feel that power. That's something we are going to really fight hard for."

• • • • •

Brian Evans, a former IU All-American who played for the Hoosiers from 1993-96, is typical in many ways when it comes to his feelings about the Indiana program. Basically, he just wants a coach who is going to do things the right way and find a way to get IU basketball back to that sustained level of winning.

"I just want this program to have sustained success," Evans said. "I'm not looking for a free ticket. I'm not looking for rose pedals when I come to town, I just want this program to succeed. Yes, I was a former player but I'm a fan. I was a fan as a little kid. I'm a fan of the program."

Evans said he likes a lot of the things he has seen and heard about Miller in the first few months on the job. He likes that Miller wants to have a family atmosphere. He likes that Miller stresses fundamentals, playing solid defense and valuing the basketball. In fact there's even a few things that Miller DOESN'T DO that Evans is happy that's the case.

"There was one thing I found out in the first month or whatever and I absolutely love this," Evans said. "And I love it because coach Miller doesn't do this. It's all the updating and the social media crap that I have no interest in. To me that has no part of the job. Go out and do your job because that's not part of it. I haven't seen him do any of that and I love it.

"And this is going to sound like a huge crack on coach Crean and maybe it is but it wasn't my favorite part of him being our coach. And I really hope that coach Miller is able to stay away from that in the future, too. Coaches have enough things to worry about without all of that hoopla."

Evans said he has an appreciation for what college basketball coaches do even though he has never coached at that level himself.

"Myself, I've never worked in that profession but I know these guys work really hard," Evans said. "They don't sleep and they just bust it all the time. I know they have three different cellphones on their arm at all times and they're expected to know the names of 2,500 kids in the back of their heads all the time. And they have a staff that is working their asses off, too. I think it's a really hard job.

"But here is my sense with Archie Miller. I really believe coach Miller knows the job. He has been a head coach. When coach Davis followed coach Knight he had never been a head coach and that made it that much more difficult. Coach Miller has been a head coach. And I believe this guy really knows what it's going to take to win here."

Pat Graham said from all of the early signs he personally is sold on Miller.

255

"I think we got a good one," Graham said. "I really do."

A.J. Guyton was a senior guard on Bob Knight's final team at Indiana in the 1999-2000 season. He said he likes what he sees with the hiring of Archie Miller.

"Once I read what he was about as a coach, I knew it was similar to the way I view basketball and the way I think it should be played," Guyton said. "I've always been a fan of his Dayton teams and how hard they play. I believe in their style of play. The enthusiasm they play with and their intensity defensively are what stands out.

"I just think he is the kind of coach that can take Indiana not only to Sweet Sixteens but farther than that."

Guyton said on the day that Miller was hired the first thing he thought of was how if Miller could do good things at a place like Dayton, just what could he do with the resources he'll have in place at Indiana.

Guyton also liked the fact that Miller is not just a coach but was once a player.

"He played the game at North Carolina State and had a good four year career and was a contributor," Guyton said. "He is a guy who knows exactly what the collegiate athlete goes through, what motivates them and what doesn't motivate them and I just think that was an added bonus to his hire.

"I just think that was something that Indiana basketball needed. They needed someone who had an understanding of everything as a whole."

When Todd Meier, one of three seniors on Indiana's 1987 national championship team, met Miller for the first time about a month after he was hired, he said IU's young coach in some ways reminded him of Bob Knight.

"To me he reminds me of kind of a modern day coach Knight style guy," Meier said. "He's no nonsense, we're going to beat your ass on defense and we're going to run an efficient offense. And I think the ability to sustain success is getting players that buy into the idea that 'I love playing defense and

Archie Miller

I'm going to shut your ass down.' We're going to run a good open offense and players today like scoring.

"It just sounds like he has a great mix it's just a matter of getting the right players. Maybe the players he has (his first year) will buy in and there will be a quick transition."

Lance Stemler, whose two seasons at Indiana were under Kelvin Sampson in 2007 and 2008, is eager to see what Archie Miller does in terms of style of play. He thinks that will be the area where Miller has th most success at Indiana.

"I think he'll build a defensive buy-in from the team," Stemler said. "I think that was one of the biggest things that coach Sampson did when he took over was he had to get Rod Wilmont and Earl Calloway and those guys coming from coach Davis's style to buy into his way of playing. And obviously recruit guys to his style of play, too. I think if coach Miller does that you'll see more of a style that Indiana fans appreciate."

Stemler said it will always come back to how good you are on the defensive end.

"A lot of people like to see a team score a hundred points a game but the problem is if you don't score 100 points how are you going to win?" Stemler said. "That's kind of where coach Crean's teams fell off. There were no grind out games as far as winning a game and only scoring 60 points."

Kirk Haston said the key to recruiting in this day and age is to be visible and to make sure the recruit knows that you're there to watch him.

"I think it's more than a phone call," Haston said. "I think you just have to be seen and obviously follow the rules in that regard but you have to physically go to these places and get in these towns and go to these camps. Now maybe more than ever it's a salesman job and it's pretty political and you've just got to be a people person. And maybe all of the former IU coaches have done that but all I know in talking with assistants and talking with people heavily involved with recruiting is that a big part of it is being there in person, making eye contact with these coaches and these players and working tirelessly to get things done."

As has been discussed in this chapter, the expectations are going to be high on Archie Miller at Indiana. But he has made it clear it's the neighborhood that he wants to reside in and he knows what he is getting himself into.

Stemler said the expectations from the fan base are fair based on the kind of program that Indiana tries to field year in and year out.

"Does it put pressure on coaches and players? Sure," Stemler said. "But that's kind of what you sign up for when you play basketball at Indiana or agree to coach. And I don't think someone like Archie Miller would take that job without knowing that the expectation was there."

About the Author

Terry Hutchens knows Indiana University football and basketball. Beginning in the fall of 2017, he begins his 20th season as a beat writer covering the two Indiana University sports. He now works for CNHI Sports Indiana and his work is syndicated in 13 newspapers in the state of Indiana every day including Anderson, Kokomo, Terre Haute, Jeffersonville/New Albany, Logansport, Greensburg, Goshen, Lebanon, Zionsville, Batesville, the Hendricks County Flyer, Zionsville and Washington. Previously, Terry spent 22 years at the Indianapolis Star including 15 seasons covering the Hoosiers.

This is Terry's 11th book and the fourth he has self-published. Other titles include *An Indiana Hoosier Fans Bucket List*, published by Triumph Books out of Chicago and also released in the fall of 2017. *Hoo-Hoo-Hoo Hoosiers*, a children's book that came out in 2016, *Hoosiers Through and Through, Missing Banners, So You Think You Know Indiana University Basketball, So You Think You Know Indiana University Football, Rising From The Ashes, Hep Remembered, Never Ever Quit* and *Let 'Er Rip*. He has also written two revisions for the *Indiana University Basketball Encyclopedia*, originally written by Jason Hiner.

Terry and his wife, Susan, live in Indianapolis. They have two grown sons, Bryan and Kevin.